Bloom's Modern Critical Interpretations

Bloom's Modern Critical Interpretations

Stephen Crane's
THE RED BADGE
OF COURAGE

Edited and with an introduction by
Harold Bloom
Sterling Professor of the Humanities
Yale University

CHELSEA HOUSE
PUBLISHERS
A Haights Cross Communications Company
Philadelphia

©2004 by Chelsea House Publishers, a subsidiary of
Haights Cross Communications.

A Haights Cross Communications Company

Introduction © 2004 by Harold Bloom.

Printed and bound in Malaysia.

10 9 8 7 6 5 4 3 2 1

Library of Congress Cataloging-in-Publication Data applied for.

ISBN: 0-7910-7578-8

Contributing editor: Pamela Loos

Cover design by Terry Mallon

Cover: Library of Congress, digital ID 3g03194

Layout by EJB Publishing Services

Chelsea House Publishers
1974 Sproul Road, Suite 400
Broomall, PA 19008-0914

www.chelseahouse.com

Contents

Editor's Note

My introduction centers on Crane's originality in his representation of battle, particularly in his ironics.

Donald Pease argues that Crane's mode demands "battles as elaborations and justifications of already narrated events," after which Frederick Newberry posits that *The Red Badge of Courage* owes a literary debt to Nathaniel Hawthorne's *The Scarlet Letter.* Henry Fleming's battle-fury is seen by Chester L. Wolford as a proof of Crane's control of the contest that epic tradition requires.

In a remarkable essay, Michael Fried brings Crane together with the painter Eakins, showing that both equate aesthetic recognition with processes of disfiguration.

Donald Pizer reflects upon the novel's ambivalences, while Donald B. Gibson analyzes the opposition between nature and Henry Fleming's development.

The question of character in Crane's novel is raised by Lee Clark Mitchell's account of the personages as "gazing subjects," after which Kevin J. Hayes meditates upon Crane's shaping of Henry Fleming.

James M. Cox memorably discovers in Crane's vision of war a curious "purity," while John E. Curran, Jr. ponders the book's ironies.

The aura of Henry's invulnerability is evoked by Joseph Urbas after which Daniel Shanahan closes this volume with a Marxist probing of the origins of Crane's sense of an army in capitalism.

HAROLD BLOOM

Introduction

I

Stephen Crane's contribution to the canon of American literature is fairly slight in bulk: one classic short novel, three vivid stories, and two or three ironic lyrics. *The Red Badge of Courage*; "The Open Boat," "The Blue Hotel," and "The Bride Comes to Yellow Sky"; "War is Kind" and "A Man Adrift on a Slim Spar"—a single small volume can hold them all. Crane was dead at twenty-eight, after a frantic life, but a longer existence probably would not have enhanced his achievement. He was an exemplary American writer, flaring in the forehead of the morning sky and vanishing in the high noon of our evening land. An original, if not quite a Great Original, he prophesied Hemingway and our other journalist-novelists and still seems a forerunner of much to come.

 The Red Badge of Courage is Crane's undoubted masterwork. Each time I reread it, I am surprised afresh, particularly by the book's originality, which requires a reader's act of recovery because Crane's novel has been so influential. To write about battle in English, since Crane, is to be shadowed by Crane. Yet Crane, who later saw warfare in Cuba and between the Greeks and the Turks in his work as a correspondent, had experienced no fighting when he wrote *The Red Badge of Courage*. There is no actual experience that informs Crane's version of the Battle of Chancellorsville, one of the most

1

terrible carnages of the American Civil War. Yet anyone who has gone through warfare, from the time of the novel's publication (1895) until now, has testified to Crane's uncanny accuracy at the representation of battle. *The Red Badge of Courage* is an impressionist's triumph, in the particular sense that "impressionist" had in the literature of the nineties, a Paterian sense that went back to the emphasis upon *seeing* in Carlyle, Emerson, and Ruskin. Conrad and Henry James, both of whom befriended Crane, had their own relation to the impressionist mode, and each realized that Crane was a pure or natural impressionist, indeed the only one, according to Conrad.

Pater, deftly countering Matthew Arnold, stated the credo of literary impressionism:

> The first step towards seeing one's object as it really is, is to know one's impression as it really is, to discriminate it, to realize it distinctly.

Pater's "object" is a work of art, verbal or visual, but the critic here has stated Stephen Crane's quest to see the object of experience as it is, to know one's impression of it, and to realize that impression in narrative fiction. Scholarly arguments as to whether and to what degree *The Red Badge of Courage* is naturalistic, symbolist, or impressionist, can be set aside quickly. Joyce's *Ulysses* is both naturalistic and symbolist within the general perspective of the Paterian or impressionistic "epiphany" or privileged moment, but juxtapose the *Red Badge* to *Ulysses* and Crane is scarcely naturalistic or symbolist in comparison. Crane is altogether an impressionist, in his "vivid impressionistic description of action on that woodland battlefield," as Conrad phrased it, or, again in Conrad's wording, in "the imaginative analysis of his own temperament tried by the emotions of a battlefield."

If Crane's impressionism had a single literary origin, as to some extent is almost inevitable, Kipling is that likely forerunner. The puzzles of literary ancestry are most ironical here, since Kipling's precursor was Mark Twain. Hemingway's famous observation that all modern American literature comes out of one book, *Huckleberry Finn*, is only true of Crane, the indubitable beginning of our modern literature, insofar as Crane took from Kipling precisely what the author of *The Light That Failed* and *Kim* owed to Twain. Michael Fried's association of Crane with the painter Eakins is peculiarly persuasive, since Crane's visual impressionism is so oddly American, without much resembling Whistler's. Crane is almost the archetype of the writer as a child of experience, yet I think this tends to mean that then there are a few strong artistic precursors, rather than a tradition that makes itself available.

Associate Crane with Kipling and Eakins, on the way to, but still a distance from, Conrad and the French Postimpressionists, and you probably have stationed him accurately enough.

II

The Red Badge of Courage is necessarily a story about fear. Crane's Young Soldier, again as Conrad noted, "dreads not danger but fear itself.... In this he stands for the symbol of all untried men." Henry Fleming, as eventually we come to know the Young Soldier, moves ironically from a dangerous self-doubt to what may be an even more dangerous dignity. This is the novel's famous yet perhaps equivocal conclusion:

> For a time this pursuing recollection of the tattered man took all elation from the youth's veins. He saw his vivid error, and he was afraid that it would stand before him all his life. He took no share in the chatter of his comrades, nor did he look at them or know them, save when he felt sudden suspicion that they were seeing his thoughts and scrutinizing each detail of the scene with the tattered soldier.
>
> Yet gradually he mustered force to put the sin at a distance. And at last his eyes seemed to open to some new ways. He found that he could look back upon the brass and bombast of his earlier gospels and see them truly. He was gleeful when he discovered that he now despised them.
>
> With this conviction came a store of assurance. He felt a quiet manhood, nonassertive but of sturdy and strong blood. He knew that he would no more quail before his guides wherever they should point. He had been to touch the great death, and found that, after all, it was but the great death. He was a man.
>
> So it came to pass that as he trudged from the place of blood and wrath his soul changed. He came from hot plowshares to prospects of clover tranquilly, and it was as if hot plowshares were not. Scars faded as flowers.
>
> It rained. The procession of weary soldiers became a bedraggled train, despondent and muttering, marching with churning effort in a trough of liquid brown mud under a low, wretched sky. Yet the youth smiled, for he saw that the world was a world for him, though many discovered it to be made of oaths and walking sticks. He had rid himself of the red sickness of battle. The sultry nightmare was in the past. He had been an

animal blistered and sweating in the heat and pain of war. He turned now with a lover's thirst to images of tranquil skies, fresh meadows, cool brooks—an existence of soft and eternal peace.

Over the river a golden ray of sun came through the hosts of leaden rain clouds.

More Hemingway than Hemingway are these very American sentences: "He had been to touch the great death, and found that, after all, it was but the great death. He was a man." Is the irony of that dialectical enough to suffice? In context, the power of the irony is beyond question, since Crane's prose is strong enough to bear rephrasing as: "He had been to touch the great fear, and found that, after all, it was still the great fear. He was not yet a man." Crane's saving nuance is that the fear of being afraid dehumanizes, while accepting one's own mortality bestows upon one the association with others that grants the dignity of the human. How does Crane's prose find the strength to sustain a vision that primary and normative? The answer, I suspect, is the Bible and Bunyan, both of them being deeply at work in this unbelieving son of a Methodist minister: "He came from hot plowshares to prospects of clover tranquilly, and it was as if hot plowshares were not." The great trope of Isaiah is assimilated in the homely and unassuming manner of Bunyan, and we see the Young Soldier, Henry Fleming, as an American Pilgrim, anticipating when both sides of the Civil War "shall beat their swords into plowshares, and their spears into pruning hooks."

III

Crane's accurate apprehension of the phantasmagoria that is battle has been compared to Tolstoy's. There is something to such a parallel, perhaps because Tolstoy even more massively is a biblical writer. What is uniquely Crane's, what parts him from all prior visionaries of warfare, is difficult to define, but is of the highest importance for establishing his astonishing originality. Many examples night be chosen, but I give the death of the color sergeant from the conclusion of chapter 19:

Over the field went the scurrying mass. It was a handful of men splattered into the faces of the enemy. Toward it instantly sprang the yellow tongues. A vast quantity of blue smoke hung before them. A nighty banging made ears valueless.

The youth ran like a madman to reach the woods before a bullet could discover him. He ducked his head low, like a football player. In his haste his eyes almost closed, and the scene was a wild blur. Pulsating saliva stood at the corners of his mouth.

Within him, as he hurled himself forward, was born a love, a despairing fondness for this flag which was near him. It was a creation of beauty and invulnerability. It was a goddess, radiant, that bended its form with an imperious gesture to him. It was a woman, red and white, hating and loving, that called him with the voice of his hopes. Because no harm could come to it he endowed it with power. He kept near, as if it could be a saver of lives, and an imploring cry went from his mind.

In the mad scramble he was aware that the color sergeant flinched suddenly, as if struck by a bludgeon. He faltered, and then became motionless, save for his quivering knees.

He made a spring and a clutch at the pole. At the same instant his friend grabbed it from the other side. They jerked at it, stout and furious, but the color sergeant was dead, and the corpse would not relinquish its trust. For a moment there was a grim encounter. The dead man, swinging with bended back, seemed to be obstinately tugging, in ludicrous and awful ways, for the possession of the flag.

It was past in an instant of time. They wrenched the flag furiously from the dead man, and, as they turned again, the corpse swayed forward with bowed head. One arm swung high, and the curved hand fell with heavy protest on the friend's unheeding shoulder.

In the "wild blur" of this phantasmagoria, there are two images of pathos, the flag and the corpse of the color sergeant. Are they not to some degree assimilated to one another, so that the corpse becomes a flagpole, and the flag a corpse? Yet so dialectical is the interplay of Crane's biblical irony that the assimilation, however incomplete, itself constitutes a figure of doubt as to the normative intensities of patriotism and group solidarity that the scene exemplifies, both in the consciousness of Henry Fleming and in that of the rapt reader. The "despairing fondness" for the flag is both a Platonic and a Freudian Eros, but finally more Freudian. It possesses "invulnerability" for which the soldier under fire has that Platonic desire for what he himself does not possess and quite desperately needs, but it manifests even more a Freudian sense of the ambivalence both of and towards the woman as object of the drive, at once a radiant goddess sexually bending her form though imperiously, yet also a woman, red and white, hating and loving, destroying and healing.

The corpse of the color sergeant, an emblem of devotion to the flag and the group even beyond death, nevertheless keeps Fleming and his friend from the possibility of survival as men, compelling them to clutch and jerk at the pole, stout and furious. Life-in-death incarnate, the corpse obstinately tugs for the staff of its lost life. Homer surely would have appreciated the extraordinary closing gesture, as the corpse sways forward, head bowed but arm swung high for a final stroke, as "the curved hand fell with heavy protest on the friend's unheeding shoulder."

Crane is hardly the American Homer; Walt Whitman occupies that place forever. Still, *The Red Badge of Courage* is certainly the most Homeric prose narrative ever written by an American. One wants to salute it with Whitman's most Homeric trope, when he says of the grass:

And now it seems to me the beautiful uncut hair of graves.

DONALD PEASE

Fear, Rage, and the Mistrials of Representation
in The Red Badge of Courage

In the April 1896 issue of *The Dial*, Army General A. C. McClurg, in a critical document interesting less for the general's insight into the novel than the direction of his criticism of it, bitterly denounced *The Red Badge of Courage* as a vicious satire of army life. "The hero of the book, if such he can be called, was an ignorant and stupid country lad without a spark of patriotic feeling or soldierly ambition," the general wrote. "He is throughout an idiot or a maniac and betrays no trace of the reasoning being. No thrill of patriotic devotion to cause or country ever moves his breast, and not even an emotion of manly courage." And after noting the work is that of a young man, and therefore must be a mere work of "diseased imagination," the general concludes, in a catalogue informed with political as well as dramatic principles, that "Soldier Fleming is a coward, a Northerner who fled the field ... and that is why the British have praised *The Red Badge*." Suspending for a moment any question of the accuracy in the general's remarks, we cannot fail to register the force in his reaction. Nor can we fail to notice the source of the general's rage: the absence in Private Fleming's account of those virtues usually included in conventional war narratives whenever describing or justifying the excesses of war. Moreover, although the general does not explicitly mention it, his reaction to still another omission proves clear enough from the fury in his final barrage of accusations. That Crane would

From *American Realism: New Essays*. © 1982 by The Johns Hopkins University Press.

represent battle conditions frightening enough to produce cowards might perhaps be excusable, but that he would present such conditions in a context devoid of such crucial issues as the slavery question or southern secession, issues bound to inspire in the reader what they failed to evoke from Private Fleming, namely a renewed commitment to the Union cause, must in General McClurg's mind be grounds for the charge of treason.

Clearly Crane inflamed the general's ire by leaving political considerations out of his account altogether. Written at a time when the nation's historian's were characterizing the political and ideological significance of seemingly every battle in the war, Crane's power derived from his decision to reverse the procedure. By stripping the names from the battles he describes, Crane releases the sheer force of the battle incidents unrelieved by their assimilation into a historical narrative frame. And like a naive social historian, General McClurg decided to make good on the debits in Crane's account. In his critical relation to the war novel he restored to the narrative what Crane carefully eliminated from Henry Fleming's confrontation with war: a political and moral frame of reference.

By 1896, many American historians considered the Civil War the decisive moment in the nation's "coming of age." A moment's reflection on the contentions in early documentary accounts of the war should indicate the crucial role it played in providing a young nation with both a historical and a geographical orientation. For many historians viewed this war as a struggle that cross-identified ideological and geographical demarcations and finally granted a name and a sense of place to the United States of America. Given their evaluation of the crucial role the war played in the formation of national character, it was difficult if not impossible to eliminate moral questions from their accounts of the war. While few historians argued that freedom, equality, and union were decisively secured in the aftermath to the war, none denied the ideological power of these abstract principles. Indeed the moral values inherent in these principles not only affected these accounts, in some accounts they replaced battle descriptions altogether.

While Civil War narratives had developed into a flourishing enterprise capable of deflecting all considerations of the experience of the war into an ideological frame of reference intent on justifying it, Crane in registering the effects of the war innocent of the consolations of any coherent ground whatever defied the captains of the war industry. Once we acknowledge the number of reviews and critical studies that have either overlooked or scrupulously read back into *The Red Badge of Courage* what Crane has carefully eliminated, no further evidence of the pervasive hold of the typical Civil War narrative wields over the American imagination need be mentioned. What needs reiteration, however, is the threat not only against the Civil War industry but against America as a nation implicit in Crane's narrative. For if the conventional war narrative used the Civil War as a pretext for an ideological recounting of those principles that gave shape to a nation, Crane, by excluding these principles, was guilty of an assault against the American character. To register the force of this attack, however, we must read Crane through the eyes of a military officer eager to order a young nation to shape up, to conform to the features of stability and confidence delineated and secured by the war. General McClurg in his review, then, did not wish to launch a personal attack on Private Fleming but to recover those representations Stephen Crane had withheld. As the general's review vividly attests, by 1896 these representations had become ingrained enough in the American character for one of her "representative men" to take their absence as a personal affront.

By mentioning General McClurg's reaction specifically, I do not mean to isolate its eccentricity, but to suggest that in its very force his reaction represents the urgent need to recover that sense of a developing American character Crane's account has taken leave of. Whether commentators attack this lack of character directly as General McClurg does in denouncing Private Fleming as a coward, or denounce it after a manner subtle enough to remain unconscious of it, as do more recent critics, by reading a coherent line of character development into the arbitrary incidents in Henry's life, the wish remains the same in both cases, to recover the sense of exemplary continuity, integrity, and significance for those Civil War events Stephen Crane has forcibly excised from official history. Crane acknowledges the urgency of this need by never failing to drive a wedge between the sheer contingency of Henry's battle experiences and those reflections on them that never account for so much as they displace these incidents with other concerns. What results is an ongoing sense of disorientation, a knowledge of Henry Fleming's involvement in a battle that history will later turn into a monumental event, but whose dimensions never presently convert into anything more than a series of discontinuous incidents, followed by pauses whose emptiness Henry can never fill with sufficient reflections. Without adequate ideological underpinnings these battle scenes flare up as severe emotional and psychic blows without the consolation recognition brings. Instead of absorbing Henry's recollections and the experiences they are meant to describe into the continuities of a narrative, *The Red Badge of Courage* underwrites the absence of continuity in a war that never achieves the epic qualities either Henry or a nation of historians would imposed on it.

Indeed the war Henry suffers through seems, in its tendency seemingly to start from the beginning with each encounter, to lack any historical attributes whatever. Unlike the America that found its past confirmed and its

geography decisively marked by war, Henry Fleming can discover no frame
capable of situating him securely in either time or place. With each explosive
battlefield encounter, Henry discovers that the barrier against too much
stimulation has been breached, that the recognitions following these
encounters and the anticipations meant to prepare him for them are both
painfully inadequate. Confronted repeatedly with shocks utterly
disrespectful of that lag between recollection and healing forgetfulness when
experience has the time to form, Henry witnesses scenes that even when able
to leave marks in the memory do so by quite literally leaving him out. In the
following scene, for example, Henry records, with a lucidity heightened
through his fears, a series of impressions released from the control of any
fixed reference point:

> It seemed to the youth that he saw everything. Each blade of
> green grass was bold and clear. He thought that he was aware of
> each change in the thin, transparent vapor that floated idly in
> sheets. The brown or gray trunks showed each roughness of their
> surfaces. And the men of the regiment, with their staring eyes and
> sweating faces running madly, or falling as if thrown headlong, to
> queer, heaped-up corpses—all were comprehended. His mind
> took a mechanical but firm impression, so that afterward
> everything was pictured and explained to him save why he himself
> was there.

In this description, each colorful image surges up as all foreground,
with a suddenness whose intensity is unmediated by a context capable of
either subduing or containing it. Instead of settling into that relationship in
which a figure is clearly contextualized within a stable ground and which a
coherent picture is supposed to guarantee, these "firm impressions" glare out
as if in defiance of an implicit order to move into perspective. Not only the
individual impressions fail to modify one another, however; so do the
sentences in which they appear. These sentences do not describe a sequence
in which new facts are "comprehended" by an overall principle of coherence.
Without any perspective capable of sorting out the relevant from the
irrelevant, everything crowds into Henry's consciousness with all the force of
confusion. Thus the very givenness of this jumble of impressions renders
redundant Henry's concluding observation that everything was explained to
him save his own presence in the scene.

In this scene, then, the exclusion of any coherent perspective begins to
function as a perspective, one sufficiently powerful to make audible Henry's
unspoken reaction, his sensed alienation from the scene he observes. In this

account, however, Henry Fleming does not assert his alienation as a feeling of separation. If anything he seems utterly absorbed in the picture he describes. He seems so utterly consumed in a battle scene in the act of manifesting itself as to be indistinguishable from what he perceives. Because, however, what he perceives are little more than sheer impressions, unrelieved by any signification whatsoever, it would be more accurate to say that what Fleming perceives is not a conventional battle scene but the loss of any framework capable of informing this scene with significance. In this scene then he becomes absorbed not in a picture but its loss, the disappearance of what grounds a picture in a significant frame of reference.

By representing such "private" impressions unverified by either the accounts of other veterans or historians of the war, Crane depicts a character incompatible enough with the nation's self-portrait to elicit General McClurg's fear of "foreign" influence. For Henry's chance observations, in the radical incongruity of their sheer givenness, do indeed permit the past to speak in an unfamiliar voice. This voice, in the very strangeness of its inflection, unsettles both the nation's past and the character sanctioned by it. Moreover, when carefully listened to, this voice fabricates a "reality" able to invest the past with an uncanny sense of immediacy, but an immediacy interlaced with an irony unlimited enough to relegate this past to a realm of irretrievable pastness.

It would be a mistake, however, to suggest that this voice dominates the narrative line of *The Red Badge of Courage*; it cannot be accommodated by narrative conventions. Narration, in converting the mere succession of incidents into a meaningful sequence, silences the voice released in the chance encounter. Like a photograph of a battle scene with the captions cut off, this voice counts any explanation capable of guaranteeing a coherent context or selecting out the significant details among the casualties of war. It speaks *through* the impressions surviving Henry's presence at scenes of battles, and by speaking through these incidental details asserts their independence from the war story Henry has to tell. Indeed this voice sustains itself by converting Henry's statements about the war back into pieces of it, so that what gets narrated in *The Red Badge of Courage* never coincides with those incidents that can never be explained but only marked.

If in scenes like the one cited, Henry's impressions denote his awareness of everything except a rationale for his being there, his narration forcibly displaces these impressions by supplying a missing rationale. Thus, the narrative inscribes a discrepancy between the self-image Henry wishes to represent and the incidents that fail to engage any image of the self whatsoever. Given that these marked incidents occupy a different space from those narrated events Henry creates through an act of reflection, the reader must engage this work with a double vision. Once envisioned through this double perspective, however, *The Red Badge of Courage* reveals a conception of the self that is perhaps as much a victim of narrative conventions as the vicissitudes of war. Having begun this discussion with a reflection on the incompatibility between Henry's chance incidents and conventional representations of the Civil War, we are drawn by the very force of this discrepancy to another interpretation, one guided by Henry's struggles to confer a significance on events that would otherwise utterly confound him. Through such an interpretive strategy we feel the pressure first of the merely chance encounter and then the force of Henry's need to recall those incidents in the mold of a meaningful narrative. In many cases the irrational force of the war proves a sufficient rationale to justify Henry's need for a significant narration. But Crane's text is remarkable for its refusal to favor the meaningful narrative. By persistently locating Henry in the space between unrelieved contingency and imposed narrative, Crane inveigles the arbitrariness usually associated with the chance event into the orderly narrative sequence. More startlingly, however, through this organization of materials, Crane exposes the need to choose Henry's narrative instead of his experience as still another narrative convention.

Perhaps we cannot acknowledge the force of this recognition until we ascertain the daring implication of Crane's narrative strategies. In the arrangement of his plot, Crane did not use the brutality of the war as a pretext for justifying the humane values implicit in narrative conventions. Crane's chronology inverts the one we have described. In *The Red Badge of Courage*, narratives do not follow battles and provide needed explanation; instead, they precede and indeed demand battles as elaborations and justifications of already narrate events.

"Private" Fleming negotiates this "turn of events" in that moment of reflection he secures for himself in the wake of the excitement following Jim Conklin's "rumor" that the troops are about to move. In the course of his reflection Henry does not, as do so many of his fictional and nonfictional predecessors, envision himself in a project involving the liberation of slaves. The only mention of a Negro in the entire novel appears in the fourth paragraph, when Jim Conklin's tale creates a state of confusion that quite literally abandons the Negro's cause. "When he had finished, the blue-clothed men scattered into small arguing groups between the rows of squat brown huts. A negro teamster who had been dancing upon a cracker box with the hilarious encouragement of two score soldiers was deserted. He sat mournfully down." Without any "noble" causes to commandeer his martial emotions, Henry's musings fill this vacuum by turning to "tales of great movement" as opportunities for personal aggrandizement. These battles, Henry reflected, "might not be distinctly Homeric, but there seemed to be much glory in them." Having already read of marches, sieges, conflicts, Henry now "longed to see it all." His busy mind had drawn for him large pictures "extravagant in color, lurid with breathless deeds"; it remained for him to "realize" these narrated pictures with matching deeds. In the reflections that inevitably follow all of his battle experiences, then, it is obvious that Henry tries to take possession of himself as the figure he had previously imagined occupying center stage in one of these extravagant pictures. What may not be obvious, however, is that Henry's means of taking possession of himself share nothing with his battlefield ordeals. Battle narratives and conventions from these narratives provide Henry both with the practice and the position of his acts of self-reflection. Moreover, these conventions replace the battle condition Henry survives with previously narrated battle scenes. And these representations impinge on lived scenes with sufficient pressure for Henry to measure the adequacy of his response against these representations.

At this juncture, however, Henry's narrative qualifies rather significantly an earlier observation. For in disclosing the distinction between his "narrated self" and actual experiences, Henry does not elide but reveals the rift between the incidents beyond telling and the telltale narrative that displaces them. Even more remarkable, however, is what else Henry implies in his innocent disclosure of his motives for going to war. For if Henry enlisted to appropriate, upon reflection, images of his own aggrandizement, he did not really wish to see action in battle at all. Action in battle was only an alibi for his need to fulfill a preoccupation, gleaned through diligent reading of war narratives, with action at a distance, his ability to take possession of the world through images of an overwhelming effect upon it. As Henry himself indicates in his reflections following the first battle, war exists as a testing ground to prove the power to turn the world into signs of the individual's advance upon it:

So it was all over at last! The supreme trial had been passed. The red, formidable difficulties of war had been vanquished. He went into an ecstasy of self-satisfaction. He had the most delightful sensations of his life. Standing as if apart from himself, he viewed that last scene. He perceived that the man who had fought thus was magnificent. He felt that he was a fine fellow. He saw himself with even those ideals which he had considered as far beyond him.

While it will take a later scene for Henry to acknowledge the distinction between the "image" of "himself" gained after the fact through reflection, and the shocking battle incidents exceeding in their overwhelming immediacy the self's ability either to have experiences or to reflect upon them, it takes no longer than the eve of his first encounter for Henry to delineate the frightening dimensions of the terrible logic at work in war. "From his home his youthful eyes had looked upon war in his own country with distrust. It must be some sort of play affair." The double bind at work in these two starkly phrased sentences lashes out with all the force of a compulsion. Henry must go to war to realize the glories previously only narrated, but once at war he inevitably discovers the need for a narrative to displace actual wartime incidents incompatible with a reality legitimized by and *as* narration. In other words, the "play" war that Henry would "realize" by going into battle upholds no necessary similarity with actual battle conditions; only the conventions of a narrative that Henry, through reflection, can read into these insufferable conditions can confer the appearance of "reality" upon these otherwise aberrant circumstances. This is to say that Henry's reflections constitute efforts to reread narratives he had taken to heart prior to taking up the Union colors. When considered in this perspective, however, war does not seem an arbitrary congeries of contingent circumstances. Instead it imparts a sense of the necessary limit to, and indeed the reprieve from, the excesses of already narrated "reality." Crane exploits the contradictions implicit in this perspective when he suggests that Henry's motive for going to war may be nothing more than his wish to coincide with the extravagant deeds, the "*broken*-bladed" exploits attributed to the heroes of traditional war narratives. Consequently not even the "private's" wishes are even truly "his" own but migrate to him from a "generalized" subject of conventional war stories Henry, with all the secret shame of a raw recruit, tries to feel equal to. In *The Red Badge of Courage*, then, Henry Fleming must feel alienated in turn both by those incidents that portend their inaccessibility to significance but also by the very narratives intended to impose significance upon them. Thus from a vantage point quite different from Henry's we begin to understand the urgency of his need to take possession of the war in personal terms. Involved in incidents unable to be retrieved in human terms, Henry must invent a history for himself that would at least guarantee the continuity of his identity, and at best alleviate the pressure of those incidents he merely lives through. In other words, Henry's narrative does not exist as his means of recording events of war but as his principal strategy for taking possession of "his" life.

REPRESENTATIONS AND FEAR

Ironically, however, the only way he can truly possess "his" life in a narrative leads him to assert the independence of his narrative from those literally surrounding him. To prevent "his" absorption in "their" narratives, Henry, on the eve of the first battle, develops a rather perverse tactic. First he acknowledges his debt to already written war narratives by recalling the inspiration he drew from accounts of those soldiers whose extravagant deeds relieved the boredom of his days at home, but then in a curious turn he dramatizes the return to "his" senses by indulging in doubts over his ability to replicate their feats. Surprisingly, these doubts do not lessen Henry's feelings of self-regard but heighten them. Indeed Henry's musings draw a compelling line of connection between fantasies of personal failure and newly discovered personal resources sufficiently different from the conventional to authorize a "private" identity. Positioned between events that alienate him through excessive shock and already narrated events that replace his exploits with those of traditional heroes, Henry charges this space between impossible alternatives by fearing "his" cowardice. Through this fear, Henry makes a virtue of his dispossession by converting this depersonalized separation from both narrated and actual events into a personal act of choice. Without any abstract moral principle to organize and legitimize his behavior, he feels compelled to develop an ethos of fear as his basis for a unique personality. His fear asserts its distinct quality by supplanting the threat to personal integrity usually associated with an object of fear. Instead of a threat Henry discovers hidden reserves strong enough to withstand prospects that would otherwise prove utterly self-destructive.

Consequent to a series of reflections inspired by his fear, Henry feels free to conceive of himself as a figure set apart from the representations of his comrades. A "mental outcast," he must abandon all preconceptions, his own as well as those in the narratives he had earlier consumed so avidly, for "in this crisis the previously learned laws of life proved useless." Instead of a feeling of disgrace, a sense of self-discovery and a challenge to his habitual modes of understanding result from his unparalleled fear. "Whatever he had learned of himself was of no avail. He was an unknown quality. He saw that he would again be obliged to experiment as he had in his earlier youth." Confronted, in other words, with emotions that made him "feel strange in the presence" of the other men, Henry made the most of his estrangement. Refusing to conceive of himself as a fixed object of "their" derision, Henry explores the range of "his" feelings on the subject of his fear, until in the course of these reflections he decides that fear not only sets him apart from the other men but it also situates him above them. On the eve of his first battle experience, Henry invests fear with enough privilege to suggest that "he must break from the ranks and harangue his comrades.... The generals were idiots to send them marching into a regular pen. There was but one pair of eyes in the corps." Fear, in other words, enables Henry to enact a drama of his powerlessness reassuring enough in its ancillary benefits to convert his "private" sector into a position of sufficient exemplary power to make his reflections superior to those of the generals. This drama reaches its peak when Henry, in an ecstasy of rejection, imagines the other men reacting derisively not to his fear but to the "refined perceptions" resulting from it. And the advance in rank secured by this imagined humiliation enables Henry to situate himself outside the context of all previously written war narratives, as he assumes "the demeanor of one who knows that he is doomed alone to unwritten responsibilities."

Through fear, Henry discovers the power to shape what he takes to be the "original" style of his powerlessness. Consequently, when he actually takes his part in a battle and does not run away in fear, he experiences this failure to run away not as an influx of courage, the reversal familiar from conventional war narratives, but as a loss of those privileges in rank that fear conferred upon him. So instead of continuing to conceive of himself as set apart from the ranks, in battle Henry "suddenly lost concern for himself ... became not a man but a member." Surrounded by the din and roar of combat, Henry, working his rifle "like an automatic affair," cannot take the time to know fear. Rather, he feels a "brotherhood" with his comrades, yet a brotherhood that does not result from a shared sense of purpose. Deprived of a humane cause to motivate them, the members of this "brotherhood" lose all signs of human purposiveness and seem less like a group of men and more like a "firework that, ignited, proceeds superior to circumstances until its blazing vitality fades." Because preparation for this first battle is secured through the consciousness of a private who had already made much of his dispossession, what comes as the greater shock is not Fleming's reduction in stature to the level of a "beast" or an automaton but his loss of those "private" daydreams that formerly enabled him to take possession of that alienation. During this incident, Fleming could not continue to brood over his fear but "lost concern for himself" and fell into a battle sleep emptied of his dreams and witnessed all "as one who dozes."

We have already considered Fleming's first reaction to his initiation into battle. He uses it as an opportunity to appropriate from a distance representations of his ability to measure up to the "red formidable difficulties of war." As if to underscore the falsity of these representations, however,

Fleming combines them with "ideals which he considered far beyond him" and which had no influence on his decision to enlist. Following his first battle, then, Private Fleming fears his apparently courageous battle actions misrepresent him. When his reflections on the battle turn up a Henry Fleming who did not feel fear, Henry is jubilant at the discovery of an ideal representation of himself, but his joy diminishes when he considers that this ideal is sufficiently at odds with the self-image he has been manufacturing to constitute a loss of himself.

SHAME

Moreover, when he finally does run away, during the second encounter, he finds fear a sufficiently generalized response to cease to be "his" private reaction. We do not realize the significance Henry derives from this loss, however, until the very end of his narrative, when, upon reflecting on his victorious encounter, Henry once again feels gratified over his apparently heroic behavior. This time, however, after he spends "delightful minutes viewing the gilded images of memory," his thoughts return to his action on the first day, whereupon he fails to recall his initial encounter altogether. Instead of recollecting the scene in which he actually outlasted the enemy assault, he can remember only his desertion in the field, chronologically the second incident, as having happened first: "The ghost of his flight from the first engagement appeared to him and danced.... For a moment he blushed, and the light of his soul flickered with shame." This lapse of memory is understandable enough when we recall the trancelike state he continuously falls into when battles actually begin. Another context for understanding this lapse emerges, however, when we recall how effective fear was in enabling Henry to take possession of his alienation. During that first battle Henry effectively forgot his fear, so following the logic sanctioned by his psychic economy, we can infer that this fear, which underwrote Private Fleming's inscription within a coherent narrative, upon returning to consciousness erased Henry's memory of the "first engagement." Yet given Henry's former correlation of his identity with his prolonged dream of fear, this memory lapse was almost an inevitability. Indeed this lapse seems less attributable to Henry's memory than to the loss in this instance of any identity. Without fear, Henry lacks the state of mind capable of conferring the privileges of a continuous identity upon him. Moreover, as a reproduction of those heroic representations familiar from all the narratives he had previously read, Henry's reflections on that first engagement were not "his" any more than they were those of any other member of his regiment. They were postures and actions that belonged to no one precisely because they were the "commonplaces" of war stories. After he finally does run away in fear, Henry does not return to battle intent on recovering the attitude he displaced during that first battle, but to recover that great dream of fear he lost when he fell into battle sleep.

In Henry's eyes, the greatest casualty of war was the loss of those psychic resources he needed to mobilize in order to countermand the anticipated derision and consequent shame he would inevitably experience when others found out about his fear. In the moment that he runs, Henry, like the men he saw retreating from the field before his first battle experience, is not even conscious of the presence of an audience. Like the "proverbial chicken," Henry, cut off from any rationale for his actions, could only save face after the fact by reactivating his earlier daydreams of cowardice and shame. Without an abstract moral principle capable of absorbing his actions into reality, Henry is condemned to "realize" his daydreams. Involved as he is in actions irrelevant to the mastery of any human subject, Henry can only redefine himself as a human subject by willfully conceiving of himself as an object of derision. In short, Henry Fleming who was formerly subject to the delusions of fear, after the second battle engagement releases all the resources of what we might call the subject of fear.

While he runs, Henry replaces his blind fear with fear rationalized, and from this transformed position he recognizes his former deeds. For example, when he runs away from the scene of battle, Henry runs into a scene that reenacts almost precisely the conditions of his first battle engagement. In this quite literal version of a recognition scene, Henry, upon seeing the regiment hold its ground, does not interpret this behavior as a sign of valor but pities the men for being "methodical idiots, machine-like fools." With this recognition, however, Henry does not merely replace the earlier role of hero with the role of deserter, though his ability to play both roles with equal reason does expose the interchangeability of the roles of hero and deserter. In judging as mechanical an earlier version of his activity that might otherwise be interpreted as courageous, he displays the privileges released by desertion. Instead of feeling judged by the men in the field he finds them to be merely elements engaged in strategic maneuvers. By co-opting their accusation, he thereby defuses in advance any judgment these men might level against him. Ironically enough, it is only when Henry is in a position of defensive reaction that he feels in sufficient command of himself to speak with authority.

At this point in the narrative, however, an even deeper irony intervenes. For the only discourse that Henry feels sufficiently powerful as a defense of his desertion is a discourse that has already been spoken. Unable to defend his desertion alone, he must enlist the support of a Nature who "would die if its timid eyes were compelled to see blood." On the eve of the first battle scene, Henry prepared himself for the inadequacy of this attribution of a maternal role to nature. Prior to going to battle he had primed himself for a beautiful scene of departure, one wherein his mother, like the mothers of the Greek epics, was to respond with great pathos to the tragic news of his departure, but not even his mother proved sufficiently maternal to fulfill his superstitions; "she had disappointed him by saying nothing whatever about returning with his shield or on it." We need only recall Henry's earlier "flash of astonishment," the irreconcilability between the apparent indifference of Nature to War and the concern Nature should be demonstrating, to see the wishful thinking in this conception. After all the noise and din of that first battle, Henry looked up at the blue sky and realized that "Nature had gone tranquilly on with her golden process in the midst of so much devilment." Whenever Fleming looks to Nature for signs of grief or solace, Nature responds not with a look of indifference but with the demeanor of one who has already completed the work of mourning for a lost beloved. Instead of functioning as a support system, Nature, like Henry's mother, seems to have subscribed to a series of representations enabling it to explain Henry's death as a commonplace occurrence. If anything, this scene only visually reenacts what Henry's mother had said much earlier: "'If so be a time comes when you have to be kilt ... why, Henry, don't think of anything 'cept what's right, because there's many a woman has to bear up 'ginst sech things these times, and the Lord'll take care of us all.'"

In such scenes as these, Crane takes pains to separate Henry's wish to envision Nature as "a woman with a deep aversion to tragedy" from the enlistment of Nature to underwrite and hence "naturalize" such totally contradictory sentiments as those expressed by Henry's mother. Henry dramatizes this need, to use Nature as a mode of legitimizing action when, upon seeing a squirrel "run chattering with fear" from a pine cone thrown by him, he interprets this behavior as Nature's sign corroborating his desertion. Then, inspired by this unlooked for support, he intensifies the authority of this sign until it reads like a mandate. "There was a law, he said.... The squirrel, immediately upon recognizing danger, had taken to his legs without ado." In the very next paragraph, however, Henry records a sign that fails to reenforce his argument but seemingly reenacts his feeling of being helplessly trapped. So when he sees "out at some black water, a small animal pounce in and emerge directly with a gleaming fish," Henry cannot assimilate this action to his theme of Nature's sympathy for his plight. Like the battle incidents before it, then, this scene flashes into consciousness as an impression closed to reflection, not so much an empty perception as a perception inimical to the categories of representation enlisted to convert perception into cognition.

Henry's desertion is of course no more sanctioned by the "nature" of things than is the war he flees, but the need to seek this sanction is the same in both cases. And the moment Henry uses Nature to justify his desertion marks a turning point in the narrative. In the incidents prior to his flight, Henry converts his fear into *unrealized* fantasies of desertion and thereby recovers an identity by making the most of *his* dispossession. But the moment he wishes to justify his actual desertion he must use the favorite strategy of the forces mobilized against him: the enlistment of Nature as a principal agent in a narrative designed to justify a course of action. In choosing a narrative to justify his actions, however, Henry abandons his charged position between battle incidents and already related events. For instead of continuing to resist them, he chooses to appropriate preexistent narratives as signs of the validity of his choice. Henry's choice of Nature, rather than Slavery or Union or martial heroism, as the final arbiter for his action proves more telling than any use to which he might put Nature. By definition the most fundamental because the least derivative of the narrative discourses at Henry's disposal, Nature and representation sanctioned by the discourse of Nature promise to be the most reliable arbiters of action and perception. So when Henry entertains a "natural" perception, like that of the trapped fish, irrelevant to the discourse of Nature he has been pursuing, he must either register that perception but take no notice of it or force it to cohere with the narrative he has been elaborating. In view of his efforts to include all of Nature within a uniform framework of representation, however, a perception uninformed with the privileges of that representation must have impinged on Henry's consciousness like a wound, a mark of what has been cut away from an organized whole.

RAGE

In *The Red Badge of Courage*, Crane focuses less on Henry's attempts to recover coherence by imposing an interpretation than on his failures. For, as we have seen, in these failures Henry repeatedly recovers the force of his character as its inaccessibility to preexistent forms. Whereas Henry formerly elaborated this inaccessibility into compelling dreams supervised by fear, in the course of the desertion that realizes "his" dream, Henry confronts a visionary figure terrifying enough to make even his dream of fear seem ghostly by comparison. Possessed by the need to justify his desertion, Henry happens upon the figure of a dying soldier who should have provided just the occasion Henry needs to give desertion a persuasive rationale. Turned into a ghost of himself by the battle incidents that converted him into just another casualty of war and the war narrative that sacrificed his life to its purposes, this "spectral soldier" effectively marks the point of intersection of the two great forces of alienation Henry equally fears. As the horrible double effect of both battle and battle narratives, Conklin's death should have the power to provide Henry's fear with the justification even Nature failed to supply. When confronted, however, with this horrible justification, Henry does not find still another corroboration for his desertion but a limit to all attempts to justify any activity whatever. Faced with the figure swelled with the redoubled force of alienation, Henry discovers the inadequacy of every attempt at justification. When we recall that it was Conklin, waving his arms in enthusiastic sympathy with the exciting news of troop movement, who awoke Henry's earliest fears, we get a sense of the full extent of their loss. Moreover, when we perceive the spastic arm movements released by his death as after-images of the arm-waving enthusiasm that earlier accompanied Jim's tales of war, we get an uncanny sense of witnessing in this literal correlation of narration and existence not simply the destruction of Jim Conklin but the loss of the power of narration to inform existence. In this scene, Henry mourns both the loss of his friend and the loss of a narration intended to represent this loss. Upon recognizing the identity of the "spectral soldier," Henry comprehends through this terrible recognition the shadowy limitations of his great dream of fear. Conklin's death interrupts Henry's attempt to rationalize his fear at the very moment Henry needs it most urgently, or rather it permanently separates the shock enveloped within his fear from any recognition capable of relieving it. Conklin's death, as the intersection of alienating forces released by battles and narratives, thereby supplants Henry's cowardice in that charged place between actual and narrated events. Henry recovers this space, however, when he turns his urgent need to supply the rationale for his fear into rage over the absence of any rationale whatsoever. This rage expresses itself not through the constraints of discursive narratives but through the breakdown of any attempt to constrain it into meaning:

> The youth turned with sudden, livid rage toward the battlefield. He shook his fist. He seemed about to deliver a philippic.
> "Hell—"
> The red sun was pasted in the sky like a [fierce] wafer.

Instead of being discharged into a "philippic," a convention that socializes rage into a manageable expression of loss, Henry's rage breaks down into a threatening impression, one that glares back at him with all the fury of its inaccessibility to his context. In registering this impression at this moment, Crane does not secretly subscribe to the doctrine of naturalism. As a cultural movement, naturalism only justified man's advance upon nature by reflecting back the force of his encroachment as if it were the course of Nature. Nor does this impression "symbolize" Henry's reaction. Like the color that dominates it, this impression renders visible only a glaring surface. Henry's registration of this perception in place of the philippic marks a transformation in his mode of accommodating himself to events. Formerly, Henry actively ignored events and scenes his representation could not appropriate. After emptying Henry's perception of such vast ideological issues as the liberation of the slaves and the recovery of the Union, Crane investigates perception reduced, as it were, to its least common denominators. In the absence of abstract moral and political principles, fear and shame restore coherence and significance to perception even as they circumscribe its locus. Disrespectful of the seeming irrelevance of Private Fleming's apperception to the events surrounding him, fear and shame intervene and replace Fleming's sense of the sheer contingency of what actually transpires with a conventional drama, proceeding from fear and into desertion but holding out the promise of a triumphant recovery of courage.

By holding out the promise of a recovered mastery, the discourse of fear installs Henry in a position to record and reflect upon his perceptions; thus he can later narrate his adventures. Neither the discourse of fear nor that of shame proves innocent of ideological consideration. By underwriting every other representation they constitute the least common denominators, the constraints of ideological representation. Unlike either fear or shame, rage acts out the loss of what can never be possessed. Utterly inimical to the claims for coherence and privileged responsibility formerly secured through shame and fear, rage replaces their reflective appropriation of perceptions and actions after the fact with the loss of any fact whatsoever to reflect upon. When enraged, Henry no longer fears being gazed at by another any more than he feels ashamed before the judgment of his projected ego ideals. Instead he becomes so completely absorbed in the loss of any representation capable of doing justice to what he perceives that all of the energy of perception seems to have been redirected. In such scenes as that of the interrupted phillipic, Henry does not speak from the position of one who reflects upon a scene. Unable to begin a philippic on the injustices of war, Henry instead notices that "the red sun was pasted in the sky like a [fierce] wafer." And he seems so utterly identified in this remark with what would otherwise sanction a thoughtful outburst of despair and frustration as to fail in his official duties as a subject. Instead of looking at the red sun, he seems to be looking out from its red surface with all the intensity of a glaring rebuke. Consequently the sentence does not express so much as it restores the rage generating it, nets the loss of what grounds it. Through this impression, Henry acknowledges both the undischargeable force of an event that cannot be assimilated to the Nature of things, and all in Nature that cannot be accommodated to man's need to impose an interpretation. And he accompanies this dual recognition with all the fury of an unmet demand.

In this scene, rage displaces fear and shame as Henry's response to his failure to be assimilated by either actual or narrated events. Through rage, however, Henry does not rest content with a recovery of his sense of dispossession as was the case with the prolonged dream of fear. Rage turns Henry's feelings of impotence into an overwhelming power, for when he is enraged his sense of total loss makes absolute demands on the world. Rage, as the power released through a reaction to power's loss, effectively separates the power of alienation from its cause. When Henry discovers the power released by rage, it is impossible to distinguish the power Henry fights with from the power Henry fights against. This is not to say as was the case with his fear that Henry identifies with either preexistent narrations or battle conditions as his means of justifying his rage. Rage disrupts the line of demarcation between agent and action, system and circumstance, throwing everything into a state of confusion.

When I suggest that Henry replaces cowardice with rage in that charged space between equally alienating alternatives, I do not mean that Henry never fears cowardice again. Earlier Henry's fear that he would fail to measure up released a compensatory belief in the superiority of his perspective. He needed to believe his fear was privileged because "he" felt anonymous, a veritable unknown soldier in the midst of vast actions performed by vast collections of men. Through fear he converts his suspicion that "he" will never be recognized into a discovery of a previously unknown element in his psyche, a cowardice that distinguishes him by setting him apart from his fellows. In the course of events, Henry makes the desertion implicit in this feeling of being apart explicit when he actually runs from the field. When he seeks to render his desertion privileged by articulating its unique rationale, he identifies with all the conventional narratives that justify war by aligning it with the nature of things he earlier found so oppressive. After his confrontation with Jim Conklin, however, he not only recognizes the limitations of this rationale but also fears this limit. In other words, the fear of cowardice that led him to flee the field has become differently valenced. Without any effective rationale to recover the superiority in his former position of "mental outcast," Henry can only identify with a rage that acknowledges total loss and transforms loss into power.

Having experienced the absolute loss of all his former claims, Henry reactivates his fear of being judged a coward not in order to secure the sense of his superior rationale but in order to react with rage against the inadequacy of all rationales. His fear of being judged a coward, in other words, once the sole motivating force for his actions, becomes a pretext for his rage against any viable motivation whatsoever.

After the Conklin incident, Henry no longer feels shame. Shame after all presupposes a prior feeling of belonging to a community capable of making one feel alienated by shame. In his discovery of the limits of his rationale, Henry also discovers the limits of the community justified by it. Through various narrative devices, Crane suggests that the basis for this socializing process is not a shared purpose but a common fear of becoming a figure of public shame. As has been suggested, the ideological power of this process derives from Henry's belief that fear confers a "private" identity upon him. But throughout the narrative, Crane signals the "general" state of this fear by interrupting his "private" fantasy of cowardice with its implicit expressions by others. When every soldier seems engaged in the same "private struggle," this struggle cannot be "his" but must be "theirs" or no one's. After Henry's long reverie of shameful fear prior to that first incident, to offer only the most salient example, the "loud soldier" Wilson indicates his participation in the same "privileged" drama of fear as Henry's when he blurts out a plea that Henry send home, after Wilson's death in the field, packets of letters to his mother. Crane suggests that the very feelings of fear and cowardice capable of releasing the illusion of "privacy" have already been overcoded and directed toward common military aims. And Crane signals this abuse by turning what should be a "private" first-person form into a third-person narrative. For through this narrative strategy Henry's most private thoughts turn out not to be his but "theirs" after all.

After his encounter with Conklin, Henry attempts to regain his shame, but now he knows only "the ghost of shame," the rage he has not been socialized out of. Following the Conklin incident, Henry needs to feel the shame he earlier feared. Shame, after all, would make him feel the inadequacy of some judgment. But Henry always finds the position of shame preoccupied by his rage over its inadequacy. That is why he reacts with such violence when the tattered soldier asks him where he is wounded. A wound would be a justification for leaving the field, and Henry, in discovering the inadequacy of all attempts at justification, has carried his desertion too far. So when he runs back to the field he does not wish to prove himself to the other soldiers—that would only corroborate the adequacy of their categories—but to represent to them the "magnificent pathos" of his rage by dying right in front of them. In short, he wishes to bring "their" judgment up against "his" rage.

Paradoxically, however, Henry's means of reentering the military world is not through a demarcation of his rage but through an apparent identification with that world's ability to judge. A head wound, received when he grabs a deserter and asks for an explanation of his desertion, facilitates this turn of events. The head wound, in its openness to ambiguous interpretation, is what the deserter gives Henry instead of what he asked for, an explanation for desertion. This wound, like the sheer contingency of the battle scenes, is utterly unassimilable to the moral discourse of courage or cowardice. As the record of what gets perceived once privileged representations lose their power to master an event, this wound marks on Henry's body the equivalent to the locus of those losses "the red sun pasted in the sky like a wafer" burned into his consciousness. However much the other men might try to impress this wound to the scale of judgment adjudicated by either courage or cowardice, this wound fails to represent anything but the breakdown of the procedures of judgment. As the mark on his body not of any particular moral code but of his having been *cut off* from these codes, Henry's wound turns every attempt to interpret it as a sign of courage into avast charade of judgment. Through an identification with this wound, Henry can return to his regiment not as a "member" reincorporated into the "body" of men, but as a wound, a mark of what has already been cut off from the body.

This is not to say that upon returning Henry refuses to engage in judicial exchanges, but that the resultant charade of justice differs significantly from Henry's earlier experience. When in order to forestall Wilson's harsh rebuke of him for fleeing the field, Henry calls Wilson a coward and points to that packet of letters as proof, he performs that same activity of co-optation of judgment enacted earlier in the day. When he delivers this judgment, however, a judgment he himself fears, he does not judge Wilson so much as he converts the feeling of being judged wrongly into a judgment—a judgment whose inadequacy he knows from within the position of the judge. Thus Henry's secret revenge against it disrupts the very judicial system he seems in the service of. To socialize this behavior Henry reactivates that same narrative of the gifted man protected by Nature he used earlier to rationalize his desertion. But neither discourse brings his rage to justice. Each instead leaves a residue, a reaction against his distortions, and recovers for Henry the anger he can only discharge through the fury of his actions in battle.

Upon his return, as a more profound outcast, a figure all the more tellingly "cut off" from his peers than the man who deserted, Henry does not recover his place but reactivates his rage against all that displaces him. Nor does he actually fear the judgments of others, but demands these judgments as excuses for vengeance. When a general curses Henry's regiment for a pack of mule drivers, Henry is grateful for the chance to localize his rage on the general. When he fights on the field he does not fight Confederate soldiers but wages war on the discourses that formerly placed him so securely as a private in the military: he wounds his fear of cowardice with a fury in excess of any judgment and destroys his fear of shame with actions outrageous enough to make all the other soldiers feel ashamed by contrast. Henry, who earlier felt cursed and ashamed by his inability to live up to the heroics demanded by war, displays such extravagant brutality on the field that he becomes a general's means of cursing and shaming other men into battle. But Henry is no longer inspired by heroic representations. His apparent courage derives from the sense that he has already been marked as a casualty of war. Having formerly identified himself with all the representations gleaned from his battle narratives, once he loses those representations Henry fights with all the reckless abandon of one who has already been lost in battle.

Neither cowardly nor courageous, in his elemental fury and rage he arouses the need of those around him to reduce him to this code. Henry has already despaired of a world that the dialectic of courage and cowardice would idealize him back into. In battle he does not discover a personal identity resistant to the mutual dispossession of both actual and narrated events, but revenges himself against the delusions of a private identity and replaces identity with the force of its abandonment. His rage preoccupies every position, whether on the battlefield, in society, or in the narrations that "realize" them all, with a vengeance over the inevitability of their loss. By the end of the novel, then, rage has ceased to be a mere theme and has replaced shame and fear, the principal agents of ideological construction, with the power of its destruction.

When in rage, Henry performs actions that cannot be assimilated by any narrative: they emerge with all the accidental force of battle incidents. Rage replaces duration with immediacy, reflection with "glare," appropriation after the fact with loss as what takes the place of fact. After his final battle scene, when Henry accepts the description of his behavior as courageous, his frame of acceptance does not silence his rage, nor does his memory of the moment of desertion repress his fury. In this moment of acceptance, when fear and shame return with all the force of repressed representation, however, Henry does reveal the opposition between courage and rage, and the narrative that implements it, to be the official means of being absorbed back into the world.

Some of Henry's rage reappears, however, when we recall what Henry does not: that Henry earlier felt alienated by this traditional narrative into which he now willingly reinscribes himself. By way of conclusion, we could begin a list of the many shocks of representation, its inadequacy to the situations it should inform with meaning. We could begin this list, moreover, with shock at our recognition of the completely different social worlds separating the dialect Henry Fleming uses when he actually speaks in the novel from the refined discourse of moral discrimination representing his frame of mind throughout. Whenever we begin such a list, however, we cannot fail to include Henry's decision at the end of the novel apparently to continue to rehearse the discourse that unfailingly misrepresents him throughout. If almost a century of critics have cushioned this shock by subscribing to the conventions of "character development," "fear overcome," "recovered responsibility," and "mature judgment," authorized by Henry's final narrative, we begin to recover some of its force when we recall General McClurg's fierce denunciation. Unlike most commentators, the general does not feel persuaded by Henry's final narrative. Instead of commending him for returning to his duty, the general needs to call Henry a coward, a Northerner who fled from the field, and a British sympathizer. The overreaction implicit in the general's ideological overcoding indicates that he, like Henry Fleming, feels the inadequacy of these terms to account for the experiences of war. Thus, however thoroughly he may repudiate Henry's actions, he finally feels persuaded enough by Henry's rage to use his denunciation of Henry's actions as his means of sharing that rage. Indeed his rage does not emanate from disagreement over Henry's actions in battle but from the failure of his own ideology to do justice to experiences in battle. Moreover, when we reread Henry's decision to use guilt and shame as his own private debriefing ceremony from the general's perspective, another implication of Henry's choice comes into view. Henry always deployed guilt and shame as his means of making moral claims on events utterly beyond the control of any individual. At the end of the novel, however, the guilt Henry feels cannot be ascribed to his failure to measure up to a battle narrative. The source of his shame, the tattered soldier, is not a representative of moral responsibility. Neither a coward nor a hero, the tattered soldier remains etched in Henry's memory as a man who did not desert but was deserted on the field. Haunting the boundary lines of traditional war narratives, this spectral figure delineates the extent of what they failed to include. But if Henry's guilt originates from this shadowy figure, it will not, as General McClurg correctly intuits, facilitate his reentry into a conventional ideological framework. Motivated as it is by the specter of the tattered soldier unrepresented by any narrative convention, Henry's guilt does not reactivate representations guaranteed by shame and fear, but acts out the inability of those representations to reabsorb him into the world.

   As we have seen, Crane set out to reduce the Civil War narrative to its barest essentials. He stripped the names from the war battles and emptied out the frame of referents enabling the war to confirm for Americans a sense of their place in the history of nations. By driving a wedge between authorized versions of this war and experiences alien to them, Crane caused a fissure to form in the nation's self-conception, which not even the ideology of union would be sufficient to heal.

FREDERICK NEWBERRY

The Red Badge of Courage
and The Scarlet Letter

It might seem on the face of it entirely too fanciful to claim that Stephen Crane drew upon Hawthorne's *The Scarlet Letter* for *The Red Badge of Courage*. Such a claim would surely find no support among Crane's biographers, since no evidence has yet been found to prove that Crane ever read Hawthorne. Then again, it must be stressed that very little direct evidence has been discovered showing Crane's knowledge of any writer, especially, for my point, up to the period when *The Red Badge* was composed. Not that there has been a shortage of source studies; they have continued to reach print regularly over the years. It is appropriate to remark, however, that most of these studies are admittedly tentative and nearly all bear upon Crane's knowledge of the Civil War.[1] As far as his artistry and ideas are concerned, we know scarcely more about his sources today than did readers fifty years ago. Through *The Red Badge* period, at least, Crane almost never quotes from predecessors, does not obviously refer or allude to them, whether in fiction, correspondence, or miscellaneous works. This situation largely accounts for the bafflement and, in effect, virtual annoyance of some commentators. John Berryman, for example, says that "it is not easy to think of another important prose-writer or poet so ignorant of traditional literature in English as Stephen Crane was and remained."[2] James B. Colvert essentially agrees with this view, while Daniel Hoffman says even more

From *Arizona Quarterly* 38, no. 2 (Summer 1982). © 1982 by the Regents of the University of Arizona.

sweepingly that Crane was ignorant of nearly all the usual literary sources available to late nineteenth-century poets who received a University education.[3] Nevertheless, no one seriously believes that Crane conceived himself, or that he suddenly appeared on the literary scene as ready equipped to write a masterpiece as Frederick Jackson Turner's frontiersman once stepped forth to advance democracy. He had his roots, incurred literary debts, as any writer must. My theory, based on accumulated internal evidence richly suggestive, is that *The Red Badge* owes a fairly substantial debt to *The Scarlet Letter*.

While the contents of the two novels bear little obvious surface resemblance, the red and scarlet emblems in their titles nevertheless invite comparison, as does the exploitation of colors throughout both—especially red, black, and gold.[4] And one critic, though not arguing for a source, compares the "careful symmetry" of the two works and their arrangement in twenty-four chapters.[5] Beyond these immediate similarities in emblems and colors and structure, however, a closer study reveals significant links between the two which, in sum, argue for something other than fortuitous analogies. Hawthorne's "tale of human frailty and sorrow"[6] and Crane's treatment of Henry Fleming's initiation into a world of pain and struggle present the question of guilt and remorse in nearly identical psychological fashion. Involved in his flight from battle and desertion of a fellow soldier who needs help are Henry's efforts to deal with estrangement and hidden guilt, "the consequences of his fall."[7] The case is much the same with Arthur Dimmesdale's attempts to acknowledge his remorse. This similarity R.W. Stallman has observed for his own purposes, saying, "Henry's plight is identical with the Reverend Mr. Dimmesdale's plight in Hawthorne's psychological novel *The Scarlet Letter*."[8] But we may further observe that the ironies involved in Henry's attempts to face guilt in the company of fellow soldiers have more than coincidental resonance with the open and hidden "badges" that shape Hester and Dimmesdale's relationships to their community. Resonance, analogies, similarities—these hardly amount to the stuff from which sources can be indisputably claimed. But if Daniel Knapp is correct, as I believe he is, they add up to all that Crane probably thought his readers needed to unriddle sources he deliberately meant to obscure.[9]

Young and perhaps not yet graduated from "seminary" (*RB*, p. 8), Henry is no intellectual match for the Oxonian Dimmesdale, who is "wise beyond his years" (*SL*, p. 65). Henry is, however, a youth of imagination, nervous and highly sensitive to the threats his own nature poses to his sense of self, much as Dimmesdale is. This sensitivity is evident from the outset in Henry's fear that he might turn tail and run from his first battle. During the second wave of that battle, he does run, overturning the fragile self-image he has built from heroic legends and his initial, largely unconscious submersion in a "subtle battle-brotherhood" when first under fire (*RB*, p. 35). Later, after rejoining scattered and wounded Union troops, he is not unlike Dimmesdale at Hester's ignominious public exposure in the opening scaffold scene, desperately guarding a sanctified role that jars sharply with an inner recognition of his own weakness and guilt. Being "amid wounds" (*RB*, p. 54) without a wound himself intensifies Henry's fear; and following a question from the tattered soldier dogging his heels—"Where yeh hit?" (*RB*, p. 53)— Henry nearly panics, sensing his exposure: "... he now felt that his shame could be viewed. He was continually casting sidelong glances to see if the men were contemplating the letters of guilt he felt burned into his brow" (*RB*, p. 54).

The "letters of guilt" quite tellingly recall the central image of *The Scarlet Letter*, a public emblem exposing private sin to community vision. Henry's belief in the *visibility* of these letters ironically counterpoints the *invisibility* of the wound that would justify his presence among the injured troops; and his testy response to repeated questions about his physical condition reveals the extent to which his frayed nerves sense this irony: "He was enraged against the tattered man and could have strangled him. His companions seemed ever to play intolerable parts. They were ever up-raising the ghost of shame on the stick of their curiosity" (*RB*, p. 61). Guilt makes Henry more than usually self-conscious, even paranoid, and he obsessively misconstrues the good intentions of the tattered soldier, seeing him as the type of a society having a metaphysic designed to expose his shame:

> The simple questions of the tattered man had been knife-thrusts to him. They asserted a society that probes pitilessly at secrets until all is apparent. His late companion's chance persistency made him feel that he could not keep his crime *concealed in his bosom*. It was sure to be brought plain by one of those arrows which cloud the air and are constantly pricking, discovering, proclaiming those things which are willed to be forever hidden. He admitted that he could not defend himself against this agency. It was not within the powers of vigilance. (*RB*, p. 62, emphasis supplied)

The echoes of *The Scarlet Letter* here are most striking, particularly I should think to one who has recently read the two novels and can detect, beyond the shared ideas, the kinship in language and style. The letters of guilt Henry first imagines burned in his brow are transferred, by allusion, to his bosom—concealed there, as is Dimmesdale's shame and the imagined or self-inflicted scarlet letter representing it. Henry's fantasized "society that probes pitilessly at secrets until all is apparent" is precisely the kind of Puritan community Hawthorne delineates, one that takes seriously and punishes individual sin as a matter of public import. This is a society, as Hawthorne describes it in "Endicott and the Red Cross," which "search[es] out even the most secret sins, and expose[s] them to shame, without fear or favor, in the broadest light of the noonday sun."[10] Such is the case with Hester in the beginning of *The Scarlet Letter* as she is examined and publicly humiliated at noonday; and such is the case, significantly reversed, with Dimmesdale in the ironic "noon" of his midnight scaffold scene (*SL*, p. 154). Standing by as witness to that latter scene is Chillingworth, who, with malignant curiosity and force of will, probes the minister's heart throughout the book. In terms of the discovery plot that Henry imagines, the tattered soldier, benign though he is in fact, is evidently Crane's substitute for the hateful physician. Certainly Henry reacts to the tattered man with the same kind of revulsion and dread as Dimmesdale intuitively reacts to Chillingworth.

Finally, Henry's "arrows which cloud the air" suggest that Crane's conception of his character's response to guilt is notably like Hawthorne's portrait of Dimmesdale. Preoccupied as Henry is with his guilt, he naively translates his obsession into the concerns held by a cosmic world: vigilance will not avail against a metaphysical design to expose him. When in his "midnight vigil" Dimmesdale perceives an "A" emblazoned in the sky, he also lapses into a solipsism so immense that he imagines Providence writing his private guilt upon the scroll of heaven. Hawthorne's comment on the minister's preoccupation with self applies just as fittingly to young Henry, however brief the latter's agony: "... it could only be the symptom of a highly disordered mental state, when a man, rendered morbidly self-contemplative by long, intense, and secret pain, had extended his egotism over the whole expanse of nature, until the firmament itself should appear no more than a fitting page for his soul's history and fate" (*SL*, p. 155).

Now of course Dimmesdale's reading his own soul's trouble into the celestial "A" is only an exaggerated version of the Puritan community's habit of interpreting "all meteoric appearances, and other natural phenomena, ... as so many revelations from a supernatural source" (*SL*, p. 154). Henry Fleming's egotistical projections reflect this habit, an essentially religious sensibility, no doubt acquired, from religious instruction, which looks to nature for signs of justification or doom.[11] Whether for good or ill, Henry feels singled out by a universe having something special in store for him. He is therefore quick on the uptake whenever natural events lend themselves to pressing psychological needs. For example, since Henry broods far ahead on the possibility that he might run, and since he checks prior to the first battle "to make sure that the rear was unmolested" for a clear route of escape (*RB*, p. 34), it comes as no surprise when he eventually does run; but especially noteworthy is Crane's labeling the immediate cause of the flight a "revelation" (*RB*, p. 41). No specifics appear defining the nature of this revelation, but it evidently involves permission to run from imagined powers greater than Henry's weak and desperate self. Confirmation from such powers rushes to aid Henry again, when, concealed in the woods and needing to rationalize his smarting guilt, he throws a pinecone at a squirrel and, seeing it run, thinks with satisfaction that "Nature had given him a sign" and "that nature was of his mind" (*RB*, p. 47).

At this early point in the novel, Henry wants to believe that his destiny matters, not only to him but to nature and the universe. In looking to nature for signs much as any good Puritan, he looks for ways to accommodate his cowardice with a preorganized design favoring his election, not his damnation. Yet he has no consistent view of the design or the designer. Nature might justify his act at one moment but in the next something else makes him feel "ill-used" and "trodden beneath the feet of an iron injustice" (*RB*, p. 46). This modern, Kafkaesque intuition, so different from Dimmesdale's unquestioning acceptance of his sin and the "iron framework" of Puritan dogma (*SL*, p. 123), merely launches Henry into hazier abstractions: "He searched about in his mind for an adequate malediction for the indefinite cause, the thing upon which men turn the words of final blame. It—whatever it was—was responsible for him, he said. There lay the fault" (*RB*, p. 64).

Alternately seeming to conceive a benevolent and malevolent God, Henry will later discover that there is no God at all, no "it" to blame—responsibility rests with him alone. He will also learn that teleology is a fiction betraying his shaky self-importance in the "celestial" battle which frightens and makes him feel insignificant (*RB*, p. 49). And the truth in his mother's earlier warning against egotism is part of the lesson. His mother says: "Don't go a-thinkin' you can lick the hull rebel army at the start, because yeh can't. Yer just one little feller amongst a hull lot of others..." (*RB*, p. 7). Romantic visions of heroic deeds, along with notions of special dispensation, lead solely to isolation. Put to a test in the everyday embattled world and failing it, the self is stranded, the ego helpless.

Thus is Henry helpless when he latches on to a fleeing Union soldier and receives a fortunate knock on the head; for with this wound, he gets an apparent red badge of courage. With it, too, begin further parallels to *The Scarlet Letter*. Initially, the badge ironically substitutes for the letters of guilt

Henry earlier felt on his brow. Just as the scarlet letter becomes a focal point for community observation, so too the red badge makes Henry a center of attention when he returns to camp. And much like Hester, who prevents well-meaning people from getting close to her by pointing to the letter, Henry wards off questions about his absence by exploiting the ostensible meaning of his wound. The wound also defines and establishes Henry's new relationship with the regiment; in the same manner as Hester's badge, it shapes his behavior during the second day of battle when, in the eyes of the regiment, Henry fights bravely.

Hester, of course, behaves in such charitable ways that the Boston community eventually perceives new meanings in her symbolic badge; Henry must try to live up to the acknowledged public meaning of his. However antithetical their methods, both characters are not quite consciously involved in the same issue: the discrepancy between inner and outer realities. The assigned public meanings of their badges inadequately describe this discrepancy since they entail metaphorical, one-to-one correspondences between a sign and its denotation. Both characters, psychologically, need wider latitudes of interpreting their badges—Hester to account for herself in other terms than adulteress, Henry to account for his cowardice in paradoxical relation to his wound. They need what Hawthorne and Crane offer their readers, the flexible connotations of symbols.

Although Henry is relieved to find the regiment automatically believing his courageous pose, accepting the wound as a customary metaphor, the relief is not complete. Because with that posture, he supplements his shame with hypocrisy; and this deceptive complication in his mental life relates to a comparable one in *The Scarlet Letter*. During the opening scaffold scene, Dimmesdale acknowledges the full implication of concealing his part in Hester's public shame when, however disingenuously, he urges Hester to name her lover. It would be better for him, the minister argues, to have his sin exposed than "to hide a guilty heart through life. What can thy silence do for him, except it tempt him—yea, compel him, as it were—to add hypocrisy to sin?" (*SL*, p. 67). Effectively admitting his weakness by wanting Hester to do what he hasn't the courage to do himself, intellectually at least Dimmesdale knows that unconfessed sin will take revenge upon the heart.

Henry may not have a conscious urge to confess and thereby relieve the shame lodged in his "bosom," but his shame nags him to such an extreme that he fears he cannot prevent it from showing forth in his behavior, an idea which brings to mind not only Dimmesdale but a large cast of Hawthorne's Puritanic characters. "With his *heart* continually assuring him that he was despicable, he could not exist without making it, through his actions, apparent to all men" (*RB*, p. 67, emphasis supplied). In its own way, this fear may also admit the psychological benefit brought on by confession, that benefit which would bring into more reasonable conformity, as Dimmesdale puts it, the despairing "contrast between what I seem and what I am!" (*SL*, p. 191).[12] But the fear of public exposure continues to dominate Henry as it does Dimmesdale, despite the minister's certainty that it is "better for the sufferer to be free to show his pain ... than to cover it all up in his heart" (*SL*, p. 135).

Mutual concern over a guilty heart and potential outside threats made upon it are further affinities between Henry and Dimmesdale. When at one point below the clergyman's window the infant Pearl affixes burrs to Hester's scarlet letter and then throws one in Dimmesdale's direction, "The sensitive clergyman shrunk, with nervous dread, from the light missile" (*SL*, p. 134). Dimmesdale apprehends that Pearl has made the connection between Hester's visible letter of guilt and his invisible one. This apprehension has its correspondence in Henry's own fear just before rejoining his regiment around the campfire. "He had a conviction that he would soon feel in his *sore heart* the barbed missiles of ridicule. He had no strength to invent a tale; he would be a soft target" (*RB*, p. 75, emphasis supplied). Henry is a soft target, as indicated by his guilty reaction to chance remarks, at first from the tattered soldier and later from comrades; and, much in the manner of Dimmesdale, he does more than simply cringe and shrink at these remarks.

The manifestation of Dimmesdale's guilt and "nervous dread" of exposure is the habitual gesture of placing a hand over his heart. By this action alone, the preternatural Pearl comes to identify the minister. This gesture of guilt is similar to one of Henry's. When the tattered man first asks the youth where he is wounded, Henry's "fingers were picking nervously at one of his buttons. He bended his head and fastened his eyes studiously upon the button [on his chest, I take it] as if it were a little problem" (*RB*, p. 53). The problem, however, is no minor one. Returning to his comrades with the false wound of bravery, Henry feels as much a hypocrite as does Dimmesdale after attempting hollow confessions of sin to the reverential congregation. Henry cannot comment upon his friend's observations that "A shot in th' head ain't foolin' business" but, once again, nervously begins "to fumble with the buttons of his jacket" (*RB*, p. 79). These two gestures associated with Henry's guilty heart metaphorically indicate the location of his real wound.

It is to his heart that Henry looks in the last third of the novel as he prepares for and then enters into ferocious battle. Up to this point, he has been a match for Dimmesdale in the degree of his "self-hate" (*RB*, p. 66).

With the failure of comrades to interpret correctly his head wound, however, Henry affects to believe that his heart is safe and thus recovers his former "self-pride" (*RB*, p. 86), a quality the minister evidently lacks until his determination to preach the concluding Election Day Sermon. But Henry, "In the shade of" his pride's "flourishing growth, ... stood with braced and self-confident legs, and since nothing could now be discovered, he did not shrink from an encounter with the eyes of judges, and allowed no thoughts of his own to keep him from an attitude of manfulness. He had performed his mistakes in the dark, so he was still a man" (*RB*, p. 86). Secrecy, at least for the moment, has its advantages. Akin to the bold way Dimmesdale returns to Boston after imbibing Hester's spirit in the forest, Henry is no longer afraid of a probing and judgmental society. Nor is he afraid of any metaphysical design to expose and punish him. The lessons of his first day of war, he now thinks, are that "retribution was a laggard and blind" (*RB*, p. 86). With an extreme effort to suppress any thought of his cowardice, there is not even a question, at this stage, of psychological retribution. Instead, Henry considers his possibilities in the second day of battle, and he decides that "chance," not a vengeful Calvinistic God, determines who gets stung by the dragon of war. Coupled with this idea is Henry's perception that the war dragon does "not sting with precision" (*RB*, p. 86). His chances seem pretty good. All he must do, as must Dimmesdale if he is to escape to Europe with Hester, is shed a tremulous heart and adopt a stout one, for a "stout heart often defied; and, defying, escaped" (*RB*, p. 86).[13]

Henry is perhaps hoping that with a stout heart he can escape from more than the bullets and shells of battle. But once the second day of fighting begins, Crane suspends commentary on Henry's guilt. Physical action, for the most part, replaces psychological study; or, more precisely, Crane observes how events of war have their own psychology, how they usurp the mind to such an extent that levels of thought take over which may not be considered thought at all, but what might be termed instinct or "battle-madness" (*RB*, p. 128). Henry not only can submerge himself in this madness, but also live out the role implied by the fake red badge. Inasmuch as he can overcome the immobilizing effects of guilt, as well as the false bravado enacted the morning after he rejoins the regiment, Henry reveals a world of possibility foreign to the fixed role of guilt and hypocrisy in Dimmesdale's world, notwithstanding the Puritan's becoming a more effective minister because of his sin.

If *The Red Badge* simply concluded with Henry's successfully emerging from battle, it would be as unsatisfying a novel as *The Scarlet Letter* if it concluded with Dimmesdale's fading on the Atlantic horizon, arm in arm with Hester. For despite Dimmesdale's splendid Election Day Sermon, heartened by the apostasy and sexual energy of Hester, who is paradoxically his "angel" (*SL*, p. 201); and despite Henry's brave actions in battle, heartened by the Union banner, which is his "goddess" (*RB*, p. 108), neither Hawthorne nor Crane will let their subjects off the guilty hook. The last two pages of *The Red Badge* bring together the whole novel in a climactic "procession of memory" (*RB*, p. 133). Henry sees his "public deeds ... paraded in great and shining prominence" (*RB*, p. 133); and from them he concludes that he is "good" (*RB*, p. 134). Yet immediately after these happy reflections return thoughts of his first day's cowardice and, now significantly added to it, of his abandoning the wounded tattered man. Retribution may well be a "laggard," as Henry thought only a few hours before, but at this crucial juncture it clearly has caught up to him. Crane speaks of these thoughts in psychological terms that recall the haunting spirits in Hawthorne's work: the flight appears to Henry as a "ghost"; the reproach he feels for deserting the tattered soldier comes to him as a "spectre"; no matter what he thinks, he is dogged by "the sombre phantom of the desertion in the fields" (*RB*, p. 134). just as Dimmesdale finally sees that going away with Hester could only be a brief palliative, so Henry sees that action cannot provide any final escape from facing the self.

Heroic feats notwithstanding, then, Henry's consciousness is once again defined by shame, not the least remote from the "ruined wall" psychology of human fallibility and guilt which describes Dimmesdale's condition during the forest interview with Hester (*SL*, pp. 200–01). The shift in weight of guilt for Henry's own twice-ruined wall, from cowardice to abandonment of a fellow soldier in need, indicates a key change in his values. A revised form of brotherhood, which is related to but different for its humaneness from the "battle brotherhood," is Henry's moral gain once the battlesmoke has cleared. He is now as much afraid of being "detected in the thing" (*RB*, p. 134), of having others read in his face the phantoms of guilt over the tattered man, as he previously shuddered over their potentially divining his cowardice. Crane gives only brief attention to this shift, but Henry's anguish is no less for it, and probably more, since this particular guilt results from "sin"—the sole appearance of this term in the novel (*RB*, p. 135).

The most important aspect of the shift is Henry's implicit acknowledgment that his deeds on the battlefield cannot offset his "vivid error" (*RB*, p. 135). And as Marston LaFrance has said, "Henry never entirely banishes this ghost [of the tattered man]—an attainment which would be as impossible in Crane's world as it would be in Hawthorne's...."[14] Henry's thinking parallels, in its own secular way, that of his guilty prototype, Dimmesdale. The issue, as Hester states it, is good works. She tries to persuade the minister that, after seven years from the time of sin, his "present life is not less holy, in very truth, than it seems in people's eyes. Is there no reality," she somewhat rhetorically asks, "in the penitence thus sealed and witnessed by good works?" (*SL*, p. 191). Dimmesdale denies the argument. "There is no substance in it!" he declares (*SL*, p. 192); and he has in mind not only his hypocritical penitence but also the ineffectiveness of good works in clearing his conscience.

Henry's heroics on the battlefield, there can be little doubt, bring him great comfort as a corrective to his initial flight.[15] And probably there is no irony in Crane's point that Henry "had been to touch the great death and found that, after all, it was but the great death" (*RB*, p. 135). But when it comes to abandoning the tattered soldier, none of Henry's heroics serves to cancel the act. No wonder, then, that he gives "vent to a cry of sharp irritation and agony" (*RB*, p. 134) in an identical way that Dimmesdale shrieks aloud in the midnight scaffold scene when he can see no escape from his sin. And no wonder, too, that Henry fears his guilt "would stand before him all of his life" (*RB*, p. 135).

To argue that Henry's guilt will indeed stand before him all of his life would be to distort Crane's text. For just as Henry casts aside his cowardice during the second day of battle, so "gradually he mustered force to put the sin [of abandoning the tattered man] at a distance" (*RB*, p. 135). There will be no public confession or expiation as in the climax of *The Scarlet Letter*; and herein lies a major distinction between Henry's late nineteenth-century and Dimmesdale's seventeenth-century worlds. Henry will simply have to live with his guilt (hiding "the inmost Me behind its veil" [*SL*, p. 4] as Hawthorne says of his nineteenth-century narrator), whereas Dimmesdale finally confesses and dies—thereby reuniting inner and outer realities, self and community, self and God, at least in his view. Henry will always be partially isolated; and there is no reason to suppose that he will not be revisited by guilt in his subsequent life.[16] True, Henry turns in the closing lines "to images of tranquil skies, fresh meadows, cool brooks; an existence of soft and eternal peace" (*RB*, p. 135). These are images, however, that Henry pointedly longs for with a "lover's thirst," not those that actually exist or that Henry seems to perceive, as he actually does perceive out of desperation earlier in the novel. What he wants and what he will get are two different things, or they are as mixed as the closing lines of the novel depicting a "golden ray of sun ... [coming] through the hosts of leaden rain clouds" (*RB*, p. 135).

The concluding fate of Henry, so greatly different from that of Dimmesdale, should not obscure the similarities between the two characters elsewhere, similarities that seem much more than archetypal. While it would be useful someday to examine how the major ideas representing the development of American intellectual history alternately influence and confuse Henry—from Calvinism to the Enlightenment and Transcendentalism and Darwinism and beyond—I have been concerned with how closely Henry can be identified with the Calvinistic stage in the psychological and symbolic ways Hawthorne represents them. Henry may or may not consciously arrive at Crane's view that reality is highly indeterminate; but along the way, the revelation of guilt, teleology, symbolic perception and manipulation so closely resemble counterparts in *The Scarlet Letter* as to suggest that Crane was indebted to Hawthorne for their treatment.

NOTES

1. Rather than itemize the long list of source studies on *The Red Badge*, almost all of which are hypothetical, I refer the interested reader to the fine list in Milne Holton, *Cylinder of Vision: The Fiction and Journalistic Writing of Stephen Crane* (Baton Rouge: Louisiana State University Press, 1972), pp. 305–06, n. 32. Studies more recent than Holton's citations, of course, can be found in the annual MLA Bibliography, in *American Literary Scholarship*, and in *The Stephen Crane Newsletter*.

2. John Berryman, *Stephen Crane* (New York: William Sloane Associates, 1950), p. 24. Berryman goes on to say: "Less than any other American writer of the century had he a sense of tradition or continuity in letters, whether English or American; the sense grew in him intermittently only toward the end of his life" (p. 25).

3. James B. Colvert, "The Origins of Stephen Crane's Literary Creed," *Texas Studies in English*, 34 (1955), 181; and Daniel Hoffman, *The Poetry of Stephen Crane* (New York: Columbia University Press, 1957), p. 11. If Crane had been better than the erratic student he was, and if records of his course work in schools survived, tracing his early reading might be facilitated. Lacking the appropriate records, scholars must, as does Thomas A. Gullason, "re-create" Crane's education—see "The Cranes at Pennington Seminary," *American Literature*, 39 (1968), 530–41.

4. Jay Martin is the only critic to equate the titles. See "*The Red Badge of Courage*: The Education of Henry Fleming," in *Twelfth Yale Conference on Teaching English, 1966* (New Haven: Yale University, 1966), p. 76.

5. Eric Solomon, *Stephen Crane: From Parody to Realism* (Cambridge, MA: Harvard University Press, 1966), p. 77. Although he does not claim sources, Solomon also draws parallels between *The Red Badge* and Hawthorne's "The Minister's Black Veil" (p. 87) and "Roger Malvin's Burial" (p. 89).

Holton, p. 305, equating the chapel scene in *The Red Badge* with "My Kinsman, Major Molineux" (and citing Seymour L. Gross, "Hawthorne's 'My Kinsman, Major Molineux': History as Moral Adventure," *Nineteenth-Century Fiction*, 12 [1957], 97–109), all but claims a source when he says: "Neither Professor Gross nor I am offering Hawthorne as a source for Crane's war novel, ... although to resist such an offering is exceedingly difficult...."

6. *The Scarlet Letter*, Centenary Edition, ed. William Charvat et al., I (Columbus: Ohio State University Press, 1962), 48. Hereafter, references to this work will be cited in the text as *SL*. Other volumes of this edition will be cited by title, volume number, and date.

7. *The Red Badge of Courage*, University of Virginia Edition, ed. Fredson Bowers, II

(Charlottesville: The University Press of Virginia, 1975), 67. Hereafter, references to this work will be cited in the text as *RB*.

8. Robert Wooster Stallman, ed., *Stephen Crane: An Omnibus* (New York: Alfred A. Knopf, 1952), p. 198.

9. Knapp's sensitive reading of Crane is indispensable to anyone who wants to see with what care Crane draws on and transforms literary sources, in this case biblical ones. See "Son of Thunder: Stephen Crane and the Fourth Evangelist," *Nineteenth-Century Fiction*, 24 (1969), 253–91.

10. "Endicott and the Red Cross," *Twice-told Tales*, Centenary Edition, IX (1974), 436.

11. By claiming that Henry has a religious sensibility, I do not mean to slight other influences on his mind that color and distort his perceptions. Nor do I mean to endorse a religious interpretation of the novel and enter the critical debate over that issue. As I see it, part of Henry's mind has been influenced by Calvinism, similar to, if not identical with, Hawthorne's treatment of Puritanism. Crane's own experience with moderate and, especially, extreme forms of Methodism, acquired in the former case through his clergyman father and in the latter through his mother and her clerical forebears, is consonant with this Calvinistic influence revealed by Henry. Having this connection in mind, Amy Lowell offers an acute interpretation of Crane, in the spirit of which I believe Henry might profitably be seen: "Crane was so steeped in the religion in which he was brought up that he could not get it out of his head. He disbelieved it and he hated it, but he could not free himself from it." See her Introduction to *The Black Riders and Other Lines* in *The Work of Stephen Crane*, ed. Wilson Follett, VI (New York: Alfred A. Knopf, 1926), xix. Hoffman, pp. 43–99, has dealt most thoroughly and perceptively with evangelical Methodism, or hell-fire Calvinism, in Crane's background.

12. In keeping with his religious interpretation of *The Red Badge*, Stallman links Henry to Dimmesdale in reference to confession: "Redemption begins in confession, in absolution.... Henry's wounded conscience is not healed until he confesses the truth to himself and opens his eyes to new ways..." (p. 198).

13. In such defiance, Henry adopts yet another experimental role to pose against the guardian powers of judgment and damnation. The absolute existence of these powers is not nearly as germane as Henry's fear that they exist, a fear apparently resulting from long exposure to evangelical Calvinism. Both in his fear and defiance, Henry parallels Crane's own struggle with natural depravity and a vengeful God, ideas which Crane took seriously enough not to dismiss but to utilize and then rebel against them. The transformation of Henry's guilty heart to a defiant one is a case in point. As Daniel Hoffman sees it, Crane was raised on the notion that the heart is the repository for all that is vile in depraved man. See especially pp. 54–56.

14. Marston LaFrance, *A Reading of Stephen Crane* (Oxford: Clarendon Press, 1971), p. 122.

15. When, after he becomes the color-bearer in the second day's battle, Henry "passed over his brow a hand that trembled" (*RB*, p. 113), is he not symbolically erasing the imaginary letters of guilt for his first day's flight while also subconsciously remembering the head wound whose courageous meaning he wants to justify retroactively?

16. One must be cautious in drawing upon Crane's "The Veteran" (1896), in which Henry Fleming makes another appearance, now a wizened grandfather and cracker-barrel celebrity. But it is worth mentioning that in this story Henry admits to running from his first battle, much to the crestfallen awe of his romantic grandson, yet says nothing about the deeper shame of abandoning the tattered soldier. Nevertheless, as if that shame has taught him the value of charity, Henry sacrifices his life in an effort to save two colts from a burning barn.

CHESTER L. WOLFORD

The Anger of Henry Fleming:
The Epic of Consciousness &
The Red Badge of Courage

The immense poetry of war and the poetry of a work of the imagination are two different things. In the presence of the violent reality of war, consciousness takes the place of the imagination.... It follows that the poetry of war ... constitutes a participating in the heroic.

—WALLACE STEVENS[1]

War is a teacher who educates through violence; and he makes men's characters fit their conditions.

—THUCYDIDES

*T*he *Red Badge of Courage* establishes Stephen Crane as a writer formally and solidly within the great tradition established and fostered by Homer, Virgil, Milton, and others. While including many of the trappings and conventions and much machinery of formal epic, *The Red Badge* also shares with the epic a more essential quality: the tradition of epic competition. Although greatly oversimplified, a broad review of that tradition would read rather like a social history of Western society over the last twenty-five hundred years.

Because it began traditionally with Homer and historically sometime before 400 B.C. in the eastern Mediterranean, the tradition of epic

From *The Anger of Stephen Crane: Fiction and the Epic Tradition.* © 1983 by the University of Nebraska Press.

competition is as old as any in Western literature. One version of an ancient romantic work called "The Contest of Homer and Hesiod," for example, relates how Homer and Hesiod competed to determine who was the best poet.[2] A comparison of the recitations, as well as the judgment of the audience, indicates that Homer was clearly the better of the two. Yet the king of Chalcis in Euboea, where the contest was reportedly held, awarded the prize to Hesiod, saying that "he who called upon men to follow peace and husbandry should have the prize rather than one who dwelt upon war and slaughter."

While demonstrating the antiquity of epic competition, the story makes another point vital to the tradition and to *The Red Badge*: epics and epic poets do not always compete over literary values. Although the reputations of Virgil and Milton as epic poets rest in part upon how well they compare aesthetically with Homer, nonliterary factors such as cultural and religious values also claim the attention of these men. The most important of these values for the epic is the different ideal of heroism held by each poet, particularly regarding the object of man's duty. The Homeric epics may be termed "individual" because they tend to glorify the individual man. Virgil's is a "group" epic because it glorifies Rome and defines the state as a more worthy object of duty than the individual. Milton attempts, among other things, to glorify a Puritan God and to justify worthiness in his sight as the object of man's duty. To the degree that Milton saw man's task as an attempt to reproduce God's kingdom in the self and community of Christians, *Paradise Lost* and *Paradise Regained* become "group" epics. One way, then, to look at the history of the West is as a movement from man being accountable only for himself—man as individualistic and ego-centric—to man as part of something larger, more enduring and significant than himself.

Each of these views finds an embodiment in a great epic poet's notion of heroism, for heroism consists of fulfilling the demands of duty. The Homeric hero ascribes to the code of *areté*, which demands that he strive ceaselessly for the first prize. The driving force behind all the hero's actions, *areté* often connotes values different from Roman and Christian virtue. Virtues lauded over the last fifteen hundred years and more—loyalty, honesty, charity, fair play—are simply not part of the code of *areté*; Achilles deserted the field and his friends and spent much of the war in an adolescent funk and Odysseus was a liar and a cheat, but both were great warriors and so have the highest *areté*.[3]

What distinguishes Virgil's Aeneas from Homeric heroes is not the greatness of his deeds but the reasons for performing them. Virgil's epithet for Aeneas is "pius," a term denoting more than "pious" for Aeneas is also "dutiful." Careful to pour appropriate libations for the gods, Aeneas also is concerned for his family and his destiny. Seeker of peace, invincible in war, believer in law, Aeneas is the heroic ideal of the *Romanum Imperium* of Augustus.

To explain how Aeneas, a second-level Homeric hero in the *Iliad*, became a metaphor for Rome in the *Aeneid* would require several volumes of social, intellectual, and literary history that would carry one from Attic to Roman civilizations. The problem for Virgil, however, was that Homer still dominated the genre in Augustan Rome and his heroes were still revered. As a result, Virgil was forced to compete unevenly with Homer. If Rome were superior to Homeric Greece, then the great Roman epic would have to be superior to the Homeric epics. Virgil succeeded, at least politically, by elevating the Roman hero and debasing the Homeric, elevating *pietas* and debasing *areté*. Thus Turnus, *alius Achilles*, embodies *areté*, and when Aeneas kills him in the poem's final fines, Virgil metaphorically "kills" Achilles, *areté*, and the Homeric epic. Later Christian epic poets such as Tasso, Camoens, Dante, and Ariosto also despise *areté*—which they saw as almost identical to hubris—and show their contempt by assigning it as a quality belonging to their heroes' enemies. Milton's Satan belongs to this type, and in spite of his attractiveness as a Homeric or Shelleyan hero, he is nevertheless a personification of evil.[4] Milton's concept of heroism and duty is as complex as his use of the epic medium, but it is also clear that genuine heroism lies in "true patience and heroic martyrdom." The real Christian hero seeks glory by following the New Testament and dedicates his deeds *ad majoram gloriam Dei*. How one plays the game determines whether one wins or loses.

When Crane includes these notions of heroism and duty in *The Red Badge*, he undertakes a task crucial to writing epics. Because these concepts of heroism and duty are among the most influential in Western history, when Crane denigrates and replaces them, he rewrites, in a very real sense, the cultural history of the West.

Inward Repudiations

The first chapter of *The Red Badge* presents heroic ideals in the mind of Henry Fleming, a "youth" inclined by instinct toward *areté*, but checked by "religious and secular education" so that he feels himself to be a part of something much larger than himself. Henry is introduced into the story and is immediately engaged in a debate with himself over "some new thoughts that had lately come to him" (2:4). On the one hand, he sees himself in expressly Homeric terms, with "peoples secure in the shadow of his eagle-eyed prowess" (2:5). In retrospect, he remembers having "burned several times to enlist. Tales of great movements shook the land. They might not be distinctly Homeric, but there seemed to be much glory in them. He had read of marches, sieges, conflicts, and he had longed to see it all. His busy mind had drawn for him large pictures extravagant in color, lurid with breathless deeds" (2:5). On the other hand, his mother, the voice of Christian-group ideals, "had discouraged him." Her advice upon his enlistment is the advice of the group: "Don't go a-thinkin' you can lick the hull rebel army at the start, because yeh can't. Yer just one little feller amongst a hull lot of others, and yeh've got to keep quiet an' do what they tell yeh" (2:7). Contrary to Henry's Grecian mood—he would rather have heard "about returning with his shield or on it"—his mother's relationship to Christianity is everywhere apparent. Her only remark upon hearing of Henry's enlistment is "The Lord's will be done," and when he leaves she says simply, "The Lord'll take keer of us all" (2:7).

As a surrogate mother, the army too puts a damper on his heated individualism. Before leaving home, "he had felt growing within him the strength to do mighty deeds of arms," but after spending "months of monotonous life in a camp," Henry comes "to regard himself as part of a vast blue demonstration" (2:8).

Throughout the first half of *The Red Badge*, the competition between the individualism of Henry's *areté* and the collectivism of *pietas* and "heroic martyrdom" swings between extremes. In his first engagement, Henry seems finally to give in to the standards of the group: "He suddenly lost concern for himself and forgot to look at a menacing fate. He became not a man but a member. He felt that something of which he was a part—a regiment, an army, a cause, or a country—was in crisis. He was welded into a common personality which was dominated by a single desire" (2:34). Soon, the group becomes even more important to him than the causes: "He felt the subtle battle brotherhood more potent even than the cause for which they were fighting. It was a mysterious fraternity" (2:35).

Much has been made of Henry's joining the subtle brotherhood, but few remember that when the enemy makes a second charge against the regiment, the mysterious fraternity dissolves under an individuality revived by Henry's sense of self-preservation. He turns tail and runs. Although Achilles has more grace and style, the effect is the same in either case: both Henry and Achilles desert their friends in the field. To say, as many do, that Henry should be damned for his desertion is to speak from an historically narrow perspective; from an Homeric standpoint, one cannot be so quick to judge. In fact, no moral judgments necessarily result from Henry's flight. If Henry can get away with it (he does), if no one finds out about it (no one does), and if later he can perform "great deeds" (he does), then that is all that matters. By the end of the sixth chapter, Henry's individualism, his Homeric sense, seems to have won a limited victory—victory because Henry has escaped being subsumed by the group, limited because his sense of shame dogs him throughout the novel.

In the novel's first half the battle for Henry's allegiance to Homeric or Christian-group values occurs in Henry's mind. In the first six chapters, Henry's conflicting feelings need little prodding; in the second six, the action of the novel intensifies, as do attacks on his individualism. In this quarter of the novel, Henry enters the "forest chapel," sees Jim Conklin die in a Christ-like way, and is mentally and verbally assaulted by the "tattered man." Here, too, he receives his "red badge of courage."

It should not be surprising in light of the epic structure that this section of *The Red Badge* is filled with religious imagery. Much critical ink has been spilt in a controversy over whether or not Crane, given his naturalistic bent and nihilist vision, intends Jim Conklin, for example, to represent Christ, or the tattered man to represent the Christian-group ideal; many feel that Crane himself was confused about it and that the novel fails because he fails to resolve the problem. From the standpoint of examining the traditional epic qualities of the book, there is no problem. These chapters mark what ultimately becomes a failure of the Christian-group value system—with two thousand years of indoctrination behind it—to make Henry Fleming return to the fold. It is not Crane's intent to have the reader see things in a religious way, but to see Henry succumb to the pathetic fallacy of Christian-colored glasses.

Arriving at a spot deep in the woods, Henry hears the trees "sing a hymn of twilight.... There was a lull in the noises of insects as if they had bowed their beaks and were making a devotional pause. There was silence save for the choruses of trees" (2:49). Henry now sees things through a "religious half light," and the forest seems to form a "chapel" complete with "arching boughs," "green doors," and a "brown carpet."

When Crane places more emphasis on character and action than upon natural scenes, Christian morality and group ethics are even more strongly merged. Both value systems require humility, love, awe, and admiration for something perceived as greater than and outside of the individual. In chapters six to twelve, the screw is tightened on Henry's conscience, demanding both complete subjection and unqualified support. The first person Henry sees after leaving the forest is the tattered man, who, for Henry, embodies the Christian-group ideal. The tattered man is introduced by a dignified and classical anaphora as if he were the subject of an ancient fable: "There was a tattered man...." This archetypal follower listens to an officer's "lurid tale" with "much humility." Rough as the ragged private looks, his voice is as "gentle as a girl's," and when he speaks it is "timidly." His "pleading" eyes are described in a simile bearing a Christian symbol that could not have escaped Crane; they are "lamblike." With a general "air of apology in his manner," the tattered man is so humble, timid, and conventionally feminine that he becomes a caricature of a Christian-group member. Even his physiognomy betrays an overwhelming love for the group. "His homely face was suffused with a light of love for the army which was to him all things powerful and beautiful." Crane here takes standard emotional slither from the rhetoric of nineteenth-century religious writers' descriptions of people saved at camp meetings and attaches it to the army. All of the tattered man's questions are uttered "in a brotherly tone," and his "lean features wore an expression of awe and admiration." In short, he must have been meant to be a caricature, for even his breathing has in it a "humble admiration."[5]

It is also clear that Henry sees Jim Conklin in a "religious half light." Stallman's original reading of Conklin as Christ is fundamentally correct if one understands that it is Henry and not Crane who sees Conklin as Christ.[6] Few figures in American literature have a better claim to the trappings of Christ's Passion than does Jim Conklin. His initials are J. C., he is wounded in the side, he dies on a hill, he is a "devotee of a mad religion," and his death stirs "thoughts of a solemn ceremony." Those who deny that Conklin is a Christ-figure usually do so by pointing out that Conklin is a loud, cracker-crunching, rumormonger. Such evidence is specious, since these qualities are part of Jim only before he became "not a man but a member" by staying on the line during the battle.[7] Some also forget that Crane's intent is to show that Henry sees Conklin in this way, not that Conklin is that way.

One way to place the various episodes of the first half into a perspective of the moral and social competition between Christian-group values and the Homeric ideal of individualism (areté) may be to describe that epic competition as a representation of the psychology of Christian conversion from an egocentric individualism to an altruistic membership in the flock. The pattern is familiar; as a moral being, man in Christian process moves from the commission of sin to guilt, to alienation, to a desire for expiation, to confession, and finally to redemption.[8] In the end, the process fails to redeem Henry for Christianity, but it does give him a rough time of it, and it organizes the epic competition and psychology of the novel's first half.

Three particular episodes are representative of this psychological movement. The episodes with Mrs. Fleming, Jim Conklin, and the tattered man each appear to bring Henry steadily closer to rejecting his Homeric individuality while ultimately functioning ironically to force his acceptance of areté. By the time he is hit on the head and receives his "red badge of courage," Henry has sloughed off the Christian-group concept of heroism. His red badge is, however, not ironical in that he receives it for an act of cowardice; rather it is an outward sign—what the Greeks called *geras*—of his accomplishment in rejecting two thousand years of social and religious indoctrination. An epic feat.

Occurring in the first chapter, the "Mrs. Fleming" episode serves to increase Henry's feelings of sin and guilt over his Homeric sense of selfish individuality which encompasses egoism, insensitivity, and the pursuit of personal glory at all costs—*areté*. The episode opens with Henry in his hut (and *in medias res*) remembering his earlier thoughts about "breathless deeds," his "burning to enlist," and his having "despaired of witnessing a Greeklike struggle."

Mrs. Fleming is a stereotype of the pious, hard-working, long-suffering, farm boy's mother. Her views are Christian-group oriented and come from "deep conviction." Her "ethical motives" are "impregnable." Guilt and remorse over his insensitivity toward his mother work on Henry as he remembers a scene from his leave-taking: "When he had looked back from the gate, he had seen his mother kneeling among the potato parings. Her brown face, up-raised, was stained with tears, and her spare form was quivering" (2:7–8). The effect on Henry is predictable: "He bowed his head and went on, feeling suddenly ashamed of his purposes" (2:8). Significantly, he is not so much ashamed of enlisting as he is of his purposes, his longing for the glory road of individual heroism that scatters the hurt feelings and genuine needs of others along the roadside. Christians would accuse Henry of *hubris*; Augustan Romans would not chide him for enlisting but for having done so without thought to duty and family; Homeric Greeks would have wondered what all the fuss was about, shrugged their shoulders, and remarked that while the action might be a little sad, it was also probably necessary: how else become a hero? Unlike Homeric heroes, however, Henry leaves for war carrying in his soul the cultural burdens of twenty centuries of self-condemnation for succumbing to *areté*.

It is important to emphasize the universal qualities of the novel in general and of Henry Fleming in particular. He is at once common and uncommon; he is Man rebelling against his Mother, Mankind (or at least the archetypal American in the archetypal American novel) attempting to slough off the Past. In the American experience this last action ties Henry closely to the transcendental movement, as well as to such archetypal figures as Huck Finn, Natty Bumppo, Rip Van Winkle, and a host of other American heroes. The difference is that unlike Twain, Cooper, and Irving, Crane is using the formal epic ironically to destroy the traditions of heroism, and epic competition is used because its very purpose is to disparage what the past has considered to be the highest expression of man's duty, courage.

The Jim Conklin episode carries Henry a step further in the process by adding to sin and guilt the anguish of alienation and the desire for expiation through good works. After deserting the regiment and wandering through the forest, Henry joins a band of wounded men moving toward the rear. These men have stood their ground—for God and country possibly, for the group certainly. Their wounds seem to symbolize their sacrifices and their devotion to duty. Seeing them in this way, Henry feels alienated: "At times he regarded the wounded soldiers in an envious way.... He wished that he, too, had a wound, a red badge of courage" (2:54). Such a badge would grant to Henry membership and acceptance in the group, would assuage his guilt and close the gap between himself and the others caused by his alienation. Henry's anguish is now greater than during the earlier episode: "He felt his shame could be viewed. He was continually casting sidelong glances to see if the men were contemplating the letters of guilt he felt burned in his brow" (2:54). At this stage Henry is Stephen Crane's Dimmesdale, and the only difference between the two is that Crane's character ultimately is able to "put the sin at a distance." Hawthorne's protagonist never can.

Feeling that he bears the Mark of the Beast, Henry is then confronted by Jim Conklin's wounds, and in his already anguished state, Henry is quite ready to see in Jim an exceptional Christian devotion to duty and sacrifice for the group. Jim's actions, however, deny Henry expiation and even serve further to heighten his anxiety. Henry's attempts to receive absolution are repulsed, for Jim only wants to be left alone to die: "The youth put forth anxious arms to assist him, but the tall soldier went firmly on as if propelled.... The youth had reached an anguish where the sobs scorched him. He strove to express his loyalty.... The youth wished his friend to lean upon him, but the other always shook his head and strangely protested. 'No—no—no—leave me be—leave me be—'.... and all the youth's offers he brushed aside" (2:56). Henry's view of Jim as a Christ is Henry's alone. The youth's attempts to assuage his guilt in a bath of atonement fail; although he asks, he does not receive—Jim Conklin will have none of it. All that remains is Henry's very real and painful desire for redemption. Redemption itself is as far away as ever.

Henry's Christian-group consciousness is pushed to its limits in the "tattered man" episode. There are two "sins" here: one is Henry's refusal to confess his earlier desertion of the regiment, and the other is his desertion of the tattered man, an act which redoubles his guilt. When Henry meets the tattered man, the latter repeatedly asks him, "Where yeh hit?" This question, asked over and over again, causes Henry to feel the "letters of guilt" burned, Dimmesdale-like, into his forehead. Instead of causing Henry to repent, however, the letters merely force him to desert the wounded tattered man and leave him to wander off into the fields to die. Immediately after deserting the tattered man, Henry's guilt reaches almost unbearable proportions: "The simple questions of the tattered man had been knife thrusts to him. They asserted a society that probes pitilessly at secrets until all is apparent.... He could not keep his crime concealed in his bosom.... He admitted that he could not defend himself" (2:62). Believing that "he envied those men whose bodies lay strewn" on the field, he explicitly wants to be redeemed: "A moral vindication was regarded by the youth as a very important thing" (2:67).

Confused, guilt-ridden, and afraid that the group may discover his "sin," Henry's mind goes through, as in the first chapter, the same metronomic movement between the demands of the group and the desires of the individual, but with more pain. Henry's anguish remains severe throughout the eleventh chapter. In the twelfth chapter, however, this changes.

Chapter 12 is the last chapter of the first half of *The Red Badge*. Like the end of the first half of the *Iliad*, the *Odyssey*, the *Aeneid*, *Paradise Lost*, and other epics, it includes both a culmination of the first half and a preparation for the second. In the twelfth book of the *Iliad*, the Trojans have broken into the Greek encampment. They are never again so close to victory. In the *Odyssey*, the hero nears the end of his wanderings and sets off in the next book for a final successful junket to Ithaca, where he will lay plans to set his house in order. In the *Aeneid*, Aeneas is about to land in Italy, thus putting himself in a position to fulfill his destiny by founding the Roman nation. In *Paradise Lost*, the battle in Heaven ends; Satan and his angels have fallen into Hell, and the stage is set for the second half: the fall of man. Similarly, in *The Red Badge*, Henry completes his epic of return by sloughing off his Christian-group conscience: he accepts his individuality, and he is then prepared to battle the group in the second half.

Henry is "reborn" after being hit on the head in chapter 12.[9] The language of the episode is carefully, even poetically, rendered to represent rebirth. After watching a group of retreating soldiers, Henry runs down from a rise, grabs one of the soldiers, and is clouted for his trouble:

> [*The other soldier*] *adroitly and fiercely swung his rifle. It crushed upon the youth's head. The man ran on.*
>
> *The youth's fingers had turned to paste upon the other's arm. The energy was smitten from his muscles. He saw the flaming wings of lightning flash before his vision. There was a deafening rumble of thunder within his head.*
>
> *Suddenly his legs seemed to die. He sank writhing to the ground. He tried to arise. In his efforts against the numbing pain he was like a man wrestling with a creature of the air.*

> *There was a sinister struggle.*
>
> *Sometimes he would achieve a position half erect, battle with the air for a moment, and then fall again, grabbing at the grass. His face was of a clammy pallor. Deep groans were wrenched from him.*
>
> *At last, with a twisting movement, he got upon his hands and knees, and from thence, like a babe trying to walk, to his feet.... he went lurching over the grass.*
>
> *He fought an intense battle with his body. His dulled senses wished him to swoon and he opposed them stubbornly, his mind portraying unknown dangers and mutilations if he should fall upon the field. He went tall soldier fashion. [2:70–71]*

Structurally, the passage focuses first on the falling away of the old in a metaphorical death. Henry loses his sight, his hearing, and then his ability to stand erect. In the middle is a five-word, one-sentence paragraph describing a "sinister struggle" between life and death. From there, the reborn Henry gets up on his hands and knees "like a babe," and finally is able to walk. In spite of the almost allegorical nature of the passage, its essence remains one of a very physical, almost literal, and, most important, quite individual rebirth.

One cannot help but think that the anthropological cast of the passage is intentional. At least, it demonstrates that Crane, however unconsciously, was aware of the consequences for thought of the Darwinian revolution. For Henry, as for mankind, the traditional past could no longer provide solace. Indeed, as the second half of *The Red Badge* shows, the traditional past had to be rolled up and replaced by naturalism and impressionism. These terms, given Holton's appraisal of elements shared by definitions of the former and Nagel's definition of impressionism, can be seen in some fights as nearly synonymous and as twin effects of *Origin of the Species* and of the dissemination of other scientific discoveries.[10]

The action reported in this passage is unlike anything else in the book. Except for a later instance when he pushes another fellow, it is Henry's only hostile physical encounter in the novel. Certainly this is not Christian-group combat; it is especially unusual for those engaged in modern warfare. Prior to this point all battles have been described as remote from the individual. Cannons roar at each other, and men shoot at "vague forms" shifting and running through the smoke of many rifles. Always the action has been described in terms of one group charging toward or retreating from another. Moreover, his adversary fights under the same flag as Henry.

Here, for the first time, is a representation of a "Greeklike struggle" that once had been merely a part of Henry's dreams. It has not developed as Henry had expected, and may not be distinctly Homeric, but it is close to primitive hand-to-hand combat, and bears little resemblance to the "mighty blue machine" of the group. For the first time, Henry struggles with another man. Further, Henry's wound is unusual for participants in a modern, group war. Henry's wound is not from a bullet, but from the butt end of a modern weapon used as the most ancient of weapons; as one fellow observes, "It's raised a queer lump as if some feller lammed yeh on the head with a club" (2:77).

Henry's wandering off "tall soldier fashion" after receiving the blow on the head does not mean that Henry has been converted to a group view of things. To see Jim as a Christian-group figure is to make the same mistake Henry made. Strip away the dramatic symbolism of Henry's former vision of Conklin and one is left with a man dying, alone, unwilling to be helped, and as afraid of mutilation as any Homeric hero. Speech and action are "real"; Henry's interpretation of them may not be. When Henry thus goes "tall soldier fashion," it is not necessarily as a Christ-figure. Henry is in no shape at this point to interpret events; in this instance, the information comes directly from the narrator.[11] The dying Jim Conklin and the wounded Henry Fleming are linked, or seem to be linked, only by a desire to escape the group.

Wandering in the gathering darkness, Henry is finally given direction by an epic guide. Like the role of the captain in "The Reluctant Voyagers," the function of the "cheery man" is traditional to the machinery of epic. As Ariadne helps Theseus, Thetis comforts Achilles, Athena aids Odysseus, Venus supports and guides Aeneas, and Virgil leads Dante, so the cheery man helps Henry to gain self-control, and, as Gibson points out, places him in a position to confront those forces which he otherwise would have little power to oppose but which he must overcome in order to complete his epic task.[12] The cheery man leads Henry back to the regiment.

Unlike the two men in "The Reluctant Voyagers," Henry appreciates, albeit somewhat after the fact, the cheery man's help. And well he should, for as he staggers towards the campfires of his regiment in the beginning of the second half of *The Red Badge*, he has nearly done the impossible. In a sense, he has performed more courageously than Achilles. Peliades had only to reach his goal of *areté*, while Fleming had first to throw off his sense of sin and alienation. On one level, he has suffered all the slings and "arrows of scorn" that can be shot at an individual by the archers of conscience, guilt, and alienation from the group. On another level, Henry has forced his way back through two millennia of nationalism and Christianity. Such an act is impossible for an ordinary man. To oppose and overcome, even to a limited degree, the teachings of secular and religious culture is an almost incredible, even epic, feat.

Outward Wars
Yet the battle is only half won. As the first twelve chapters are concerned with
Henry's struggle to gain individuality of mind, the second half of *The Red
Badge* concerns Henry's conflict with the same forces in the externalized,
"outside" world. In terms of the epic of consciousness, the first half concerns
Henry's escape from the cave, his coming to consciousness, and his gaining
self-control, that is, coming to terms with alienation from the other—the
group and the rest of the material world—and the fact of death. Having
come to terms internally in the first half, he is ready to confront the other
externally in the second half. Here, as in the *Aeneid*, the hero is confronted
with a competition between his new-found values and an externalized
embodiment and proponent of the value system he has recently overcome
internally. In the second half of the *Aeneid*, Aeneas must confront, battle, and
finally defeat the Roman version of the Homeric ideal of *areté* embodied in
Turnus. In the last half of *The Red Badge*, Henry must confront, engage, and
overcome Wilson, who has not only been "converted" and initiated into the
group, but also has become the embodiment of Christian-group
consciousness and its value system.

When Henry returns to confront the group, to enter into the midst of
the "subtle brotherhood," he manages to resist its attempts to "initiate" him
into membership. Henry seems aware at this point of the nature of this
confrontation, because "there was a sudden sinking of his forces. He thought
he must hasten to produce his tale to protect him from the missiles already
at the lips of his redoubtable comrades." The "information" is a baldfaced lie:
"Yes, Yes. I've—I've had an awful time. I've been all over. Way over on the
right. I got separated from the regiment. Over on the right, I got shot. In the
head. I never saw such fighting" (2:75–76). The he works, and Henry seems
to become the lost sheep returned to the fold.

Wilson, the sentinel who recognizes Henry staggering into camp,
seems remarkably changed. Henry now views Wilson much as he had viewed
the tattered man, only with colder eyes. In the first chapter, Wilson acted the
part of a *miles gloriosus*, a parody of Achilles. In that chapter, which mirrors
the first book of the *Iliad*, Wilson engaged Jim Conklin in an argument. Like
Achilles and Agamemnon, "they came near to fighting over" their
differences. Wilson also spent much time bragging about his prowess in
battle. Now, however, Wilson seems to embody Christian-group values.
When first seen in chapter 13, he is standing guard over the regiment. Upon
recognizing Henry, he lowers his rifle and welcomes the youth back: "There
was husky emotion in his voice" (2:75). Later, while dressing Henry's wound,
Wilson acts out the feminine role of the soothing and ducking mother hen
who welcomes one of her lost chicks back to the coop: "He had the bustling

ways of an amateur nurse. He fussed around" (2:78). When Wilson puts his cloth on Henry's head, it feels to the youth "like a tender woman's hand" (2:79).[13]

Because he didn't run, Wilson was subsumed by that "regiment, army, cause," or country; he joined the "subtle brotherhood," the "mysterious fraternity born of the smoke and danger of death." At the beginning of the battle neither Henry nor Wilson had gained a genuine sense of individuality; both at that point were vulnerable to the group. Because he ran, Henry was excluded from the ego-annihilating forces which Wilson joined.

As a result, Henry and Wilson are now two very different kinds of men. Wilson, who had earlier jumped at any chance to get into an argument or a fight, now stops a fight between two men; he explains to Henry, "I hate t' see th' boys fightin' 'mong themselves" (2:84). Henry, however, feels no such obligation to become a peacemaker; he laughs and reminds Wilson of an earlier fight the formerly loud soldier had had with "that Irish feller." Certain that he would be killed, Wilson had given Henry a packet of letters before the first battle with instructions that they be sent home after his "imminent" death. The contrast between Wilson's new-found humility and Henry's arrogance appears when Wilson asks for the letters back. Wilson flushes and fidgets, "suffering great shame." When Henry gives them back, he tries "to invent a remarkable comment upon the affair. He could conjure up nothing of sufficient point. He was compelled to allow his friend to escape unmolested with his packet. And for this he took unto himself considerable credit. It was a generous thing.... The youth felt his heart grow more strong and stout. He had never been compelled to blush in such a manner for his acts; he was an individual of extraordinary virtues" (2:87). There is a double irony here. On one level, the passage mocks Henry, but on another, Henry is essentially correct. He has not been "compelled" to undergo the humility of confession. He has overcome in large measure the need for communal redemption of guilt and shame. He does, indeed, have extraordinary "virtues," but they are the "virtues" of *areté*, pride, and individualism.

As they begin the second day of battle, Henry and Wilson are very soon recognized by the group as entirely different kinds of heroes. First, Henry is transfigured by *menos*, the animallike battle-rage of Homeric heroes: "Once, he, in his intent hate, was almost alone and was firing when all those near him ceased. He was so engrossed in his occupation that he was not aware of a lull" (2:96). One man derides him for not stopping when the others had, but the lieutenant (whose "voice" had been described as expressing a "divinity") praises Henry in animistic terms: "By heavens, if I had ten thousand wild-cats like you I could tear th' stomach outa this war in less'n a week!" (2:97). Finally, Henry receives the recognition from the group that Homeric heroes seek. He is viewed as someone separate, distinct, and most important, superior: "They now looked upon him as a war-devil" (2:97), they are "awe-struck."

Wilson is a hero of a different age. Henry does not incite the group to action; his only concern is for his own heroism. Wilson, the hero of the group, serves this purpose: "The friend of the youth aroused. Lurching suddenly forward and dropping to his knees, he fired an angry shot at the persistent woods. This action awakened the men. They huddled no more like sheep ... they began to move forward" (2:106–7).

Wilson has become the leader of his flock, and Henry has become an Homeric "war devil."

There are a number of confrontations between Henry and Wilson in their respective roles as individual and group heroes. The morning after Henry's return to camp, for example, Wilson "tinkers" with the bandage on Henry's head, trying to keep it from slipping. Friendly, consoling, and helpful, Wilson is berated by an unfriendly, arrogant Henry: "Gosh-dern it ... you're the hangdest man I ever saw! You wear muffs on your hands. Why in good thunderation can't you be more easy? ... Now, go slow, an' don't act as if you was nailing down carpet." Henry seems already to have gained superiority over his counterpart: "He glared with insolent command at his friend" (2:81).

Later when Henry remembers the letters Wilson had given him, he again feels his superiority and thinks in terms of dominance: "He had been possessed of much fear of his friend, for he saw how easily questionings could make holes in his feelings.... He now rejoiced in the possession of a small weapon with which he could prostrate his comrade at the first signs of cross-examination. He was master" (2:85). Wilson remains a symbol to Henry of Christian-group conscience throughout the second half, and Henry never completely overcomes his own Christian-group sense. It dogs him.

The crucial confrontation between the two heroes is a face-to-face physical encounter on the battlefield. It occurs, fittingly, in a contest to determine who will carry the flag across the field in the charge. For Wilson, the traditional approach to the flag as a symbol of a group is most appropriate. Possession of the flag would mean that Wilson had reached the goal of all group epic heroes: to become the idealized symbol of the group. For Henry, the flag is also a symbol of the group. But Homeric heroes strive after *geras*, the prize, the symbol by which they are acknowledged by the group as superior. Possession of the flag would mean that he had fulfilled the aspect of *areté* that demands that he achieve supremacy over the group. Consequently, the flag becomes for Henry "a goddess, radiant, that bent its form with an imperious gesture to him. It was a woman ... that called to him with the voice of his hopes" (2:108).

Since the flag is a symbol both for the group and for the superior individual, it is natural, when the bearer is shot, that both Henry and Wilson should go after the flag. It is also inevitable, although slightly contrived, that they should reach it at the same time: "He [Henry] made a spring and a clutch at the pole. At the same instant, his friend grabbed it from the other side" (2:108).

Neither Henry nor Wilson relinquishes the flagpole and a "small scuffle" ensues. For Henry, however, possession of the flag means so much in terms of dominance over his peers that he has no compunctions about using force against his comrade: "The youth roughly pushed his friend way" (2:110).

In gaining the flag, Henry has defeated his Christian-group rival and the value system Wilson champions. Henry has gained supremacy over his peers, achieving his *areté*. Yet the victory is not complete: there is still the enemy's flag. Were Henry to claim that flag as well, he would be proven superior not only to his peers, but also to the collective body. Henry fails. Although there is much heroism in becoming individual, one is never completely freed from the group. Its influences, physical and mental, remain forever. Although Henry has equaled or surpassed the deeds of Achilles and Odysseus, although he has overcome in large measure the long stony sleep of Christian-group culture and heritage, he fails to gain a complete victory. It is as if Henry knows what its possession would mean: "The youth had centered the gaze of his soul upon that other flag. Its possession would be high pride" (2:129). But Wilson, that champion of the group, had dogged Henry across the battlefield and beat Henry to it by springing like Christ the Panther:[14] "Me youth's friend ... sprang at the flag as a panther at prey. He pulled at it, and wrenching it free, swung up its red brilliancy with a mad cry of exultation" (2:130).

In terms of the epic tradition, Henry's possessing the other flag could have meant possibly a complete victory for the Homeric epic over the social epic after two thousand years. It might also have meant a winning back of the heroic, individual "soul" after two millennia of suppression by Christian-group value systems, both political and spiritual. But, as the later Scratchy Wilson of "The Bride Comes to Yellow Sky" and the Swede of "The Blue Hotel" discover, such a victory is fleeting at best and always illusory. Wilson may have lost an individual encounter with Henry, but he has also proven that the group cannot be completely defeated by the individual.

Victories

The epic tradition demands that a writer replace former concepts of epic heroism with his own if he wishes to be more than a mere imitator. In nearly all of Crane's best work, his idea of heroism is his ideal of personal honesty. Repeatedly, Crane measures his characters against this standard; Henry Fleming measures as well as any.

More than any other sort of writer, one whose work has epic dimensions lends to his fictional heroes his own supreme ambition; so much is this so, in fact, that the poet himself may be considered the ultimate hero of his own epic, and is sometimes difficult to separate from the fictional hero. For millennia the epic poet has been set apart from his fellows by his abilities, but especially by the intensity of his vision and by the degree to which he believes in it. For Crane, keeping close to his vision, in terms both of apprehension and of comprehension, is the standard not only of honesty but of heroism as well.

The desire to see clearly runs through *The Red Badge of Courage*. Henry in particular seeks continually to perceive with his own eyes. There are more than two hundred references in *The Red Badge* to Henry seeing, not seeing, or trying to see. However, his sight tends always to be obscured either by the group, which limits what the individual can see, or by a kind of Homeric hero complex in which Henry feels that an individual can see everything. Each is a form of blindness and each corresponds to one of the two epic value systems. There is an implication throughout most of the novel (the implication becomes explicit in the last chapter) that history is little more than an individual interpretation of events raised to a level of cultural reporting and collective interpreting. Both as individual and as representative man, Henry makes his own specific interpretations of events. On the other hand, those interpretations are also colored by epic concepts. If the individual's interpretation is deluded, so is the epic's, and vice-versa.

Since Crane uses "vision" as a metaphor for his own particular notion of heroism, former notions of epic heroism are first debased and then replaced by the use of images and references to seeing. One of the value systems attacked in *The Red Badge* is the Christian-group view, which obscures and distorts the attempts of the individual to "see." The group, in the form of the army or the brigade or the regiment, is constantly associated with smoke or fog. As Henry is about to move into his first engagement, he identifies the fog with the army; indeed, the fog seems to emanate from the group: "The youth thought the damp fog of early morning moved from the rush of a great body of troops" (2:22). The same image is used in the opening sentence of the novel: "The cold passed reluctantly from the earth, and the retiring fogs revealed an army stretched out on the hills, resting" (2:3). Smoke is even more often associated with the group. Although realistic in a novel about war before the invention of smokeless powder, the image is used for much more than verisimilitude. At one point the position of an entire brigade is identified only by reference to the position of a blanket of smoke: "A brigade ahead of them went into action with a rending roar. It was as if it had exploded. And, thereafter, it lay stretched in the distance behind a long gray wall that one was obliged to look twice at to make sure that it was smoke" (2:28). Not only is smoke identified with the brigade, but smoke also seems to give it protection.

The group is also seen in terms of darkness, snakes, and monsters, which in epics and archetypes of the unconscious are usually identified with evil. As the army is forming to march into battle, Henry perceives the group: "From off in the darkness, came the trampling of feet. The youth could occasionally see dark shadows that moved like monsters" (2:15). As the "monsters" moved off in columns, "there was an occasional flash and glimmer of steel from the backs of all these huge crawling reptiles" (2:15). And the "two long, thin, black columns" appear "like two serpents crawling from the cavern of the night" (2:16). The men of the group themselves sometimes appear "satanic" (2:18) to Henry.

Most often, however, the smoke of the group obscures and distorts Henry's vision. With the smoke of "the war atmosphere" around him in his first engagement, Henry had "a sensation that his eye-balls were about to crack like hot stones" (2:35). His desire to see is constantly getting in the way of his assimilation into the group, but he can never get an unobstructed view and his other senses are stifled, almost annihilated by the physical and metaphorical "smoke" of the group. Against this smoke Henry directs more of his anger than against a charging enemy: "Buried in the smoke of many rifles his anger was directed not so much against the men whom he knew were rushing toward him as against the swirling battle phantoms which were choking him, stuffing their smoke robes down his parched throat" (2:35).

The group has the ability to hide reality from the individual. The group takes away the individual's unobstructed use of his senses—the only means he has of perceiving the world around him. While surrounded by "smoke," a man cannot "see," and will behave in the way the group wants him to behave. Shortly before Henry becomes "not a man but a member," for example, he and the regiment are moving rapidly forward to a "struggle in the smoke": "In this rush they were apparently all deaf and blind" (2:31).

After he has run, been hit on the head, and returned to the group, Henry sees the regiment in a more sinister aspect. After spending the night in sleep Henry awakes and it seems to him "that he had been asleep for a thousand years" (2:68). This "sleep," of course, takes him back in time, not forward, and so he sees "gray mists," and around him "men in corpse-like hues" with "limbs ... pulseless and dead." If every epic hero must visit hell, then, for Henry, being in the middle of the group is just that: he sees "the hall of the forest as a charnel place. He believed for an instant that he was in the house of the dead" (2:80).

If the group influence which Henry has resisted and over which he has gained some dominance causes the individual to see less than he is able, the Homeric view of man purports to allow the individual to "see" more than he actually can. Crane renders the Homeric view meaningless by showing that it too is clouded. That is, if Wilson, the group hero, is given "new eyes" and now apparently sees himself as a "wee thing" (2:82), then Henry, the Homeric hero, becomes so caught up in his individual desires that his eyes are reduced to "a glazed vacancy" (2:96). He becomes a "barbarian, a beast" (2:97). He sees himself as a "pagan who defends his religion" (2:97), and he sees his battle-rage as "fine, wild, and, in some ways, easy. He had been a tremendous figure, no doubt. By this struggle he had overcome obstacles which he had admitted to be mountains. They had fallen like paper peaks, and he was now what he called a hero" (2:97).

The whole of chapter 17 describes Henry as being in the grip of the blind battle-rage of Homeric heroes. He forgets that he is merely a private engaged in a small charge on one day of one battle. He thinks of himself as colossal in size and of the other soldiers as "flies sucking insolently at his blood" (2:95). Although his neck is "bronzed" and he fires his rifle with a fierce grunt as if he were "dealing a blow of the fist with all his strength" (2:96), he is essentially what one soldier calls this "war devil": "Yeh infernal fool" (2:96). Heroic Henry certainly is, even in a traditional way, but a bit foolish as well.

Henry soon gains a truer vision. Going with Wilson to get some water, Henry, as well as his image of himself as a Homeric hero, is deflated by a "jangling general" who refers to Henry's regiment, and implicitly to Henry himself, as a lot of "mule drivers" (2:101). Henry, who had earlier viewed nature as a sympathetic goddess in language filled with Virgilian pathetic fallacy and Christian symbolism (the forest-chapel, for example), and later as a capricious, sometimes malevolent beast much as Homer saw it, now has "new eyes" and sees himself as "very insignificant" (2:101). This is not necessarily a Christian sense of insignificance, nor even a completely naturalistic one, but simply a realization that compared with more powerful forces, including the regiment, he is powerless. Moreover, since officers are often associated with gods, the sun, and other natural and supernatural entities, Henry's discovery can be seen as developing from his earlier views of nature.[15]

After discovering his insignificance, Henry is in a position to receive a new heroism, a new vision, a "real" vision. In his charge across the field on the second day of battle, it "seemed to the youth that he saw everything":

> *Each blade of the green grass was bold and clear. He thought that he was aware of every change in the thin, transparent vapor that floated idly in sheets. The brown or gray trunks of the trees showed each roughness of their surfaces. And the men of the regiment, with their starting eyes and sweating faces, running madly, or falling, as if thrown headlong, to queer, heaped up corpses—all were comprehended. His mind took a mechanical but firm impression, so that afterward everything was pictured and explained to him, save why he himself was there. [2:105]*

A "mechanical" impression of some blades of grass, tree trunks, and sweating, frightened, dying men: that is all one can ever hope to see. The process of epic has been reversed.

Virgil had expanded Homer's view of ten or twenty years of glory on the plains before a small town in Asia Minor to include a long-lived empire encompassing the known world. Similarly, the Christian epics of Charlemagne and the crusades are described as world wars. Milton extended the epic beyond human time and farther out than human space. Crane doubled back upon the epic tradition, gradually narrowing space until the epic vision includes only a minute perception and compressing time until that perception exists only for a fleeting instant. It is epical in its achievement and heroic only because Crane has shown it to be the only vision possible for man that remains "bold and clear."

Tiny but unobscured by the smoke of the group or the blinding *menos* of *areté*, Henry's vision has made him Crane's version of the best epic hero. Trying to "observe everything" in his first battle, but failing to "avoid trees and branches," Henry now sees only *something*. Gone is the Roman vision of national destiny and the Miltonic perception of a Puritan God's universe. Heroism is defined in *The Red Badge* as one man's limited but perhaps illusionless vision: grass blades, tree trunks, dying men.

This vision has dominated the literature of the twentieth century and has allowed writers who followed Crane to make the first tentative steps toward a new supreme fiction based upon consciousness of a materialistic universe while discarding the old fictions based upon the imagination. It is upon this vision that Wallace Stevens, for example, built his poetic edifice, and it is because of the new tradition inaugurated by *The Red Badge* that Stevens could write that "in the presence of the violent reality of war, consciousness takes the place of the imagination."[16] That is precisely what happens in this novel.

The epic of consciousness in *The Red Badge* is clearly set forth. Henry begins the novel in his hut, emblem of the enclosed violence of his mind. In this enclosure, cluttered by cracker boxes, clothing, and utensils, he gives vent to his cluttered and conflicting fears and anxieties. "Convicted by himself of many shameful crimes against the gods of tradition" (2:14) and feeling "alone in space," he has "visions of a thousand tongued fear," and admits that "he would not be able to cope with this monster" (2:20). When he first goes into combat, he sees "that it would be impossible for him to escape from the regiment. It enclosed him. And there were iron laws of tradition and laws on four sides. He was in a moving box" (2:23). After escaping from the regimental enclosure, he enters a succession of archetypes for the unconscious—the forest, a swamp, "deep thickets"—each enclosing those which follow, until he reaches "a place where the high, arching boughs made a chapel" (2:47). Here is a different sort of cave, for this is not at first the enclosure of unconscious fears, nor an enclosure of transcendence, but rather a false cave, like the den of Error (book 1, canto 1) and the cave of Mammon (book 2, canto 7) in the *Faerie Queene*, where the hero is lured toward a false transcendence. In Henry's case the promise comes in the form of religious transcendentalism. While the insects are praying and the trees are whispering, Henry pushes open the "green doors" and enters the chapel. In a paragraph or two Crane both anticipates W. W. Hudson and Edgar Rice Burroughs and parodies the Schianatulander and chapel scenes of *Parzival*, for Henry has no sooner entered and is standing "near the threshold," when "he stopped horror-stricken at the sight of the thing."

> He was being looked at by a dead man who was seated with his back against a column-like tree. The corpse was dressed in a uniform that once had been blue but now was faded to a melancholy shade of green. The eyes, staring at the youth, had changed to the dull hue to be seen on the side of a dead fish. The mouth was opened. Its red had changed to an appalling yellow. Over the grey skin of the face ran little ants. One was trundling some sort of a bundle along the upper lip. [2.47]

The stark clarity of this paragraph, with its excruciatingly painful materialism, provides a perfect contrast to the "religious half-light" leading up to this description. While the description is faintly reminiscent of Thoreau's mock epic paragraphs on ants in *Walden*, its main purpose seems to be to pose starkly the problem that Henry and other epic heroes must face. Somehow, the pathetic fallacy, the religious rose-colored glasses, must be removed, and Henry must still be able to face the "thing"—the fact of death. At this early stage, the contrast is too great for Henry and he responds by screaming and fleeing from the enclosure, which promised transcendence but delivered only death. Another way of saying it is that he was lulled by the imagination and then confronted by pure consciousness. He heads back to the regiment. Only later, after facing death in the field, does Henry accept a classical, almost Lucretian materialism with respect to mortality.[17] This seems to be what Henry learns: "He knew that he would no more quail before his guides wherever they should point. He had been to touch the great death and found that, after all, it was but the great death" (2:135).

Before this, however, Henry has other caves to face. It may be said that after he crosses the river in chapter 3, Henry is subterranean for nearly the remainder of the novel, much as Dante is throughout the *Inferno*. The others are merely caves within caves, hells within Hades. One of these is the night camp of the regiment in chapter 13. Here Henry catches "glimpses of visages that loomed pallid and ghostly, lit with a phosphorescent glow" (2:77). Another enclosure of failed transcendence, this camp is like that to which the captain brings the reluctant voyagers. This too contains a window on the stars: "Far off to the right, through a window in the forest could be seen a handful of stars" (2:77). Managing to resist the temptations of even this "charnel house," Henry subsequently overcomes the numerous enclosures formed by the smoke of the regiment's many rifles and achieves his "bold and clear" vision.

Defeats

The latest episode in the long controversy about the quality of *The Red Badge* begins with Henry Binder's 1978 articles and 1979 edition of Crane's novel for *The Norton Anthology of American Literature*—articles in which he proposes restoring, and an edition in which he does restore, several manuscript passages to the printed text. Restoring these passages, Binder claims, makes a muddled novel clear and consistent. The controversy regarding whether or not Henry "grows" is resolved: he does not; the novel is clearly ironic. While agreeing that the original Appleton edition poses problems, Donald Pizer contends that the traditional text is the best we have until evidence stronger than Binder's appears. Pizer takes issue with Binder on essentially two points: first, that because there is no evidence suggesting that Crane was pressured into making the cuts, it can only be assumed that he freely chose to make them; and second, that Binder errs in assuming that "a clear and consistent novel is better than an ambivalent and ambiguous one."[18]

Because it involves an entire chapter, the longest of Binder's additions must be addressed in some detail by anyone discussing the structure of *The Red Badge*. This is especially true of a discussion of classical epic structure, where arithmetical divisions are significant and the notion of a twenty-five-chapter epic poses some problems. The restored chapter is the original manuscript's chapter twelve, coming after the Appleton chapter eleven. Traditional epics are structurally divided in half. A twenty-five-chapter novel based on epic would be divided somewhere near the middle of chapter thirteen, leaving twelve and a half chapters on either side. Chapter thirteen in the new Norton edition is chapter twelve of the traditional Appleton edition, The middle of this chapter describes Henry receiving his wound, a description already discussed as pivotal to the work. Since Henry is in no position to do much on his own between the time he is wounded (the middle of the Norton) and the time the Cheery man deposits him with the regiment (ending the traditional text's first half), the different editions have little effect on the validity of the novel's epic structure.

The content of the added chapter does little more than reaffirm the metronomic quality of Henry's thoughts and emotions as they move between extremes of Nietzschean egotism and Paulean self-flagellation. On one hand, "it was always clear to the youth that he was entirely different from other men; that his mind had been cast in a unique mold. Hence laws that might be just to ordinary men, were, when applied to him, peculiar and gaffing outrages."[19] On the other hand, when "his mind pictured the death of Jim Conklin" and in it "he saw the shadows of his fate," he felt himself to be "unfit": "He did not come into the scheme of further life. His tiny part had been played and he must go."[20]

The additions appearing in the 1979 Norton edition of *The Red Badge* do little to enhance or diminish the notion of *The Red Badge* as having structural and thematic roots in classical epic. At the same time, since the passages do little more than reaffirm the greatness of *The Red Badge*, the classical dicta of economy and simplicity ought to apply, and one giving a supposedly classical reading of a work ought to side with his sources.

The final chapter of *The Red Badge* presents perhaps the greatest critical problem in the Crane canon. Many of the critical reservations about Crane's importance and abilities rest in the complexities and supposed inconsistencies (even inanities) of this chapter.[21]

The last chapter is both complete and consistent. It is a deliberate reversal of all that has gone before. Throughout the largest portion of *The Red Badge*, Henry is in the process of sloughing off both the Christian-group "walking-sticks" of Stallman's interpretation and the Homeric "creeds" of this reading. If the final chapter of *The Red Badge* is naturalistic, it is so only within the context of Crane's conception of the epic.

That a man may learn and then forget, as Holton says, pervades Crane's writings; in terms of the epic nature of *The Red Badge*, a man may forget and then remember. In the first twenty-three chapters, Henry proceeds to "forget" all previous cultural notions and epic concepts about the way life is. Having "forgotten," he finally achieves an impressionistic vision of the individual man unencumbered by epic and cultural trappings. In the final chapter, however, Henry "remembers"; his former epic value systems sweep back over him, and he is left at the end dreaming dreams he had dreamt in the beginning.

Throughout twenty-three chapters of the novel the major concern is to discover the true nature of heroism. In the final chapter, however, all epic values are specifically refuted. Because he forgets the vision that he has found, and the limited heroism he has discovered, Henry becomes a nonhero. *The Red Badge*, too, is negated, a nonepic. Unlike Milton, Virgil, and Homer, Crane does not wait for his particular notion of heroism to be satirized by others; he mocks it himself.[22]

The Red Badge of Courage ends by mocking the epic genre and its heroic ideals. But the novel, so saturated with epic tradition, cannot be exiled from the epic province. Its exploitation of epic conventions attests to the lingering vitality of the genre, but its annihilation of heroism—Homeric, Virgilian, Catholic, or Miltonic—at the same time exposes the genre's vulnerability. The novel marks a transition from the formal epic tradition to all that is Homerically nonepic in modern fiction: triumphant chaos and successful deceit.

The last chapter is an ironic recapitulation of each epic value system present in the remainder of the book. Homeric *areté* is savagely mocked, as is Christian-group heroism. The primary target, however, is that final concept of heroism, Crane's own, which Henry has achieved earlier: that concept based only on the individual's ability to peer into the pit of reality with a gaze unclouded by cultural and epic notions of what the world is like. Throughout this final chapter, Henry's (and Crane's) perception-based, impressionistic heroism is mocked by means of an ironic significance attached to images of and references to the sense of sight. Henry enters the chapter a cleareyed hero; he exits blind and deluded.

As the chapter opens, the battle has begun to wane and the sounds of war have begun "to grow intermittent and weaker." Henry's newfound vision soon runs the gamut of perception from egotistical pride to cringing guilt and humility, and is, in effect, also becoming "weaker." As the regiment begins to "retrace its way" like a snake "winding off in the direction of the river," Henry is with it, recrossing the Stygian stream he had crossed in chapter 3. Similarly, Henry's mind is "undergoing a subtle change": "It took moments for it to cast off its battleful ways and resume its accustomed course of thought. Gradually his brain emerged from the dogged clouds and at last he was enabled to more closely comprehend himself and his circumstance" (2:133). After "his first thoughts were given to rejoicings" because he had "escaped" the battle, Henry's vision becomes distorted. First, he contemplates his "achievements." With Homeric eyes he sees his deeds as "great and shining." His deluded vision is so distorted that he dresses those deeds in the royal "wide purple and gold," which, on Henry, give off sparkles "of various deflections."

Next, he assumes Christian eyes, and his visions of Homeric glory, of *areté*, are destroyed by an exaggerated guilt brought on by the memory of his crime against the tattered man. The tattered man had tormented his unmercifully, but all Henry sees is a grotesquely distorted image of the gentle tattered man transmogrified into a weird Christian version of some apostle of revenge who visits on Henry a "vision of cruelty." One delusion displaces another, so that Henry's previous vision, as well as his heroism, becomes changed and meaningless, because no longer is it his alone. Homeric pride makes Henry a strutting fool, and Christian-group guilt betrays him as a coward.

Images of and references to vision provide further ironic commentary on the quality of "perception" inherent in the two traditional epic value systems. For example, Crane mocks three specific aspects of *areté* in the final chapter by proving them to be false or wildly exaggerated visions of reality. The first mocks the lack of any firm moral sense in the ancient Greek battle code. At times, Henry has done less than his *areté* demands of him, but he rightly ignores this when contemplating his great deeds and he even feels "gleeful and unregretting." Another aspect of *areté* mocked by Crane is the all-important result of the Homeric hero's desire for glory, "public recognition of his *areté*: it runs through Greek life."[23] Henry tends to exaggerate the quality of his *areté*, and consequently the recognition it deserves, in a sort of daydream vision, a "procession of memory" in which "his public deeds were paraded in great and shining prominence" (2:133). The final mockery concerns that aspect of heroism lying at the heart of *areté*: the recognition of the hero's superiority over his peers. If we remember the soldier's comic, even ridiculous speech concerning "Flem's" bravery and the somewhat qualifying and dubiously conferred title "jimhickey," Henry's recollections seem to be all out of proportion: "He recalled with a thrill of joy the respectful comments of his fellows upon his conduct" (2:134).

Henry's progression toward heroism during the first twenty-three chapters reverses and inverts itself in the last chapter, for Henry's vision is a distortion that destroys his notion of Homeric bravery and of *areté*. Henry's semi-sin of leaving the tattered man haunts him.[24] Crane here employs a parody of nineteenth-century Protestant tracts, much as he has described Henry's Homeric deeds in the language traditionally used to depict the victory marches of great warriors: "A specter of reproach came to him. There loomed the dogging memory of the tattered soldier—he who gored by bullets and faint for blood, had fretted concerning an imagined wound in another; he who had loaned his last of strength and intellect for the tall soldier; he who, blind with weariness and pain, had been deserted in the field" (2:134). Henry is then "followed" by a "vision of cruelty" which clings "near to him always" and darkens "his view of these deeds in purple and gold." This "somber phantom" heightens Henry's guilt; he becomes "afraid it would stand before him all his life." Thus, "he saw his vivid error." After recognizing that he had sinned, Henry receives partial expiation in the form of partial forgetfulness: "Yet he gradually mustered force to put the sin at a distance. And at last his eyes seemed to open to some new ways. He found that he could now look back upon the brass and bombast of his earlier gospels and see them truly. He was gleeful when he discovered that he now despised them" (2:135). Henry here exchanges one false view of himself for another. The Homeric vision has given way to a Christian-group one. Crane, with beautiful, lyric irony, moves Henry away from the war and from the battle in his mind: "So it came to pass that as he trudged from the place of blood and wrath his soul changed" (2:135). Henry now believes that "the world was a world for him," as a Christian-group hero should.

There is yet another way, however, in which Crane sets about to destroy the epic. By ironically disparaging the epic view of man's history, Crane ridicules the concept that readers have of the epic genre. The epic has long been one of the more revered forms of historical interpretation and cultural expression. Through epic poetry Homer presents man as a godlike animal struggling to gain a measure of immortality through the public recognition of great deeds. But the Homeric man was like Lear in the storm—alone, naked, and "unaccommodated"—and this is probably why Crane preferred this view more than other traditional views: it was closer to his notion, expressed in "The Blue Hotel," that "conceit is the very engine of life." Virgil gave man more hope by giving him the opportunity to identify and merge with the immortality of a national group. By interpreting history in terms of a great empire, he was also in some measure espousing a kind of immortality. Medieval and Renaissance epic, including *The Song of Roland* and Tasso's *Gerusalemme liberata*, glorified the church militant, ordained to victory. Milton went even farther. He regarded man as completely unworthy of immortality, but acknowledged man's hope in a merciful God's love; man's earthly history spans the interval between creation and final redemption.

Crane felt that these interpretations of history were, to one degree or another, part of a giant hoax willfully perpetrated on man by man. At times he could be downright Aeschylean: "Hope," as Berryman quotes him, "is the most vacuous emotion of mankind."

The Red Badge is a denial of the epic view of history, which Crane felt creates an absurd, illusory, and vacuous emotion.

In the first twenty-three chapters of *The Red Badge* an epic fable is presented which carries the reader back through history. Henry begins *in medias res*, confused and torn between the two major epic views of history, and between two epic value systems as they have filtered through the epic into and out of culture. One of Henry's great accomplishments is his success in throwing off, if only for a short time, the Christian-group view that has dominated the long history of the social epic—indeed of all intellectual life in the West. Next, Henry rejects the rest of history, as recorded by the individual epic, by sloughing off the hope of being an immortal, Homeric "war devil." Finally, past all Christian doctrine, beyond the emotional slither of patriotism and breast-beating brass and bombast, this young man finds a vision in some blades of grass and the grooved bark of a few trees. He is, for an instant, free as few have ever been free; he is loosed from the illusions of history. Perhaps, because it is so limited in duration, Crane is mocking his own illusion, and that of Americans from Franklin to Ginsberg, that man can indeed throw off the process of history and the illusions it etches into the brain.

However, those twenty-three chapters may not be a fairy-tale epic. Crane may have felt that through catalytic and catastrophic experiences like war, man can scrape the scales of history from his eyes. Perhaps all the teachings of history are reduced to absurdity in the midst of the immense experience, if one tries hard enough to see for himself. Perhaps one can universalize Crane's statement that "a man is only responsible for the personal quality of his honesty" of vision. "A man is sure to fail at it," he said, "but there is something in the failure." Although the paucity of the vision may make it ironic, there is some heroism involved in the sheer ability to perceive reality. In either case, however, the last chapter of the novel indicates that Crane felt heroism to be impossible beyond the immediacy of experience.

This aspect of the last chapter functions by way of a metaphorical equation: memory is to the individual as history is to the species. As Henry moves away from the immediate experience, his memory creates lies and delusions about that experience. The ironic laughter from Crane results from his belief that man cannot really learn from experience, even when he can reach an illusionless view of reality through that experience. Once it is over, once one is no longer staring at the face of red death, then memory, or history, distorts that experience all out of any recognizable proportion.

In the last chapter, history becomes what memory becomes—a mechanism for man to build his self-image. Through the two main thrusts of the history of Western civilization, as expressed by the epic genre, man is deluded into believing himself to be either more or less than he actually is. In the end, Henry is led by his memory to believe with conviction all the mad, distorted hopes of epic history. Ironically, "at last his eyes opened on some new ways" (2:135). These are new ways only for Henry; they are as old as history. Darwin mounted on Mather.

These "new ways" are a collation of Homeric and Christian-group values. There is still much pride in Henry, but also much humility. Together, they form a paradoxically proud humility: "He felt a quiet man-hood, non-assertive but of sturdy and strong blood" (2:135). The sum of Henry's wisdom, apparently gained from these seemingly "new" ways, and required of epic heroes, is expressed in what becomes, upon close examination, a meaningless platitude worthy of the climax of a dime-novel adventure: "He had been to touch the great death, and found that, after all, it was but the great death. He was a man" (2:135).

The final delusion of history and memory Crane repudiated is that of "hope." Part of the reason that Virgil and Milton wrote epics was to give men hope. Beautifully parodic, and powerfully ironic, the last paragraphs of *The Red Badge* express the hopes of Aeneas and Adam, of Columbus and Hiawatha, and of people at all times and in all places, hot to cool, hard to soft, pain to pleasure, hell to heaven:

> *So it came to pass that as he trudged from the place of blood and wrath, his soul changed. He had come from hot-ploughshares to prospects of clover tranquility and it was as if hot-ploughshares were not. Scars faded as flowers.*
>
> *It rained. The procession of weary soldiers became a bedraggled train, despondent and muttering, marching with churning effort, in a trough of liquid brown mud under a low, wretched sky. Yet the youth smiled, for he saw that the world was a world for him though many discovered it to be made of oaths and walking-sticks.... The sultry nightmare was in the past. He had been an animal blistered and sweating in the heat and pain of war. He turned now with a lover's thirst, to images of tranquil skies, fresh meadows, cool brooks; an existence of soft and eternal peace. [2:135]*

No one lives a life of "soft and eternal peace," except in deluded dreams, and Crane knew it. "He was almost illusionless," Berryman said of Crane, "whether about his subjects or himself. Perhaps his only illusion was the heroic one; and not even this ... escaped his irony."

NOTES

1. Wallace Stevens, "[Prose statement on the poetry of war]," in *The Palm at the End of the Mind: Selected Poems and a Play*, ed. Holly Stevens (New York: Vintage Books, 1972), p. 206.

2. "Of the Origin of Homer and Hesiod, and Their Contest," in *Hesiod: The Homeric Hymns and Homerica*, trans. Hugh G. Evelyn-White (Cambridge, Mass.: Harvard University Press; London: Heinemann, 1967), Loeb Classical Library, pp. 565–97.

3. E. B. Castle, *Ancient Education and Today* (Baltimore: Penguin, 1961), p. 12; H. D. F. Kitto, *The Greeks* (Baltimore: Penguin, 1966), pp. 171–72.

4. Bowra, *From Virgil to Milton*, pp. 229–30.

5. M. Solomon [pseud.], "Crane, A Critical Study," p. 35.

6. R. W. Stallman, introduction to *The Red Badge of Courage* (New York: Random House, 1951), p. xxxv.

7. LaFrance, *A Reading of Stephen Crane*, pp. 100–101.

8. Cf. *Paradise Lost*, bks. 9–12, and Genesis, chap. 3. In both, a pattern of sin-guilt-alienation-repentance-promise of redemption is followed.

9. John E. Hart, "*The Red Badge of Courage* as Myth and Symbol," *University of Kansas City Review* 19 (Summer, 1953): 253; see also Joseph Campbell, *The Hero with a Thousand Faces* (Princeton: Princeton University Press, 1949), p. 30, for a discussion of heroes and hills.

10. Holton, *Cylinder of Vision*, pp. 5–11; Nagel, *Stephen Crane and Literary Impressionism*, pp. 1–35.

11. The problems of authorial or narrative veracity *versus* Henry's (or Crane's or other narrators') "dramatic impressionism" (Holton's phrase) or narrative "parallax" (Nagel's) are involved and many. Suffice it that here basic action and direct speech are usually "fact," and that in the above instance, because Henry is hurt and temporarily speechless, all information comes from the narrator.

12. Gibson, "Crane's *Red Badge*," item 49.

13. But see William P. Safrenek, "Crane's *The Red Badge of Courage*," *Explicator* 26 (November, 1967): item 21. Failing to note the difference between running from and remaining in the battle, Safrenek sees Henry's development as paralleling Wilson's.

14. Although Crane was familiar with real "panthers" (actually eastern mountain lions), he would not have missed this allusion to a standard Christian epithet for Christ.

15. This vision differs from the Christian-group notion of man's insignificance because the latter then attaches man to something that is significant; the existential and in some ways Lucretian vision of man as an "insignificant thing" is probably closer to Henry's vision here.

16. Stevens, "[Prose statement]," p. 206.

17. Lucretius, *The Way Things Are*, trans. Rolfe Humphries (London and Bloomington: Indiana University Press, 1969). In book 1, Lucretius explains that men fear death because religion tells them to fear the eternal punishment of their immortal (albeit pagan) souls for their sins. Since neither body nor soul is immortal, man has nothing to fear from death.

18. The pertinent works are these: Henry Binder, "*The Red Badge of Courage* Nobody Knows," *Studies in the Novel* 10 (Spring, 1978): 9–47; *The Red Badge of Courage* and introduction by Henry Binder in *The Norton Anthology of American Literature*, ed. Ronald Gottesman et al., 2 vols. (New York and London: Norton, 1979), 2:800–906; Henry Binder, "Unwinding the Riddle of Four Missing Papers from *The Red Badge of Courage*," *Publications of the Bibliographical Society of America* 72 (January–March, 1978): 100–106; Donald Pizer, "'*The Red Badge of Courage* Nobody Knows': A Brief Rejoinder," *Studies in*

the Novel 11 (Spring, 1979): 77–81; Henry Binder, "Donald Pizer, Ripley Hitchcock, and *The Red Badge of Courage*," *Studies in the Novel* 11 (Summer, 1979): 216–23.

19. *Norton Anthology*, 2:854.

20. Ibid., p. 856.

21. For a smattering of the considerable body of opinion on this, see James Tuttleton, "The Imagery of *The Red Badge of Courage*," *Modern Fiction Studies* 8 (Winter, 1962): 411; C. C. Walcutt, *American Literary Naturalism: A Divided Stream* (Minneapolis: University of Minnesota Press, 1956), pp. 66–88, 223; Kermit Vanderbuilt and Daniel Weiss, "From Rifleman to Flagbearer: Henry Fleming's Separate Peace in *The Red Badge of Courage*," *Modern Fiction Studies* 11 (Winter, 1965–66): 371–80; Winifred Lynsky, ed., *Reading Modern Fiction*, 4th ed. (New York: Scribner's, 1968), pp. 173–77; Norman Friedman, "Criticism and the Novel," *Antioch Review* 18 (Fall, 1958): 343–70; Binder, "*The Red Badge of Courage* Nobody Knows," p. 9; most important is R. B. Sewall, "Crane's *The Red Badge of Courage*," *Explicator* 3 (May, 1945): item 55, along with Steven Mailloux, "*The Red Badge of Courage* and Interpretive Conventions: Critical Response to a Maimed Text," *Studies in the Novel* 10 (Spring, 1978): 48–63.

22. Some see Homer and Virgil as mocking their own ideals of heroism. Virgil, for example, may be said to have betrayed *pietas* and Roman stoicism by ending the *Aeneid* with Aeneas's impassioned killing of Turnus. Even Lucretius seems to be horrified by the materialistic universe and its power to inflict pain and suffering as reflected in book 6 of *De rerum natura*.

23. Castle, *Ancient Education*, p. 12.

24. Given the moral heritage of most readers of Crane, even today, it is important to mention again that Crane felt there was "no such thing as sin, except in Sunday school." Beer, *Crane: A Study*, p. 106.

MICHAEL FRIED

Postscript: Stephen Crane's Upturned Faces

In a well-known passage early on in *The Red Badge of Courage* Henry Fleming encounters the first of several corpses that turn up in the novel:

> Once the line encountered the body of a dead soldier. He lay upon his back staring at the sky. He was dressed in an awkward suit of yellowish brown. The youth could see that the soles of his shoes had been worn to the thinness of writing paper, and from a great rent in one the dead foot projected piteously. And it was as if fate had betrayed the solider. In death it exposed to his enemies that poverty which in life he had perhaps concealed from his friends.
>
> The ranks opened covertly to avoid the corpse. The invulnerable dead man forced a way for himself. The youth looked keenly at the ashen face. The wind raised the tawny beard. It moved as if a hand were stroking it. He vaguely desired to walk around and around the body and stare; the impulse of the living to try to read in dead eyes the answer to the Question.[68]

All of Stephen Crane's formidable powers of defamiliarization are at work in this passage. The corpse is inert but active, betrayed and poverty stricken but

From "Realism, Writing, and Disfiguration in Thomas Eakins's *Gross Clinic*" in *Representations* 9 (Winter 1985). © 1985 by Michael Fried.

also invulnerable and forcing, avoided by the ranks of living men, which we imagine parting to give it a certain berth, and yet its tawny beard is manipulated by the wind in a gesture of extraordinary intimacy, which more than anything else establishes the dead soldier's uncanniness for us. As for Henry Fleming's relation to the corpse, it is at once apparently straightforward, as when we are told that the youth could see the soles of the dead man's shoes or that he looked keenly at the dead man's face, and conspicuously indeterminate, as when Crane's prose formulates thoughts that could not possibly be those of his protagonist ("And it was as if fate had betrayed the soldier....") but that seem nevertheless to follow from the latter's perceptions. Indeed the apparent straightforwardness has disconcerting aspects. Thus the succession of grammatically simple sentences in the second paragraph ("The youth looked keenly at the ashen face. The wind raised the tawny beard. It moved as if a hand were stroking it.") seems almost to imply a causal relationship, as if the youth were acting on the corpse through the agency of the wind, though characteristically the next sentence comes close to dissolving the distinction between living and dead both by virtue of the ambiguity of the initial pronoun and because we are told that the youth (i.e., "He") felt a vague desire to walk around the corpse and stare—precisely the action attributed to the corpse in the second sentence of the first paragraph. It is as though throughout the passage the separateness of the youth both from the corpse and from the narrator is palpably the accomplishment of *absolutely* local effects of writing, which here as elsewhere in *The Red Badge* suggests that we may be in the vicinity of a "sublime" scenario of fantasized aggression, identification, and differentiation not unlike the one that governs the painter's relation to the dramatis personae of the *Gross Clinic*.[69]

But my aim in citing this passage is not to insist on that affinity. Instead what I want especially to emphasize is, first, the salience in both paragraphs of a particular bodily position, that of the corpse lying flat on its back (this is what allows the wind to get at the beard); second, the characterization of the corpse's upward-staring face as an object of another character's keen attention and the related fact that something, in this case something ostensibly gentle, is done to the face or at least to a metonym, for it (the tawny beard); and third, the dramatization, through the image of the protruding foot, of an unexpected detail—that the soles of the dead soldier's shoes "had been worn to the thinness of writing paper." I won't try to gloss these matters here but will move directly on to another passage in Crane, this one from his novella *The Monster*.

The passage is taken from an astonishing scene in which the Negro Henry Johnson, who works for the Trescott family as a coachman, goes heroically into a burning house in order to save young Jimmie Trescott from certain death. Johnson rushes up the stairs and finds Jimmie having just awakened in his own room, but when he tries to carry the boy down he discovers that flames and smoke have made the route impassable. For a moment he despairs, then recalls a private staircase leading from another bedroom to an apartment that Jimmie's father, a doctor, had fitted up as a laboratory. But when Johnson finally makes his way there he discovers not only that that room too is on fire but that the doctor's chemicals are exploding in fantastic hues and forms ("At the entrance to the laboratory he confronted a strange spectacle. The room was like a garden in the region where might be burning flowers. Flames of violet, crimson, green, blue, orange, and purple were blooming everywhere. There was one blaze that was precisely the hue of a delicate coral. In another place was a mass that lay merely in phosphorescent inaction like a pile of emeralds. But all these marvels were to be seen dimly through clouds of heaving, turning, deadly smoke."). After pausing on the threshold, Johnson rushes across the room with the boy still in his arms; just then an explosion occurs and "a delicate, trembling sapphire shape like a fairy lady" blocks his path; Johnson tries to duck past her but she is "swifter than eagles" and her talons are said to catch in him as he does so. Whereupon, "Johnson lurched forward, twisting this way and that way. He fell on his back. The still form in the blanket flung from his arms, rolled to the edge of the floor and beneath the window." (Jimmie will later be saved unharmed.) The scene concludes:

> Johnson had fallen with his head at the base of an old-fashioned desk. There was a row of jars upon the top of this desk. For the most part they were silent amid this rioting, but there was one which seemed to hold a scintillant and writhing serpent.
>
> Suddenly the glass splintered, and a ruby-red snakelike thing poured its thick length out upon the top of the old desk. It coiled and hesitated, and then began to swim a languorous way down the mahogany slant. At the angle it waved its sizzling molten head to and fro over the closed eyes of the man beneath it. Then, in a moment, with a mystic impulse, it moved again, and the red snake flowed directly down into Johnson's upturned face.
>
> Afterwards the trail of this creature seemed to reek, and amid flames and low explosions drops like red-hot jewels pattered softly down it at leisurely intervals.[70]

By the end of this passage we again are presented with an unmoving body lying face-up on the ground. In this case the body is not that of a corpse and its eyes are closed rather than open; but the author's (or let us say the

novella's) stake in the body's final position becomes plain when we consider
the oddly inconclusive nature of the lurchings and twistings that produce it.
Another difference from the description of the corpse in *The Red Badge* is that
no second character is represented gazing at Johnson's upturned face. But the
passage from *The Monster* narrates the destruction of Johnson's face (we are
soon told that "he now had no face. His face had simply been burned away"),
and the remainder of the plot will turn on the dreadfulness to vision of the
non-face with which he has been left (although never described it produces
horrendous consequences whenever it is glimpsed). In addition the novella
goes on to evoke the "weird fascination" of Jimmie and his friends with
actually seeing the non-face, which for a time Johnson, the "monster" of the
title, swathes in a heavy crepe veil. And it may be too that the sheer
gorgeousness of the color imagery of the burning laboratory should be read
in part as a displacement of effects of seeing that the logic of the narrative
doesn't allow the scene to represent directly. On the other hand, something
is indeed done to Johnson's face, and this time what is done is far from gentle.
Finally, in light of the comparison of the soles of the dead man's shoes to
writing paper in the excerpt from *The Red Badge*, I am struck by the fact that
Johnson ends up lying "with his head at the base of an old-fashioned desk,"
a piece of furniture that one inevitably connects with the activity of writing;
and just in case this seems to be pushing things too far, I shall quote again
the sentence that immediately precedes the account of Johnson's appalling
disfiguration, but with two key verbs italicized: "For the most part, they [the
jars on the desk] were silent amid this *rioting*, but there was one which
seemed to hold a scintillant and *writhing* serpent." The verbs in question
evoke a third verb that comes close to rhyming, audially and visually, with the
other two.

The third and last text by Crane I want to consider is the late short tale
"The Upturned Face"; in effect it takes the motifs and preoccupations I have
identified in the passages from *The Red Badge* and *The Monster* and constructs
around them a brief, two-part narrative of tremendous force and uncertain
significance. The tale virtually defies summary and is hard to quote from
effectively, but one can at least say that it narrates the burial, under enemy
fire, of a dead officer by two fellow officers who had served with him for
years. The opening paragraphs read as follows:

> "What will we do now?" said the adjutant, troubled and excited.
> "Bury him," said Timothy Lean.
> The two officers looked down close to their toes where lay the
> body of their comrade. The face was chalk-blue; gleaming eyes
> stared at the sky. Over the two upright figures was a windy sound

of bullets, and on the top of the hill Lean's prostrate company of Spitzbergen infantry was firing measured volleys.

Two men from the company are assigned to dig a grave, and Lean and the adjutant proceed to search the corpse's clothes for "things" (as the adjutant puts it). Lean hesitates to touch the first bloodstained button on the dead man's tunic but at last completes the search and rises "with ghastly face. He had gathered a watch, a whistle, a pipe, a tobacco-pouch, a handkerchief, a little case of cards and papers." Meanwhile the bullets keep spitting overhead and the two lower ranks labor at digging the grave; their completion of the task is announced in the following short paragraph:

> The grave was finished. It was not a masterpiece—a poor little shallow thing. Lean and the adjutant again looked at each other in a curious silent communication.

The two officers proceed to tumble the dead man into the grave, taking care not to feel his body as they do so; after saying a mangled prayer, they are ready to oversee the covering-up of his remains. At this point, the first paragraph of the second part of the narrative, the motif of the upturned face returns with new force:

> One of the aggrieved privates came forward with his shovel. He lifted his first shovel-load of earth, and for a moment of inexplicable hesitation it was held poised above this corpse, which from its chalk-blue face looked keenly out from the grave. Then the soldier emptied his shovel on—on the feet.
>
> Timothy Lean felt as if tons had been swiftly lifted from off his forehead. He had felt that perhaps the private might empty the shovel on—on the face. It had been emptied on the feet. There was a great point gained there—ha, ha!—the first shovelful had been emptied on the feet. How satisfactory!

Suddenly the man with the shovel is struck by a bullet in the left arm and Lean seizes the shovel and begins to fill the grave himself; as the dirt lands it makes a sound—"plop." The adjutant suggests that it might have been better not to try to bury the body just at that time, but Lean rudely tells him to be quiet and persists at his task. The tale concludes:

> Soon there was nothing to be seen but the chalk-blue face. Lean filled the shovel. "Good God," he cried to the adjutant.

"Why didn't you turn him somehow when you put him in? This—" Then Lean began to stutter.

The adjutant understood. He was pale to the lips. "Go on man," he cried, beseechingly, almost in a shout.

Lean swung back the shovel. It went forward in a pendulum curve. When the earth landed it made a sound—plop.[71]

Obviously it is impossible to convey a sense of the tortured mood of "The Upturned Face" by dismembering it in this manner, but even so several points have been established. First, once more we find at the center of the scene a dead man lying on his back staring upward; in fact, as I have noted, we are presented with such a figure twice over, at the opening of the tale, where it is described as lying at the feet of Lean and the adjutant, and at the beginning of the second part, as the first shovelful of dirt is held suspended above it. Second, the corpse's chalk-blue upturned face is on both occasions the principal object of Lean's and the adjutant's attention, and once again something uncanny and in a strong sense disfiguring happens to that face— in fact the entire second part of the tale turns on Lean's repugnance at the prospect of having to cover the dead man's face with dirt. (The exact degree of violence this implies seems to fall somewhere between the scenes from *The Red Badge* and *The Monster*.) And third, although writing as such doesn't appear to be thematized as in the other passages we have examined, the newly excavated and still empty grave is characterized as "not a masterpiece—a poor little shallow thing," a phrase that, however ironically, deploys a vocabulary of artistic valuation that one can imagine the author applying (again ironically: Crane seems to have thought especially well of this tale) to "The Upturned Face" itself. I suggest too that the ostensible matter of the tale—the digging of a grave, the tumbling of a corpse into its shallow depths, and then the covering of the corpse and specifically its upturned face with shovelfuls of dirt—and the movement of the prose of its telling are meant as nearly as possible to coincide, as if each were ultimately a metaphor for the other: this is why, for example, the text comes to an end with the word "plop," which is nothing other than the verbal representation of the sound made when the last shovelful of dirt falls on the grave, or if not the very last at any rate the one that covers the chalk-blue face once and for all. That the chief protagonist's name, Timothy Lean, invites being read as a slightly displaced version of the author's reinforces this suggestion, all the more so in that the adjutant remains nameless and the dead man is referred to only once, by Lean, as "old Bill."[72] All this is to read "The Upturned Face" as an allegory of the writing of "The Upturned Face," which as a general proposition about a literary text is hardly earthshaking. What is interesting to consider, however, is why this particular text lends itself so readily to such a reading, or to broaden our discussion to include the other passages we have examined, what it means that motifs of an upturned face and the disfiguring of that face are in all three cases conjoined with a thematization or, in "The Upturned Face" itself, an allegorization of writing.

Here is one answer. Just as in Peale's *Graphics* a kind of primitive ontological difference between the upright or erect "space" of reality and the horizontal "space" of writing/drawing became problematic for what might be called the graphic enterprise, and just as in Eakins's art an analogous difference between the horizontal "space" of writing/drawing and the vertical or upright "space" of painting turned out to play a crucial role as regards both choice of subject matter and all that is traditionally comprised under the notion of style, so in these paradigmatic texts by Crane a fundamental contrast between the respective "spaces" of reality and of literary representation—of writing if not of writing/drawing—required that a human character, ordinarily upright and so to speak forward-looking, be rendered horizontal and upward-facing so as to match the horizontality and upward-facingness of the blank page on which the action of inscription was taking place. Understood in these terms, Crane's upturned faces are at once synecdoches for the bodies of those characters and singularly concentrated metaphors for the sheets of writing paper that the author had before him, as is spelled out, by means of a displacement from one end of the body to the other, by the surprising description of the worn-down soles of the dead soldier's shoes in the passage from *The Red Badge*. (The displacement is retroactively signaled by the allusion to reading in the last sentence of the second paragraph.)

Thus for example the size of a human face and that of an ordinary piece of writing paper are roughly comparable; an original coloristic disfiguration of all three faces, either by death making one ashen and another chalk-blue or simply by Henry Johnson's blackness, may be taken as evoking the special blankness of the as yet unwritten page; and their further disfiguration, by the wind that is said to have raised the dead soldier's tawny beard (in this context the verb betrays more aggressive connotations than at first declare themselves), by the ruby-red snakelike thing that flows down into the unconscious Johnson's visage, and by the shovelful of dirt that Lean agonizingly deposits on the last visible portion of his dead comrade, defines the enterprise of writing—of covering or filling or overlaying the blank page with letters, words, sentences, paragraphs, *text*—as an "unnatural" process that undoes but also complements an equally or already "unnatural" state of affairs.[73] In fact one way of glossing the tumbling of the body into the newly dug grave in "The Upturned Face" is as an acknowledgment that the upward-facingness of the corpse, hence of the page, is not so much a brute given as a human artifact—not precisely the result of conscious choice (Lean and the adjutant don't try to arrange the corpse face-up) but by the same token not a matter of mere impersonal necessity (literary writing is a human institution). And one way of accounting for the peculiar horror of the violence that befalls the faces in "The Upturned Face" and, especially, *The Monster* is as the writer's response *as reader* to the deathliness of the blank upward-staring page (to reverse the field of the metaphor), intuited as a sign that the natural world has died and cannot be resuscitated (this is also the burden of Crane's obsessive animism), though by the force of art—of literary writing—it can at least be consumed or buried (his solution to Romanticism).[74] (Our situation as readers of those passages seems more equivocal, caught somewhere between revulsion and interpretation.)[75]

In Eakins too, as we have seen, artistic representation is equated with a double process of disfiguration even while the contrast between the respective "spaces" of writing/drawing and of painting issues in radically different images of disfiguration from anything in Crane. And if in the *Gross Clinic* the grand surgical analogy appears more optimistic in its implications than death in combat or defacement by burning chemicals or burial under enemy fire, our reading of Eakins's masterpiece has shown that that analogy should be pressed only after a long detour that makes the work of the scalpel a figure for a division within the enterprise of painting that cannot finally be healed.

NOTES

69. These observations are incompatible with accounts of Crane as practicing a rigorous method of literary impressionism; see for example James Nagel, *Stephen Crane and Literary Impressionism* (University Park, Pa., 1980), where it is claimed that "what is unique about Crane's brand of Realism is his awareness that the apprehension of reality is limited to empirical data interpreted by a single human intelligence" (19).

70. *The Monster*, in *Prose and Poetry*, 404–6.

71. "The Upturned Face," ibid., 1283–87. According to R. W. Stallman, the tale is loosely based on a real event, the burial under enemy fire of Marine surgeon John Blair Gibbs at Guantanamo on 10 June 1898 (*Stephen Crane: A Biography* [New York, 1968], 362–64).

72. John Berryman discusses both the role of "Crane-masks" and Crane's peculiar practices of naming (and unnaming) characters in his fiction in *Stephen Crane* (1950; reprint: Cleveland and New York, 1962), which despite its somewhat reductive Freudian approach and although devoting insufficient space to the interpretation of individual texts remains the most brilliant study of that writer to date.

73. Crane's pun on the verb "raised" in the passage from *The Red Badge* is doubled by the statement in the second paragraph that "the youth looked *keenly* at the ashen face" (italics mine). In this connection see Berryman's observations on what he takes to be

Crane's oedipal imagery of knives, razors, and shaving (*Stephen Crane*, 313). Incidentally, the name of the Easterner in Crane's "The Blue Hotel" is Mr. Blanc.

74. The intuition or conviction that the natural world has died, that "we carry the death of the world in us," is attributed to Wordsworth and Coleridge and to Emerson and Thoreau by Stanley Cavell in his unpublished Beckman Lectures on Romanticism and Skepticism, delivered under the auspices of the Department of English at the University of California, Berkeley, in February 1982. The concept of animism, understood as a response to that intuition or conviction, is also a theme of those lectures (for Berryman, Crane's animism is "like nothing else in civilized literature" [ibid., 268]). The service improvised by Lean and the adjutant in "The Upturned Face" is for a burial *at sea* (a point noted by Stallman, *Stephen Crane*, 364), which suggests that the entire globe is implicated in the events of the tale.

75. Indeed one function of the extremity of the disfigurations narrated in "The Upturned Face" and *The Monster* might be to stun or otherwise temporarily disable interpretation and thereby to allow the writer, who of course lived by selling the products of his literary labors, to retain possession not so much of the meaning of those texts as of something "prior" to meaning—the written words on the page. Lean's tortured reluctance to complete the job of burial and thus to close "The Upturned Face" may also be read in this light, as may Dr. Trescott's determination, which we sense to be doomed, not to surrender the maimed and helpless Johnson for institutionalization. Obviously a great deal more remains to be understood about the workings of a problematic of writing (and reading) in Crane's fictions. In any case, I find it suggestive that the "exquisite legibility" of Crane's handwriting was remarked by his contemporaries; see for example the highly interesting anecdote with which Berryman begins his book (*Stephen Crane*, 3; the phrase "exquisite legibility" is his) as well as Joseph Conrad's recollection of how after two hours of steady work "[Crane] would have covered three of his large sheets with his regular, legible, perfectly controlled handwriting, with no more than half a dozen erasures—mostly single words—in the lot. It seemed to me always a perfect miracle in the way of mastery over material and expression" ("Introduction," in Thomas Beer, *Stephen Crane: A Study in American Letters* [New York, 1927], 27).

Special thanks to Elizabeth Scott for her help in obtaining photographs and permissions; to John Wilmerding and Darrel Sewell for information about private collections and other matters; and to the Philadelphia Museum of Art for permission to quote from Eakins's unpublished manuscripts in its collection.

DONALD PIZER

The Red Badge of Courage:
Text, Theme, and Form

During the last several years, Hershel Parker and his former student Henry Binder have argued vigorously that *The Red Badge of Courage* which we have been reading since 1895 is a defective text.[1] Crane, they believe, was forced by his editor Ripley Hitchcock to eliminate from the version accepted by D. Appleton & Co. an entire chapter as well as a number of important passages—particularly from the close of the novel—in which he underlined with biting irony the fatuousness and wrong-headedness of Henry Fleming. It is therefore the original and uncut version rather than the censored version of *The Red Badge*, Parker and Binder maintain, which we should be reading. In response to this contention Parker arranged for the uncut version of *The Red Badge* to be included in the prestigious, widely used, and in general textually responsible *Norton Anthology of American Literature* and Binder has published the version in a separate volume.[2]

This effort to rescue Crane's uncut draft of *The Red Badge* from exclusively scholarly use (the omitted portions of the novel have been known and available since the early 1950s) would have little significance except for the coincidence of Parker's editorial involvement in the Norton anthology and thus its presence in that widely circulated form. For there is no direct external evidence that Crane cut *The Red Badge* under pressure from Hitchcock. There are only inferences and assumptions derived from long-known collateral external evidence and from the critical belief that the uncut

From *The South Atlantic Quarterly* 84, no. 3 (Summer 1985). © 1985 by Duke University Press.

novel is the superior work of art—the novel which presents Crane in the form of his initially more honest and powerful intentions rather than in the emasculated and muddled form of these intentions in the first edition. The Appleton text, Parker, Binder, and yet another Parker student Steven Mailloux argue, is hopelessly flawed because of the unintentional ambivalences created in its themes and form by Crane's destruction, through his omissions, of his previously consistent and clearly evident contemptuous attitude toward Henry.[3] Thus, if we wish to read "the *Red Badge* that Crane wrote"[4] rather than the one forced upon him by Hitchcock's desire for a less negative portrait of a Civil War recruit, we must read it in the form available to us in the *Norton Anthology* and Binder's edition.

I have already discussed elsewhere the weaknesses in the argument from external evidence that Crane was forced by Hitchcock to cut *The Red Badge*.[5] I would now like to tackle the more problematical but equally vital issue of the argument from internal evidence that the ambivalences and ambiguities in the 1895 Appleton text constitute proof that Crane was forced to warp the themes of the novel through his revision and that the more immediately clear and consistent uncut draft is thereby the superior text. I have found it best in undertaking this task to concentrate initially and for a good deal of my paper on a portion of the novel which Crane wrote early in his composition of the work and which he left uncut and unrevised in its printed version—the first two paragraphs of *The Red Badge*. By demonstrating the purposeful and thematically functional ambivalences in this passage and then in the revised novel as a whole I wish of course to demonstrate that Crane's intent from the first was toward the expression of the ambivalent nature of Henry's maturation under fire and that his revision and cutting were toward the refinement of this intent. And I would also like to push on to a demonstration of the thesis that the presence of major thematic ambivalences in *The Red Badge* can be explained to a large degree by their apt relationship to major changes occurring at that time both in Crane's ideas and in the history of American thought.

Here are the first two paragraphs of *The Red Badge of Courage*:

> The cold passed reluctantly from the earth, and the retiring fogs revealed an army stretched out on the hills, resting. As the landscape changed from brown to green, the army awakened, and began to tremble with eagerness at the noise of rumors. It cast its eyes upon the roads, which were growing from long troughs of liquid mud to proper thoroughfares. A river, amber-tinted in the shadow of its banks, purled at the army's feet; and at night, when the stream had become of a sorrowful blackness, one could see

across it the red, eyelike gleam of hostile camp-fires set in the low
brows of distant hills.

Once a certain tall soldier developed virtues and went
resolutely to wash a shirt. He came flying back from a brook
waving his garment bannerlike. He was swelled with a tale he had
heard from a reliable friend, who had heard it from a truthful
cavalryman, who had heard it from his trustworthy brother, one
of the orderlies at division headquarters. He adopted the
important air of a herald in red and gold.[6]

The opening paragraph of the novel describes the coming of spring to
an army which has been in camp for the winter.[7] One major stream of
imagery in the paragraph is that of awakening—awakening both after the
cold of night and the fogs of dawn and after the brown of winter. The army
awakens eagerly and expectantly—life is more than the cold and darkness of
sleep, and in daylight and warmth passage can be made (the roads now
"proper" rather than liquid mud) in the direction of one's destiny. The
setting and its images are those of the beginning of a journey in which the
emotional cast or coloration of the moment is largely positive; something is
going to happen, and this something is better than the death in life of
coldness, darkness, and immobility. The opening of the novel thus suggests
that we are to be engaged by an initiation story, since both the initial
situation and its images are in the archetypal form of an awakening to
experience. Out of the blankness and emptiness of innocence, youth
advances through experience to maturity and manhood.

Of course, the journey will have its difficulties. Indeed, without these it
would not be an initiation journey. One is of those others in life who have
aims different from ours and who therefore appear before us as the
contradictory, belligerent principle in experience. So there is in the first
paragraph the image of a mysterious and potentially dangerous enemy whom
one sees in the night. But perhaps the greater difficulty will be in knowing in
truth both the nature of the journey as it occurs and its full meaning at its
conclusion. This difficulty is anticipated in the first paragraph by three
references to the difficulty of knowing which are expressed through images
of seeing and hearing. Fogs often obscure the landscape, the army hears only
rumors, and the river is in shadow. The only unequivocally clear image of
knowing is that the immediate avenue of movement—the roads—are now
passable. Moreover, both the awakening and opposing forces are given an
animal cast (the army "stretched out on the hills"; the "low brows" of the
distant hills where lies the enemy), which suggests the limited rational
equipment of those seeking to know.

The first, paragraph of *The Red Badge of Courage* reveals Crane in a typically complex interweaving of images. Although the images in the paragraph imply that Henry's adventures may shape themselves into an initiation story, they also suggest that Henry himself will be an inept and inadequate interpreter of what has happened to him, that he will be unable to see and know with clarity and insight. And since the narrator will choose to tell the story through Henry's sense of its nature and importance rather than with a clear authorial underlining of meaning, we as readers will be left in a permanent state of ambivalence or ambiguity. Are we to respond to Henry's experiences principally in their symbolic character as milestones in the archetype of initiation, or are we to respond to them, because of Henry's limited understanding, as fog-ridden, shadowy, and misunderstood markers on a dimly perceived road?

The second paragraph reinforces and extends the notion that we are to have difficulty fully comprehending Henry's experiences. The first paragraph rendered the distinction between a possible progressive movement through time and the difficulty of knowing what occurs in time by means of symbolic and potentially allegorical images. The second paragraph increases our sense that the conventional means of evaluating experience are not to be trusted but does so now by means of the narrator's ironic voice in his reporting of such efforts. A tall soldier goes to wash a shirt with a belief that this enterprise requires virtue and courage. (As always in Crane's narrative style, the terms describing an action—here "developed virtues" and "went resolutely"—though superficially authorial in origin are in fact projections into the third person narrative voice of the doer's own estimation of his action. It is the soldier who believes he is behaving virtuously and resolutely, not Crane.) The statement, beginning as it does with major values and ending with the minor task to which these have been applied, is couched in the classic form of ironic anticlimax. One may think that it takes virtue and courage to wash a shirt, but there is a sharp and large distinction to be made between the actual character of the act and one's estimation of it. The implication which this distinction has for the general nature of self-knowledge, for the estimation of the worth of our acts, is that we will generally both aggrandize the significance of the event and overvalue our own attributes in relation to it.

The remainder of the paragraph contains two further implications for the problem of knowledge, both of which are also expressed in habitual forms of Crane's irony. The "tale" which the tall soldier has heard is rendered suspect despite the soldier's belief in its truth by Crane's account of its distant source and by his ironic repetition of the reliability, truthfulness, and trustworthiness of each of the tellers in the tangled history of its transmission. Much of what we learn about experience from our fellows is tainted by the difficulty of communicating accurately both what has occurred and what lies in store for us. Group knowledge, in short, is as suspect as personal self-evaluation.

As a further indication of the complications inherent in the acquisition and transmission of knowledge, the tall soldier—in his belief that he has something important to tell—begins to play a traditional role. He carries a banner and adopts the air of a herald. Man, when he has something to communicate, will adopt various roles to dramatize the worth both of his information and of himself. But the role will often obscure the emptiness and valuelessness of that which is being communicated. In short, Crane appears to be saying in this paragraph, the process of gaining and transmitting knowledge is warped by powerful weaknesses within both human nature and social intercourse. And the knowledge communicated by this process—that which we believe is true about ourselves and our fellows—is thus suspect.

The two opening paragraphs of *The Red Badge of Courage* constitute a paradigm for the themes and techniques of the novel as a whole. In its events and in much of its symbolism, the novel is a story of the coming of age of a young man through the initiatory experience of battle. But our principal confirmation of Henry's experiences as initiation myth is Henry himself, and Crane casts doubt—through his ironic narrative voice—on the truth and value of Henry's estimation of his adventures and himself. And so a vital ambiguity ensues.

The initiation structure of *The Red Badge* is evident both in the external action of the novel and in a good deal of the symbolism arising from event. A young untried soldier, wracked by doubts about his ability to perform well under fire, in fact does flee ignominiously during his first engagement. After a series of misadventures behind his own lines, including receiving a head wound accidentally from one of his own fellows, he returns to his unit, behaves estimably in combat, and receives the plaudits of his comrades and officers. On the level of external action, *The Red Badge* is thus a nineteenth-century development novel in compressed form. In such works, a young man (or woman) tries his mettle in a difficult world, at first believes himself weak and unworthy in the face of the enormous obstacles he encounters, but finally gains the experience necessary to cope with life and thus achieves as well a store of inner strength and conviction. Much of the symbolism in *The Red Badge* supports a reading of the work as developmental fiction, for one major pattern of symbolism in the novel rehearses the structure of the initiation myth. Henry is at first isolated by his childlike innocence. But after acquiring a symbol of group experience and acceptance (the red badge), he is guided by a supernatural mentor (the cheery soldier) through a night journey to reunion with his fellows; and in the next day's engagement he helps gain a symbolic token of passage into manhood (the enemy's flag).

But much in the novel also casts doubt on the validity of reading the work as an initiation allegory. Chief among these sources of doubt is Crane's ironic undermining at every turn of the quality of Henry's mental equipment and therefore of the possibility that he can indeed mature. Whenever Henry believes he has gained a significant height in his accomplishments and understanding, Crane reveals—by situational and verbal irony—how shallow a momentary resting place he has indeed reached. A typical example occurs after the enemy's first charge during the initial day of battle, when Henry grandiosely overestimates the character of a minor skirmish. ("So it was over at last! The supreme trial had been passed. The red, formidable difficulties of war had been vanquished" [p. 34].) This ironic deflation of Henry's self-evaluation continues unrelieved throughout the novel and includes as well Henry's final summing up, when, after in effect merely having survived the opening battle in the spring of a long campaign (with Gettysburg to follow!), he concludes that "the world was a world for him, though many discovered it to be made of oaths and walking sticks" (p. 109).

In addition, Crane casts doubt on the depth of Henry's maturity at the close of the novel by revealing Henry's exercise in sliding-door conscience. Henry, at the end of the second day's fighting, is still troubled by two of his less estimable acts—his desertion first of his unit and later of the tattered soldier. But what troubles him most is less the intrinsic nature of these acts than that they might be discovered, and when he realizes that this is not likely, he "mustered force to put the sin[s] at a distance" (p. 109) and revels instead in his public accomplishments. It was this aspect of Henry's intellect—his conscience-troubled rationalizations of his behavior and his closely related fury at fate for having placed him in conscience-troubling situations—which Crane, after concluding the first draft of the novel, realized he had overdone and thus cut heavily in the interval between the draft and publication.

Crane also undermines the initiation structure of *The Red Badge* by including in the hovel two major counterstructures. Initiation is essentially a mythic statement of a faith in the potential for individual growth—that the forward movement of time is meaningful and productive because through experience we acquire both the capacity to cope with experience and a useful knowledge of ourselves and the world. But *The Red Badge* also contains two major structures which imply that time is essentially meaningless, that all in life is circular repetition, that only the superficial forms of the repetition vary and thus are capable of being misunderstood as significant change and progress. One such symbolic structure is that of the rhythmic movement of troops. The novel begins with the advance to battle by Henry and his regiment, it ends with their departure from battle, and the body of the work contains a series of charges and countercharges, advances and retreats. Since these movements occur in an obscure landscape in connection with an unnamed battle, and since little meaning attends the various movements aside from their impact on Henry and his regiment, significance is attached to the fact of movement itself rather than to movement in relation to a goal or direction. One of the symbolic structures of *The Red Badge* is therefore of a flow and counterflow of men, a largely meaningless and directionless repetition despite Henry's attribution of deep personal meaning to one of its minor phases, a moment of flow which he mistakes for a moment of significant climax.

Another such circular symbolic structure is even more consciously ironic in character. Henry runs on the first day of battle because of two psychic compulsions—an animal instinct of self-preservation and a social instinct to act as he believes his comrades are acting. On the next day—in a far more fully described series of combat experiences—Henry responds to battle precisely as he had on the first day, except that he now behaves "heroically" rather than "cowardly." Again an animal compulsion (that of the cornered animal made vicious and powerful by anger and fear at being trapped) is joined with a social one (irritation at unjust blame attached to the regiment) to produce a similar "battle sleep" of unconsciousness in action. These underlying similarities in Henry's battle performances reveal not only Crane's attack on the conventional notions of courage and cowardice but—in their role as "equal" halves in a balanced symbolic structure—his belief that life is essentially a series of similar responses to similar conditions in which only the unobservant mistake the superficially different in these conditions and responses for a forward movement through time.

These two powerful drives in *The Red Badge*—the initiation plot, structure, and symbolic imagery, and the undercutting of a development myth by a variety of ironic devices which imply that the belief that man can adequately interpret the degree of his maturity is a delusion—these two drives come to a head in the final chapter of the novel. The second day's battle is over, and Henry has behaved well in his own eyes and in those of his fellows. Yet he continues as well to overvalue his accomplishments and deny his failings. The imagery of the conclusion reflects this ambivalence. Henry, now that the battle is over, thinks of "prospects of clover tranquility" (p. 109). But in fact it is raining, and "the procession of weary soldiers became a bedraggled train, despondent and muttering, marching with churning effort in a trough of liquid mud under a low, wretched sky. Yet the youth smiled, for he saw that the world was a world for him ..." (p. 109). In this passage, the fatuousness of Henry's conception of what awaits him and therefore of what he has achieved is inherent in the sharp distinction between Henry's belief and the permanent condition of the group to which he belongs, of all mankind, in effect, despite his conviction that he lies outside this condition.

It might thus be argued that Crane wishes us, at this final moment, to reject completely the validity of an initiation experience for Henry. Yet, in the final sentence of the novel, added after the completion of the full first draft, Crane wrote: "Over the river a golden ray of sun came through the hosts of leaden rain clouds" (p. 109). This flat, bald imagistic statement reaffirms the essential ambiguity of the work as a whole, despite the possibility of reading the final chapter as a confirmation of one position or the other. For the image is not attributed to Henry; it occupies a paragraph of its own, and is the narrative voice's authoritative description of a pictorial moment rather than of Henry's suspect response to the moment. And the narrative voice wishes us to be left, as a final word, with the sense that life is truly ambivalent—that there are rain clouds and that there is the sun. The darkness and cold (and lack of vision) of the opening images of the novel are part of the human condition, but the promise of daylight and spring warmth and of vision which are also present in the opening images have in part been fulfilled by the ray of sunlight.

I would now like to explore the implications of Crane's ambiguity in *The Red Badge of Courage* for his career and for his place in American literary and intellectual history. Crane's career can be divided into the usual three major phases, of which *Maggie* (1893) is the principal work in the first phase, *The Red Badge* in the middle period, and the novellas of 1897 and 1898 (of which I shall discuss "The Open Boat") the most important work of the last phase.

Maggie has always been rightfully considered the most naturalistic of Crane's works. Each of its characters is locked in a prison of self-delusion from which he never escapes. Maggie believes that Pete is a chivalrous knight who will rescue her from poverty and the oppression of her home; Pete believes that he is a formidable lover and that he has behaved well toward Maggie; Jimmie believes that his family honor requires defense; and Mary Johnson believes that she has been a Christian parent to Maggie. These delusions are made so grossly evident by the distinction between a character's self-conception and the circumstances of his life—between Mrs. Johnson's notion of the home she has created and the actual nature of that home—that we are left with little doubt that one of Crane's principal intents in the novel is to depict the overpowering role of emotional self-interest in the handicapping of the capacity to see life and oneself fully and clearly. No one knows anything of truth in *Maggie*—neither what they are nor what he or she wants to believe about himself and the world at large. Some are destroyed by this limitation (Maggie goes to her death); some are in decline (Pete and Mrs. Johnson); and some continue on their way (Jimmie). But all are locked into a world of blindness which effectively thwarts any possibility of growth based on understanding. Although the physical setting of *Maggie* is a slum, its symbolic setting is a surrealistic hall of mirrors, where the characters see only grotesque versions of themselves, versions, however, which they accept as real. And since there are no exceptions to this principle in *Maggie*, it must be assumed that Crane, at this stage of his career, believed self-delusion to be the universal human condition, with only its degree and level of sophistication a matter of variation.

"The Open Boat," written some five years later, is at the other end of Crane's depiction of the human condition. The allegorical context of the story, however, does not differ radically from the slum of *Maggie*; here, too, life is principally a matter of coping with the destructiveness present in all existence. The four men in the open boat find the sea (the immediate setting of their lives) dangerous; the sky (God) empty; and the shore (society) unknowing. But unlike the characters of *Maggie* in their absolute social and emotional isolation, the four men in "The Open Boat" come to rely on each other—to lean heavily on each other in order both to bear their condition and to survive it. Much in the story details a growth in their mutual interdependence, from a sharing of duties in the boat to a sense of comradeship which all feel. In the end, after the adventure is over, Crane tells us that the men, hearing the sound of the sea at night, "felt that they could then be interpreters."

Few readers have viewed this closing line as ironic. Our sense of a successful resolution of the adventure for its survivors, of something gained through the experience, is too great to cast doubt on the "reliability" of this final statement. Thus, the principal question to be asked of the statement is what indeed can the men now properly interpret? Crane replies to this question within the story as a whole, and his answer also replies, in a sense, to the issues raised by *Maggie*. There is no God, he appears to be saying, and isolation is therefore the quintessential human condition. But within this unchanging situation men can both establish temporary communities based on mutual need and entertain compassion for those ranges of human experience which also reveal man's essential loneliness. To be more precise, the correspondent learns, within the story, that there are no temples to cast stones at in blame for their fate, but that the men can establish a "subtle brotherhood" in their mutual understanding and aid on the boat, and that his realization of these truths of experience can at last bring him to a recognition of the universal pathos surrounding the soldier of the legion, alone and dying far from home.

"The Open Boat" thus suggests that Crane has come some distance from *Maggie*. We are still battered by life, and some, like the oiler, are mercilessly destroyed. But we can now understand this condition and, to some extent, through our understanding, lessen its effect on us, both physically and emotionally. We need not all be victimized by the human capacity for self-delusion; some of us have the capacity to mature, under pressure, to understanding. Which returns us to *The Red Badge of Courage*. In relation to Crane's career, the novel, in an image appropriate to its setting, is a kind of battleground in which the two views of human nature and experience which I have identified as flourishing in *Maggie* and "The Open Boat" struggle for dominance, without either succeeding in gaining the day. The plot and a good deal of the symbolic structure of the novel imply growth on Henry's part in coping with the eternal "war" which is human experience. But Crane's ironic voice and other symbolic structures imply that Henry is as self-deluded at the close of the novel as he is uncertain about himself at the opening. The theme of the value of social union in *The Red Badge* has something of the same ambivalence. Henry does gain a sense of a "subtle battle brotherhood" (p. 31) at various times during combat, and his return to his regiment is depicted as a productive reunion. But at other times, when he opposes the blind obedience which "union" requires of him, he is described as locked into a "moving box" (p. 21) of social and psychic compulsion as viciously destructive as is the Johnson household in imposing its values and demands on its weakest members.

The Red Badge of Courage is thus a work whose ambivalences and ambiguities are an appropriate and probably inevitable reflection of those of its author at that particular moment in his career. Crane in the novel was "working out" his then divided and uncertain notion of the balance of emphasis to give to the human capacities both for self-delusion and for insight and understanding.

The Red Badge of Courage also reflects in its ambivalences a major moment of transition in the history of American belief—that of a period in American thought when, broadly speaking, there was a movement from nineteenth-century certainties to modern doubts, from a willingness to affirm large-scale notions about the human enterprise to an unwillingness to do more than represent the immediacies of experience itself.

The origins of this state of mind in the 1890s lie less in the events of the decade itself than in the realization by a generation coming of age during the decade of changes which had been occurring in the American scene and

American belief since the Civil War. In brief, and with some of the melodramatic overemphasis and overgeneralization inherent in the art of intellectual history, young writers of the 1890s were now no longer sure of two transcendent faiths which had buttressed American belief for over a hundred years. The first was a faith in human nature in general—or more specifically in the Christian notion of man as God's special creature as that notion was refined and extended by late eighteenth-century Enlightenment idealism and early nineteenth-century romantic transcendentalism. The second was a more specialized faith in America as a world in which the Edenic possibilities of man could indeed flourish—that in this new-found-land man's capacity for productive self- and national development could best be realized.

Challenging these two faiths in the 1890s were the growing awareness of the impact of a Darwinian explanation of man's origin on the belief that man was principally a reflection of God's own capacity for wisdom and goodness, and the growing awareness that American society in its present state of development was indeed an apt symbolic reflection of man as a jungle, rather than an Edenic, creature. The animal degradation of life in the slums and factories and the cut-throat character of economic life everywhere made such an endorsement of the metaphor of America as jungle so obvious than even the popular mind could grasp the analogy.

Yet always—along with these realizations—there remained a powerful vestige of a continuing faith, one that took many forms but which had in all its shapes an emotional center of belief that America was indeed a new birth for the best that was in man—that the experiment could yet succeed. It is out of this tension between old belief and new doubts that a work such as *The Red Badge of Courage* emerges in the mid-1890s. And as so often occurred in the Americanization of the nineteenth-century great debate between faith and doubt, the specific poles of tension among writers of the 1890s were less within religious or even social categories of belief than within epistemological ones: can man know and translate into experience the great transcendent truths of life? If one can posit the two extremes in the American version of the debate, they might thus be Emerson's celebration of man's capacity to grasp intuitively the large truths analogically present in experience (that is, in nature) and the early Hemingway's lack of confidence in all but the concrete immediacies of experience itself, of his immense distrust of all large abstractions which men seek to impose on life.

Henry's experiences in *The Red Badge of Courage* appear to confirm, in their symbolic analogue to an awakening at dawn and a concluding ray of sunshine after battle, the great nineteenth-century faith in the human capacity for growth and development through a self-absorbed projection into life. But the novel also contains an equally powerful edge of "modern" doubts about the capacity of man to achieve wisdom, doubts expressed in the "modern" form of an ironic undercutting through voice and structure of the protagonist's belief that the traditional abstraction of courage is real and can be gained. It is thus an irony of a different kind that in seeking to universalize his story, to have it be not a depiction of a specific battle but an expression of a permanent human condition, Crane in fact also brought his account of Henry Fleming closer to the specific state of mind of his own historical moment—to the uncertainties about the possibility for growth and self-knowledge which had begun to gnaw at the American consciousness in his own time.

The Red Badge of Courage therefore plays seemingly contradictory roles in relation to the career of its author on the one hand and its historical moment on the other. In relation to Crane's career, the novel lies between Crane's deeply pessimistic view of man's blindness in *Maggie* and his far more affirmative sense in his later novellas of man's capacity to grow in insight and moral courage through experience. In relation to American thought, however, the novel affirms an earlier nineteenth-century faith in man's ability to mature while offering as well a modernistic critique of man's fatuous belief in his own ability to evaluate correctly both himself and experience. But this paradox, this cross-stitching, so to speak, of past and present in the work, in which it looks both backwards and forwards depending on whether one adopts a biographical or historical perspective, is one of the major sources of the novel's richness and permanence. *The Red Badge of Courage* is not a work flawed in its ambivalences. Rather, as its first two paragraphs suggest, it holds them in meaningful suspension to reflect what in the end is perhaps the modern temper in its essence—not so much a reaffirmation of faith or an announcement of the triumph of doubt as a desire to explore the interaction between these two permanent conditions of man.

NOTES

1. See Binder's "*The Red Badge of Courage* Nobody Knows," *Studies in the Novel* 10 (Spring, 1978): 9–47 and Parker's comments on *The Red Badge* in his "Aesthetic Implications of Authorial Excisions," in *Editing Nineteenth-Century Fiction*, ed. Jane Millgate (New York, 1978), pp. 99–119 and "The New Scholarship," *Studies in American Fiction* 9 (Autumn, 1981): 181–97.

2. Ronald Gottesman et al., ed., *The Norton Anthology of American Literature*, Vol. 2 (New York, 1979) and Henry Binder, ed., *The Red Badge of Courage* (New York, 1982). Parker is one of the editors of the Norton Anthology.

3. See Mailloux's *Interpretive Conventions: The Reader in the Study of American Fiction* (Ithaca, N.Y.: Cornell University Press, 1982), pp. 160–65, 178–91.

4. Binder, "*The Red Badge of Courage* Nobody Knows," p. 10.

5. "'*The Red Badge of Courage* Nobody Knows': A Brief Rejoinder," *Studies in the Novel* 11 (Spring 1979): 77–81.

6. *The Red Badge of Courage*, A Norton Critical Edition, ed. Donald Pizer (New York,: 1976), p. 5. Citations from this edition will hereafter appear in the text. The text of *The Red Badge* in the Norton Critical Edition is that of the 1895 Appleton edition conservatively emended, principally to correct typographical errors.

7. The reading of *The Red Badge of Courage* which follows has been evolving in my own thinking about the novel and about Crane's career and his times for some years. See, for example, my "Stephen Crane's *Maggie* and American Naturalism" and "Late Nineteenth-Century American Naturalism" in my *Realism and Naturalism in Nineteenth-Century American Literature* (Carbondale, Ill., 1966); "A Primer of Fictional Aesthetics," *College English* 30 (April 1969): 572–80; "Nineteenth-Century American Naturalism: An Approach Through Form," *Forum* (Houston) 13 (Winter, 1976): 43–46; and my edition of *American Thought and Writing: The 1890s* (Boston, 1972). I have also drawn upon my awareness of the vigorous debate in Crane studies on the nature, role, and worth of the ambiguities in *The Red Badge*. For a survey of the debate, see my "Stephen Crane," in *15 American Authors Before 1900: Bibliographical Essays on Research and Criticism*, ed. Earl N. Harbert and Robert A. Rees (Madison, Wisc., 1984), pp. 128–84.

DONALD B. GIBSON

Nature

Another source of aid in determining how to read *The Red Badge of Courage* is attention to one of its most important elements, an element clearly central to Crane's concerns, nature. The relation of humankind to nature is a frequent and prominent concern in Crane's fiction and poetry throughout his career, a phenomenon not entirely surprising if we recall the extent to which his nineteenth-century American literary forebears were engaged with that issue. Crane, however, saw nature in a completely different way from the way that Emerson and Thoreau perceived it on the one hand and Hawthorne and Melville on the other. For Emerson and Thoreau nature is an intermediary whose existence allows access to a higher level of reality, of being. Contemplation of nature allows the possibility of transcending the natural world and at once comprehending that which lies beyond. In the first section of his essay "Nature" Emerson speaks of the woods as "plantations of God" and says that "in the woods we return to reason and faith." He says further, in the essay, "an occult relation between man and the vegetable exists.... They nod to me, and I to them."

In the fiction of Hawthorne and Melville the implications of the relations between humankind and nature are not quite so straightforward and clear, at least in the sense of being wholly positive and unambiguous. We find in Hawthorne that nature has both a good and an evil dimension (as

From *The Red Badge of Courage: Redefining the Hero.* © 1988 by Twayne Publishers.

opposed to Emerson who finds no evil in nature). In *The Scarlet Letter* nature is represented in the opening scene by weeds, "burdock, pigweed, apple peru," representing its sinister side; and by the wild rose, representing its positive side, whose relation to the human events is such that it may show the condemned prisoner emerging from the prison that "the deep heart of Nature [Hawthorne's capitalization] could pity and be kind to him." The weeds named above and other "unsightly vegetation" find "something congenial in the soil that had so early borne the black flower of civilized society, a prison." So whether nature's relation to humankind is positive or negative, the possibility exists in Hawthorne's fiction that nature is responsive to human activity, that some relation exists between nature and morality. This is further borne out later when it is suggested that a scarlet A, the symbol Hester wears throughout the novel, appears in the midnight sky. Whether it is an illusion is never made clear, but in any case the *possibility* exists that the relation between humans and nature is such that the letter A with all its multilayered symbolic human meaning could be replicated in nature.

Likewise in Melville's *Moby-Dick* nature is ambiguously related to humankind. It is never entirely certain whether the whale's maiming of Ahab is the result of an intention on the part of the whale itself or fate, or whether it occurs because of chance. Another possibility is that deity itself has malevolent purposes and interferes in the operation of nature in such a way as to influence directly the affairs of humankind. It may well be that Ahab, were he able to accomplish his will to "strike through the mask" by killing the whale, would uncover a principle existing behind nature, nature being but a veil concealing some metaphysical reality. When Ahab considers the whale to be either "principle," deity, or "agent" of deity, he at one and the same time proposes the relation between God, nature, and humankind to be a close and intimate relation whether God exists in nature as the whale or whether God directs the course of action of the whale.

Hawthorne and Melville differ considerably from Emerson and Thoreau in their view of the relation between humankind and nature. Considered together, however, they point backward and forward in a developing trend in America whose course outlines a historical sense of that relation. The legacy of the Puritans of the seventeenth century and early eighteenth is reflected in Emerson's and Thoreau's transcendentalism though surely the Puritan divines Cotton Mather and Jonathan Edwards would have found transcendentalism heretical. Be that as it may, the Puritans "read" nature no less than did the transcendentalists, finding the glory of God and evidence of His existence manifested everywhere in nature, His creation. The only thing preventing them from "finding God in the bush," as Emerson did, was their orthodox theology which said that God and nature are separate. When the orthodoxy dies away, as it eventually did through the later eighteenth century, then transcendentalism becomes possible, its Puritan origins somewhat concealed but nonetheless apparent to the close observer.

Though Hawthorne and Melville call into question whether it is possible to "read" nature, whether the human mind is capable of the objectivity necessary to interpret what it perceives clearly and correctly, they nevertheless pose the possibility. Both writers seem keenly aware of human psychology in a way that Emerson and Thoreau were not. Both are aware of the role that personality, character, and circumstance play in perception; both are aware that two people observing the same phenomenon might well perceive it differently. Emerson seems on the whole to assume that we all see the same things, that the psychology of individuals is uniform. The implication is that *any* mind through contemplation of nature will find it possible to transcend nature. Hawthorne in his short story "Young Goodman Brown" makes it clear by precept and example (by the reader's perception of the very story itself) that perception is heavily dependent upon individual psychology. Melville makes the same point in the chapter titled "The Doubloon" in *Moby-Dick*. But neither stands entirely opposed to Emerson's thinking, insofar as it rests upon assumptions about the clarity and objectivity of thought and perception. Both seem not entirely convinced of the extent to which human objectivity is possible in that they do not deny in their fictional worlds the possibility of its existence.

Crane sees nature in an entirely different way, but a way that has its own history and grows out of the same tradition from which issued the responses to nature just discussed of earlier American writers. Unlike earlier writers and even most of his contemporaries, notably Mark Twain, Crane did not entertain the notion that any kind of sympathetic bond exists between humankind and nature. In fact, he writes in such a way as to suggest firm and direct opposition to such a view. He had some support in this perspective, though he was the first American writer to carry that view into literature. He was the first American writer to write from the perspective that the human mind, consciousness, distances humans from nature. This is first apparent in Crane's first novel *Maggie: A Girl of the Streets* where the narrator's voice differs so considerably from the voices of the characters because they lack the degree of consciousness that gives the narrator the capacity to tell the story. That same distance between narrator and character prevails in *The Red Badge of Courage*, the tone of voice being a measure of the degree of consciousness separating the narrator from Henry Fleming.

For Crane neither the view of Emerson and Thoreau that nature is a manifestation of God and that God is even immanent in nature nor that, as

Hawthorne and Melville suggest, nature *may* reflect God or contain Him (and thus their ambivalence on this issue), is tenable. Crane has been influenced by Charles Darwin and in his thinking has carried the implications of Darwinism to their logical conclusion. He was driven to do this because Darwinist thought conflicted with all that his Christian, Methodist background had taught him about the origins and meaning of the universe. (Many, many others struggled with this problem after Darwin's theory became widely known.) The Bible had told him in Genesis that God created the universe, the world particularly, and nature in the span of six days. He created man and woman in his own image and breathed into them the breath of life. Darwin told a quite different story.

Darwin began to believe, as the evidence grew, that species of living things are not fixed and immutable as Genesis implies. That is, Genesis suggests that God created all living species of life at one time and they remained unchanged from that time. Darwin's evidence indicated to him that species change and develop over time. Fossil remains indicated that existing species had previously existed in prior forms. Darwin yet had questions to answer, for he did not initially understand the mechanism driving change in species, nor did he at first know the amount of time that had been involved in the development of species to their then-current state because he, along with nearly everyone else, did not know the age of the earth. Calculated from biblical evidence, the age of the earth was thought to be about six thousand years. Such a proposition can not begin to accommodate the principle of evolution. Charles Lyell, whose *Principles of Geology* Darwin began reading when he started the voyage of exploration around the world on H. M. S. *Beagle*, said that the earth was many millions of years old, and that fact alone allowed the time necessary for the kinds of mutations in species that Darwin was later to postulate; it allowed the concept of evolutionary time. The principle of natural selection triggered by the concept of the survival of the fittest was fit enough explanation of how change occurred. The *fittest* organism is that best adapted to survive in its environment; others less well equipped to survive are snuffed out over periods of time, and those characteristics responsible for promoting survival are passed on until they prevail among the species. Such an account as this of the evolution of life on the planet does not require God; Crane knew that, accepted that, and explored the implications of it.

That Crane had Darwinism in mind, that such thought was a significant component of his frame of reference, is not a matter of speculation. It might well be inferred from external evidence such as that contained in *Maggie: A Girl of the Streets* where the conflict among individuals seems to mirror the conflict of animals in nature. Better, more direct external evidence, however, is that contained in the text as we have it of *The Red Badge*, an issue for later consideration. The strongest evidence of all is contained in the chapter discarded from the novel, the original chapter 12, where Henry, after witnessing the death of Jim Conklin, escaping from "the tattered soldier," and before receiving his "red badge" ruminates about his situation: "He made a little search for some thing upon which to concentrate the hate of his despair; he fumbled in his mangled intellect to find the Great Responsibility. He again hit upon nature.... He was of the unfit then. He did not come into the scheme of further life. His tiny part had been done and he must go.... He must be thrust out to make room for the more important.... Regarding himself as one of the unfit, he believed that nothing could accede for misery, a perception of this fact" (217).[3]

What is not entirely clear here in the discarded chapter 12 is how Crane himself is seeing what Henry says. Henry is being treated ironically, for without doubt he seeks something to blame for his situation other than himself and in so doing simply rationalizes. Does the fact of his rationalizing discredit the vehicle of his rationalization? The reference is to the theory of evolution, but what attitudes toward the theory are being expressed by Crane? The question is not easily answered. The irony directed against Henry consists in his illogical uses of the theory as when he applies his sense of the notion of survival of the fittest to his flight from battle. "If his life was being relentlessly pursued, it was not his duty to bow to the approaching death. Nature did not expect submission. On the contrary, it was his business to kick and bite and give blows as a stripling in the hands of a murderer. The law was that he should fight. He would be saved according to the importance of his strength" (215–16). To the reader it is clear that Henry is rationalizing at this point; it is not clear to Henry who applies "his findings to the incident of his flight from battle," concluding, "It was not a fault, a shameful thing; it was an act obedient to a law" (216). Henry breaks his train of thought when an antithetical notion enters his head, causing him to feel that his appeal to evolutionary theory does not solve his problem, for he continues to be subject to traditional values regarding proper conduct during battle: "But he was aware that when he had erected a vindicating structure of great principles, it was the calm toes of tradition that kicked it all down about his ears. He immediately antagonized then this devotion to the by-gone; this universal adoration of the past" (216). But even this anti-evolutionary stance Crane uses to shower irony upon Henry as he embraces the past at the exact same moment he rails against its influence on the present. He even goes so far as to see himself as a new Christ, clearly an indication of his own commitment to traditional values and a measure of his inability to be objective. "He resolved to reform it all. He had, presently, a feeling that he was the growing prophet of a world-reconstruction. Far down in the untouched depths of his being, among the hidden currents of his soul, he saw born a voice. He conceived a new world modelled by the pain of his life, and in which no old shadows fell blighting upon the temple of thought" (216).

Crane uses Henry's attitudes toward a Darwinistic nature in the discarded chapter 12 as a means of commenting on the limitations of Henry's maturation. His sense of being among the unfit as the result of the operation of forces over which he has no control causes him to rail against the operation of natural process: "It was a barbarous process with no affection for the man and the oak, and no sympathy for the rabbit and the weed" (217). Nature's indifference is not simply that but a *cruel* indifference, the irony lying in the fact that Henry should presume to judge what he has insufficient knowledge or evidence to judge. Such judgments simply reflect his character and state of mind. He asserts that though "powerless and at the will of law, he yet planned to escape; menaced by fatality he schemed to avoid it" (217). How can he possibly avoid the effects on him of the survival of the fittest? Obviously he cannot, a fact emphasized by his memory of a childhood episode at the conclusion of the discarded chapter 12. He recalls hiding in an empty flour barrel in his mother's pantry while his playmates search for him, and he imagines that in a similar way he can hide from fate in a place "where an all-powerful stick would fail to bruise his life.... He saw himself living in watchfulness, frustrating the plans of the unchangeable, making of fate a fool" (217–18). Without doubt, Crane intends in *The Red Badge* to invoke the Darwinistic scheme of nature. Henry Fleming seems to believe that scheme to be a true and valid description of the working of nature. Does Crane share his belief or is Henry's interpretation of nature another of his illusions? Since the answer to this question is so terribly complicated and involves so much of what remains to say about the novel, let us postpone the answer to this question until later. Meanwhile, we will examine the question of nature as Crane handles it in the novel as he finally intends it to be published.

The great number of references to animals, because so obvious, has been frequently noted.[4] The specific character of such references, however, has been less frequently noticed. Some of those references involve direct comparisons of men to animals either in metaphor or simile. People are like this particular animal in their behavior or like that particular animal. Other references involve indirect associations of human behavior with animal behavior, as when human actions are "dogged," people "howl," "squawk," "growl," or "snarl." Considered together, the direct references to animals, whether relating to specific or indirect comparison of human to animal behavior, fall within three categories: references to, and hence direct or implied comparisons between, people and domestic animals, wild animals, and mythological animals. In all there are approximately ninety instances of direct reference to specific animals (excluding simply mention of animal qualities as "eagle-eyed," or guns "roaring," use of the word *animal* when no specific animal is mentioned, and use of the word *beast* when no specific reference makes clear what kind of beast is meant).

The greatest number of references is to domestic animals, especially the horse. These are more negative in connotation than positive, and most frequently comparisons are either explicitly or implicitly made between qualities exhibited by people, Henry or his fellow soldiers, and qualities associated with animals. For example, at one point when Henry in the third chapter feels the impulse to warn his comrades of imminent danger, he thinks: "They must not all be killed like pigs." Crane means to do several things, chiefly to express far more meanings than Henry himself expresses from his limited perspective. First of all, he creates the association between people and animals, thus giving the comparison contextual meanings it would not carry in isolation. He then expresses Henry's literal meaning and all the connotations the word *pig* evokes. Finally he comments on Henry's character at this point in that Henry's observation is in context a false conclusion. Henry's fear for his own safety determines, as it so often does, how he sees and interprets the world around him. He is not concerned about the safety of the other men at all; rather his concern is, as nearly always, for himself alone. Henry's comment also indicates his own feeling that his situation is like that of a pig before slaughter. Subsequent events prove this assessment to be untrue. The most narrowly Darwinistic reading of the novel possible still leaves space for some modicum of control over one's destiny.

The domestic animal most frequently named in the text is the horse, not surprising in view of the fact that the horse was indeed used during the Civil War as the primary mode of individual transportation. If we look at the scenes in which horses appear, we see something other than the use of horses for realistic portrayal of war during the nineteenth century. Each time a horse appears in the novel there is a clearly established relation between horse and rider, man and animal. The first appearance of the horse is in chapter 2 where it is introduced in such a way as to suggest its thematic importance, revealing one of the possible relationships between humankind and nature. A kind of tableau is described whose relation to other scenes involving men and horses becomes clear once the question is raised: "In the eastern sky there was a yellow patch like a rug laid for the feet of the coming sun; and against it, black and patternlike, loomed the gigantic figure of the colonel on a gigantic horse" (22). Again various levels of meaning are presented here. Crane presents to us what appears before Henry's eyes; hence we see what Henry sees, but since Crane's vision is more comprehensive than Henry's, Crane's understanding of the meaning of what Henry sees is greater than Henry's. Crane's consciousness, as author, is more widely pervasive. Henry sees the tableau, but he is in no position to interpret its meaning in any kind of conscious way. It may well be implied that he has some subliminal understanding of its meaning, and for that reason it registers on his consciousness.

In any case the significant factor is that the man in the tableau is in charge of himself and his circumstances. The horse, symbolic in its giganticness of the power of nature, clearly stands in a position subordinate to that of the man, the colonel, its rider. The rider is in control and is hence capable of exerting such influence on nature as to control its power, to control the direction of the flow and the extent of its released energies. In the several scenes that follow in which men interact with horses, in every case what is emphasized is not the horse as mode of transportation, but as nature controlled by man, subject to human will. Always the control of the horse by the rider is emphasized as strong verbs tell what the rider does to control the horse: "A hatless general pulled his dripping horse to a stand near the colonel of the 304th.... You've got to hold 'em back!.... The general made a passionate gesture and galloped away" (40). There exists in this case a relationship between the authority of the rider over the horse and the authority of the rider over the circumstances in which he exists. This is so in all the scenes in which men are presented riding horses. If the individual riders are not themselves high-ranking officers, they are at least the emissaries of such, and their authority is reflected in their exertion of control: "A furious order [military order] caused commotion in the artillery. An officer on a bounding horse made maniacal motions with his arms" (49). And further: "A slim youth on a fine chestnut horse caught these swift words from the mouth of his superior. He made his horse bound into a gallop almost from a walk in his haste to go upon his mission" (50). The emphasis remains the same in each such scene: "As another officer sped his horse after the first messenger, the general beamed upon the earth like a sun.... His excitement made his horse plunge, and he merrily kicked and swore at it. He held a little carnival of joy on horseback" (51). Other such scenes depicting horses and riders in chapters 18 and 21 support similar readings. Emphasis is always on the rider's control of his horse rather than on the realistic presentation of an episode of war. The implication, insofar as humans are able to exert control over nature, is that consciousness plays some role in determining the direction of the movement of humans and that there is indeed a distinction to be made between people and animals, a distinction not so clear in the terms set out in Darwin's scheme of evolutionary development.

References to wild animals may be negative or positive as are the references to domestic animals. In both cases Crane's intention is to raise the question of the character of the relationship between humankind and nature. References to domestic animals are not all as positive as the horse symbol in that many of them suggest not the power of the horse but the powerlessness or weakness of the animal and, by analogy, humans. The cow, sheep, chicken, mule or jackass, kitten, and hen suggest weakness, passivity, stupidity, or other human limitations. Some of the references to untamed animals, such as those to the worm, rabbit, squirrel, and loon, carry similar connotations. But comparable to the use of the horse as a strong positive symbol are the many references to characteristics belonging to certain wild animals and attributed to humans. Fearlessness, strength, intrepidity are implied when people are said to be like the eagle, wolf, wildcat, or panther. Whereas the horse sets humankind apart from nature, some of the references to wild animals establish animal conduct as model for human conduct. Most references to wild animals, though, function simply to establish the similarity in general between humans and animals. Interestingly enough, in the last forty or so pages of the novel there are only six references to animals. All of these references are comparisons of human prowess to animal prowess.

We have already dealt with the significance of the references to mythological or fabulous animals. In actuality only three creatures are named—the monster, the dragon, and the serpent—though they are evoked with far more frequency than the number of times their names are used would suggest. Sometimes they are referred to by the use of pronouns, "they" or "them." When Henry feels that he or his regiment is going to be "gobbled," the reference must certainly be to one of these mythological creatures. Likewise when he feels he or his comrades are going to be "swallowed," there is a submerged reference to the largest animals named in the text, the dragons or monsters. When "in the darkness he saw visions of a thousand-tongued fear that would babble at his back and cause him to flee," he must have in mind the "monster" that he names in the next sentence (27–28). It is worth observing that references of this order diminish as the novel progresses, most of them occurring in chapters 2 to 6. There are no further such references in the final fifty or so pages of the text, and if we consider that the final reference is not an expression of trepidation on Henry's part but simply a memory of his having been afraid, then the use of any of these words as representing Henry's current fears disappears from the thirteenth to the final (twenty-fourth) chapter.

Crane's pervasive employment of figures of speech involving animals is only one element of his general interest in nature and in questions of an ultimately philosophical character revolving around the issue of the relation of humankind to nature. The opening paragraph of the novel describes the

awakening army and the dawning day. Initially the reader feels that the scene
is simply the description of an objective observer, an omniscient narrator, but
that seems unsatisfactory given the third-person, limited, technical
perspective of the novel as a whole. It seems unsatisfactory because the
description is almost wholly subjective. That is, the change in temperature
from cold to warmer is not in fact a "reluctant" change; it is simply a change
involving no will of any kind as the word *reluctant* to the contrary implies.
The landscape does not in fact "change from brown to green"; it only *seems*
to. And the army does not in fact "tremble with eagerness"; it only seems an
appropriate phrase to describe a general mood and atmosphere. There must
undoubtedly be some in that body who are neither trembling nor eager. The
river can only be a "*sorrowful* blackness" (my emphasis) to a very subjective
observer. That observer, who also sees the enemy's campfires at night as
emitting an "eyelike gleam," perhaps anticipating the images of dragons and
monsters yet to come, is none other than Henry Fleming. In the very
opening paragraph of the novel he begins to "read" nature, to interpret it in
the light of his inner feelings, an enterprise in which he engages throughout
the novel from the opening sentence to the final one.

A reader is not likely, however, on the first reading to understand fully
the implications regarding nature contained in the first two chapters, at least
not before Henry is moved for the first time to acknowledge and express
feelings about his sense of his relationship to nature: "He lay down in the
grass. The blades pressed tenderly against his cheek. The moon had been
lighted and was hung in a treetop. The liquid stillness of the night
enveloping him made him feel vast pity for himself" (25). The "blades" no
more press "tenderly against his cheek" than the "cold" in the opening
paragraph "passed reluctantly from the earth." Henry's reaction is to
personify nature here as he personified the army at the novel's beginning.
"Tenderness" implies the willed expression of positive emotion, and if the
moon indeed "had been lighted" and "hung" in a tree, then someone must
have lighted and hung it. Henry feels "pity" for himself and since the grass
sympathizes with him and the moon has been lighted and hung for him, then
nature must feel sympathy for him as well. And so it appears to: "There was
a caress in the soft winds; and the whole mood of the darkness, he thought,
was one of sympathy for him in his distress" (25). Who is this imagined
"person" who expresses tenderness, hangs the moon in a treetop for him,
caresses him and feels sympathy for him in his distress? It is the only female
with whom he has experienced intimacy of the sort evoked here—his mother.
In his imagination he fuses his own conception of nature with the memory
of his own particular mother. Otherwise, what is the source of his sense of

intimacy as described above? Hence the "mother nature" here is not some fabled, fairybook figure, but a creature emerged from the innermost recesses of his own consciousness and emotions.

We may feel reasonably safe in drawing this inference because of the association of ideas Henry makes during this scene. Immediately after his imagination has conjured up this intimation of mother nature, "He wished, without reserve, that he was at home again making the endless rounds from the house to the barn ... he would have sacrificed all the brass buttons on the continent to have been enabled to return to [milk his cows]" (25–26). It is not simply his wish to return home that establishes the connection in his mind between nature and mother but his recalling the particular memory of the cows, of milking them, of anger toward them (as toward his mother), of their function as a source of nourishment. In his memory the cow displaces the figure of the mother, for he does not have sufficient access to the content of his unconscious mind to realize that he wants to return to his mother at this point. And if he did, he would hardly admit it—even to himself—committed as he is to escaping from those bonds. Nature, then, stands in antithetical relation to the impulse driving Henry to become, as he later phrases it, "a man of traditional courage." How can this be? What sense does it make to see nature as in some sense standing in direct opposition to Henry's growth and development? At this point in the novel Henry is clearly in conflict. His desire to leave home, join the army, and to fight well in battle is frustrated by his lack of knowledge and experience, his fear for his own safety and well-being, and his apprehension that he might turn and flee. When he wishes that he were home, thereby posing the possibility that he could resolve the dilemma by doing away with one of its poles (thus eliminating the tension between the two impulses), Henry firmly establishes the relation between involvement within the sphere of nature and avoidance of the necessity of heroic action. In other words, he is committed at once, perhaps alternately is more precise, to nature, home, and mother and to their opposites, consciousness, independence, and individuation. In the terms established by Crane in the novel, Henry must escape from nature if he is to become "a man of traditional courage." The notion of escaping from nature is not new in Western thought. One of many paradigms of such movement available to Crane is contained in Genesis, one of the chief myths of Western culture. Though Crane obviously knew Genesis, as suggested above, the pattern of relation between humankind and nature projected there likewise appears in countless guises in Western thought, mythology, and literature. Though there are interesting parallels between the novel and Genesis, I would not claim that Crane derived his thought directly from that source.

NOTES

1. Quoted by R. W. Stallman in *Stephen Crane: A Critical Bibliography* (Ames: Iowa State University Press, 1972), ix.

2. A list of such critics would include most who have written about the novel and would be a long list indeed. A representative sample of critics who argue the question is contained in Stanley B. Greenfield, "The Unmistakable Stephen Crane," *PMLA* 73 (December 1958): 562–63, 568–72.

3. The quotations cited here from the expunged chapter 12 are taken from the extant pages reprinted in R. W. Stallman's edition of the novel from which all subsequent quotations in this chapter derive.

4. I call attention particularly to Mordecai and Erin Marcus, "Animal Imagery in *The Red Badge of Courage*," *Modern Language Notes* 74 (1959), 108–11.

5. Chapter and verse from Genesis, King James version of the Bible, are cited in parentheses.

LEE CLARK MITCHELL

The Spectacle of Character in
Crane's Red Badge of Courage

Stephen Crane's admirers regularly deny he is a naturalist out of what appears to be a fear of linking him with a circle of "bad" writers. Instead, they invoke for him supposedly more respectable categories, like the literary "impressionism" first admired by Joseph Conrad, or the "realism" others identify with the self-conscious craft of James and Howells.[1] Yet the "Problem" of Crane persists, and it does so in part because these categories give so little sense of his singular imaginative vision, or of his obsessive fascination with behavior that lies altogether outside one's control. Repeatedly, his telltale engine of plot is an event so violent that the very possibility of agency seems precluded. Shipwrecks, blizzards, and engulfing fires, Mexican ambushes and war itself: his favored scenes insistently forestall those moments of calm reflection or deliberate choice that were, on the contrary, given such privileged status by realist authors. And like those authors described above who challenged the realists' use of language, Crane delights in the anti-mimetic techniques that so often distinguish determinist texts.

Why is an imaginative vision so compatible with that of other naturalists consistently read as if it were not, even by those indifferent to matters of taste? More precisely, why do we attribute to Crane's characters a moral capacity that we more readily withhold from the fictional figures

From *Determined Fictions: American Literary Naturalism.* © 1989 by Columbia University Press.

imagined by Norris, say, or London? The question itself sets the terms of discussion by attesting to Crane's success in getting us to disregard the absence of certain familiar human capacities. Characters in London's Arctic world may not grasp how little autonomy they have, but they realize their wills are ineffective, which contributes to our sense of their two-dimensionality. By contrast, Crane's characters are never led to doubt the strength of their wills, and this is so despite their inability to take any greater responsibility for events. Part of what makes this disjunction effective is that Crane's narratives shuttle back and forth between two basic perspectives— between external and internal views of character that reveal one's acts as either caused or motivated. The Introduction demonstrated the shaping effect of these perspectives on our understanding of plot, as either a sequence of events that seem to happen *to* people, or as personalized actions that appear instead intended *by* them. Crane masterfully explored the tension between these two by a simple expedient, lending his characters the illusion of possessing a self in a world they had not created. The very passion with which they hold to that illusion has a contagious effect, encouraging the reader to reinscribe a premise of agency into narrative contexts that are thoroughly deterministic.

Nothing is so powerful for readers and characters alike as the notion of human autonomy—of a self in control of its future because it possesses a coherent sense of its past. That comforting notion, however, is everywhere drawn into question by Crane's fiction, which anticipates prominent aspects of texts by each of the other three naturalist authors. Like London, Crane delights in contexts physically inimical to human life, and through repetition exposes the ineluctability of events and therefore the irrelevance of knowledge about them. Yet also like Norris, he foregrounds constraints inherent in our social construction of reality, which has as determining an effect on behavior as do scenes of physical violence. The heroine of his first novel, *Maggie*, for instance, is as much self-victimizer as victim, co-opted (like Vandover) by her own unself-conscious acceptance of the social morality that destroys her even more fully than does the physical deprivation she suffers in New York City's Bowery.[2] The far wiser Dr. Trescott of his late novel, *The Monster*, is more self-aware but no more capable of altering events or moderating their interpretation.

Of all the naturalists, however, Dreiser is the most akin to Crane—and this despite the notorious differences in their highly idiosyncratic styles. For what they share is a radical view of the socialized self and its construction, and what they similarly question are our conventional assumptions about personal agency. Both men deny the humanizing premises simply assumed by their characters, and do so through narrative patterns that may at first seem to be mutually exclusive: by dramatizing the extent to which deliberation is often estranged from action, making behavior seem to lie almost entirely outside one's control; and yet by also depicting the radical conflation of desires with the world, as if one's psychology was fully expressed in what one saw by merely looking around. Both authors juxtapose narrative perspectives with their characters' subjective views, revealing the gap between actual consequences and the futile intentions behind them, between impersonal events and the guilt or pride that characters mistakenly feel. Nothing more than circumstances enmesh characters in fictional worlds they are unable to alter.

Yet even more directly than Dreiser, Crane foregrounds the problem of action and agency by turning to characters who question, almost obsessively, what they will do. Which behavioral laws will govern how they act in crisis, his figures ask, expressing in fictional form Zola's single demand of the naturalist mode: i.e., to lay bare the determining logic of behavior by careful observation of events.[3] And precisely because his characters do have the capacity to address such questions, we tend to attribute further capacities to them they may not have. Despite how readily action in Crane can be explained via determining causes, characters do continue to believe in the power of a motivating will, and thereby they seize a presumption of agency from fictional worlds that deny it.

Far more than the fiction of either naturalists, Crane's sustains with equal cogency contradictory interpretations as deterministic yet free. His narratives swallow characters up in a maelstrom of events, and at crucial moments even foreground a necessitarian premise; but they also offer the illusion that characters have effective wills by tracing conventional possibilities for moral growth.[4] The contradiction between these interpretive poles cannot be easily resolved, and certainly not without acknowledging the power of assumptions we bring to any narrative. More flamboyantly than other naturalists, Crane strips his fiction of the familiar causal tissue that reinforces those projective assumptions, in order to offer a textual approximation of the experience his characters have of events. Thus, like his characters, readers regularly slip into comforting patterns of thought unsupported by the texts they read.

Claims for agency may well be no more than self-confirming, as Crane suggests, and our comforting assumption that individual psychology is a coherent process may simply mask the state of chaotic disruption in which we live. If we can never be actually sure, at least we can try for the moment to suspend assumptions that blind us to the very possibility of incoherence. And by avoiding abstract assertions of either identity or control, we will find that Crane's characters are deprived of far more autonomy than they think.

The Swede in "The Blue Hotel," like the correspondent in "The Open Boat" and Henry Fleming in *The Red Badge of Courage*: each acts only as his erratic desires happen to dictate. Each of them is further dislodged from behavior by their texts themselves, which subvert the normal connections we assume between desires and events. At times, it seems as if an orgy of incidents and feelings had melded characters together, preventing us from linking individuals to discrete experiences. More generally, even the simplest physical details are rarely used to describe a character, reinforcing a radically unconventional conception of personality—as if it were identified less with an individual body than a social system. Little as individuals are able to admit this unsettling possibility, it is everywhere established by Crane in characteristically visual terms, and perhaps nowhere more convincingly than in *The Red Badge of Courage*.

The Spectacle of War

Standing on Boston Common in the early 1830s, Ralph Waldo Emerson felt a tremendous sense of self-transcendence as he became for the moment like a "transparent eyeball." That famous and paradoxical image—"I am nothing; I see all; the currents of the Universal Being circulate through me"—has variously since been invoked, although never to describe the naturalist characters who best seem to fit the description.[5] Clyde Griffiths and Roberta Alden, Vandover and London's Arctic trekker, as well as other figures only mentioned in these pages (including Carrie Meeber, Trina McTeague, and Upton Sinclair's stockyard immigrants): all seem "transparent eyeballs," lacking the opaque material of selfhood that might obtrude between their inner desires and outer events. That deficiency helps explain their usual stance of wide-eyed staring in which they identify their incoherent energies with the worlds that bear upon them.

Few other texts, however, explore this ocular fixation as profoundly as Crane's *Red Badge of Courage*, or enact so fully the paradoxical implications of repetition in Emerson's pronouncement. The novel, that is, does more than depict the kind of visual paralysis that ensues from finding oneself in a world one has done nothing to create—the claim most often defended in Marxist analyses. Such an approach, by focusing on the alienating effects of reification, invariably bolsters our initial assumptions about subjectivity and the moral self. Accordingly, even when fictional embodiments of the full Emersonian "I" are reduced to more thinly transparent "eyes"—when, as in Crane, the coherent ego is exposed as nothing but an illusion—Marxist critics nonetheless tend to recuperate that illusion as fact. The "observer becomes a participant" in fictional texts that always, so it is claimed, subvert the self-alienation they represent.[6] Whatever the case for other authors, however, Crane's version of the "participant observer" is far less assuaging than any such reading suggests. He challenges our understanding of the primary process of vision itself, revealing through narrative repetition how fully it is transformed from what seems a literal, distinctly passive experience into an active and wrenchingly figurative one. Sight always recurs as insight that is itself determined and determining. Characters who "see all," therefore, reveal not liberating possibilities for social reform, but rather the inherent constraints that are always already shaping our vision, and enmeshing us even as we presume otherwise in a self-confirming logic.

The novel itself opens with a strikingly personified view of "the red eye-like gleam of hostile camp-fires set in the low brows of distant hills."[7] As the awakening army "cast its eyes upon the roads," the novel establishes the spectatorial activity that quickly comes to dominate. Soon after, Henry Fleming's ever-vigilant gaze is first invoked—"his youthful eyes had looked upon the war" (3)—and a day later the narrative will metaphorically assert, "new eyes were given to him." In between these opening and closing references, he is repeatedly described in distinctively spectatorial terms: "the youth stared," "the youth saw," "the youth had watched, spell-bound," a "tortured witness."[8] And at the crisis of the novel on the second day of battle, Henry appears to himself to become all-perceptive:

> It seemed to the youth that he saw everything. Each blade of the green grass was bold and clear. He thought that he was aware of every change in the thin, transparent vapor that floated idly in sheets.... His mind took a mechanical but firm impression, so that, afterward, everything was pictured and explained to him, save why he himself was there. (85–86)

After this respite from battle ends, the emotional and narrative pace again quickens and the syntax reverts once more to the endlessly reiterated form, "He saw ..."[9]

Visual activity in the novel is hardly as direct as this syntax may suggest, however, conforming instead to a pair of contradictory, alternating patterns. The first consists of an awe-struck gaze so engrossing that Henry cannot resist what he sees. Absorbed into the spectacle of martial experience, he loses all self-consciousness—a feeling powerful enough at moments to reduce him to little more than reflexive motions:

> The youth, still the bearer of the colors, did not feel his idleness. He was deeply absorbed as a spectator. The crash and swing of

the great drama made him lean forward, intent-eyed, his face
working in small contortions.... He did not know that he
breathed; that the flag hung silently over him, so absorbed was
he. (99)

Somewhat later, this ocular absorption becomes so intense an emotional
drama that it can only be presented figuratively: "The youth had centered
the gaze of his soul upon that other flag" (102). Henry has reverted to a stage
of unmediated identification with experience, and lacks any consciousness of
himself as active agent of perception. This is the reason he loses a supposedly
cowardly concern for his safety, since by the second day of battle he simply
lacks self-awareness altogether.

The long gaze of wonder in which Henry is absorbed—voided
psychologically as he is grammatically in the process of sheer perception—
occurs most frequently at severe pitches of emotional violence. Yet this forms
only one aspect of the larger process of his spectatorial dependency, since
much of the time he directs his attention obsessively at others. Under the
assumption that they are just as obsessively (if derisively) gazing at him, he
becomes reduced to their mirroring reflections of himself. This condition of
psychological enslavement to others occurs throughout the novel with an
effect that is equal to the intense private moments of perceptual absorption.
Repeatedly, Henry swings between alternate feelings of pride and shame,
both of which seem irrelevant.

Toward the novel's end, in a scene that exemplifies the first of these
responses, he amazes his comrades by the fearlessness with which he charges
into battle:

During this moment of leisure, they seemed all to be engaged in
staring with astonishment at him. They had become spectators.
Turning to the front again, he saw, under the lifted smoke, a
deserted ground.

He looked, bewildered, for a moment. Then there appeared
upon the glazed vacancy of his eyes, a diamond-point of
intelligence. "Oh," he said, comprehending.... [T]hey had found
time to regard him. And they now looked upon him as a war-
devil. (80)

In a thorough inversion of the earlier process by which Henry vanishes amid
his surroundings, he here becomes the sole object of a completely admiring
communal gaze. Yet he is no more self-constructed or autonomous than

before—as much as ever the product of constraining forces that lie beyond himself. The passage's disconnected, clausal prose confirms his slow transformation from presumed subject to manifest object, as the sequence of verbs transforms someone seeing to something seen. What at first appears simply a constraining repetition of "he saw" with "he looked" is immediately inverted by the description of what "appeared" upon "his eyes," then as immediately shifted again from ocular experience to a visual trope: "a diamond-point of intelligence." The grammatical process simply corroborates his psychological transition at the center of others' attention, as his self-conception is once again governed by the way they "regard him" and "looked upon him." With little appreciation for the power of their gaze, he now "lay and basked in the occasional stares of his comrades" (81).

Understandably, Henry is more fully aware of this communal gaze at moments when he fears he has become an object of derisive scorn. After his desertion, therefore, he suspects nearly everyone he sees, and especially the tattered man whose only fault is excessive good cheer: "The youth glancing at his companion could see by the shadow of a smile that he was making some kind of fun" (47). Odd as is the unnamed man's "chance persistency," his affable manner and genial questions hardly support Henry's paranoid interpretation—a paranoia that curiously compounds his apprehension about being seen with the fear that he may in this instance be seeing too little. No matter how carefully he trains his own gaze, he feels exposed to a damning inspection: "It was not within human vigilance" (48).

Nothing he does can help him avoid what he takes to be a Medusa-like stare, represented not simply by the tattered man but by all experience—or as he expresses it in panicked tones, "the dark, leering witch of calamity" (51). Narcissistically fearful of the "leer" being ever directed at him, he desperately imagines how to direct "the scrutiny of his companions" away from his presumed cowardice. Appearing to fail at that, however, he grimly imagines what will ensue once his dishonor is "apparent to all men":

> In the next engagement they would try to keep watch of him to discover when he would run.
>
> Wherever he went in camp, he would encounter insolent and lingeringly-cruel stares. As he imagined himself passing near a crowd of comrades, he could hear some one say: "There he goes!"
>
> Then, as if the heads were moved by one muscle, all the faces were turned toward him with wide, derisive grins. He seemed to hear some one make a humorous remark in a low tone. At it, the others all crowed and cackled. He was a slang-phrase. (54)

This humiliating vision of himself seen through the filter of others' scorn governs Henry's self-constitution, as "pictures of himself, apart, yet in himself came to him" (51).

So intense is this repeated feeling of watching himself from afar that it seems an outer-body experience, an all but literal enactment of the process of dissociated sensibility. Following his first battle, when self-consciousness momentarily vanishes, the experience is vividly dramatized: "The youth awakened slowly ... scrutinizing his person in a dazed way as if he had never seen himself. Standing as if apart from himself, he viewed the last scene. He perceived that the man who had fought thus was magnificent" (30). As Henry grows self-absorbed and increasingly complacent through the course of the novel, he will "reflect" on himself more often in versions of this posture.[10] Indeed, the passage itself anticipates the transformation yet to come in the subtle shift across an apparent repetition from literal to metaphoric sight— "he viewed" becomes "he perceived." Although the "gleeful and "unregretting" account he takes of his actions in the final chapter sharply contrasts with the sense of inadequacy he felt only a day before, the prospect from which "he saw that he was good" forms much the same external vantage: "From this present viewpoint, he was enabled to look upon [his actions] in spectator fashion and to criticise them with some correctness" (106). His fresh perspective on his newly achieved identity differs little from the old—except insofar as it blinds him further to the force of his unwilled desires.

The irony implicit in the dual forms of Henry's specular enslavement is that only when fully absorbed in battle, unaware of conforming to any behavioral standards, can he perform in accord with the judgment he would have others pass on him. Only immersed in the spectacle of war can he meet his expectations, expectations cherished in a frame of mind that itself precludes his acting that way. By losing all self-consciousness and no longer figuratively standing outside himself, he functions mindlessly in a manner that others take to be heroic. Paradoxically, heroism requires something like a state of non-being, while full self-awareness necessarily rules out any such selfless behavior: "He suddenly lost concern for himself and forgot to look at a menacing fate. He became not a man but a member.... He was welded into a common personality which was dominated by a single desire" (26). This psychological pattern, indeed the sentences themselves, are later nearly repeated when he watches others flee: "He forgot that he was engaged in combating the universe.... He lost concern for himself."[11] Of course, just as this "heroism" does, panic allows him to forget reputation, likewise enabling him to forego an external perspective on his behavior.

The Red Badge of Courage emphasizes, as do few other novels, a complex exchange between the spectacle of oneself and one's altering self-conception. While that exchange would seem to privilege powers of visual discrimination, the novel denies that one can ever control one's vision, much less ever have it effectively guide one's will. "Seeing" is either a passive process that absorbs Henry into the world, or a reactive process of responding to what he imagines others are thinking. In either case, the free-standing "self" essential to classical realism disappears, along with a self-regarding, self-conscious capacity for responsibility.[12]

Loss/Laws of Character

NO MATTER how thoroughly Henry is robbed of a self by these forms of ocular enslavement, he persists nonetheless in trying to discern the laws to his behavior that might attest to a self—a psychological structure of desires controlled by an organizing will. Of course, we tend to view him differently from the way he views himself—a tendency that fills him with apprehension, as we have just seen. And because we see more of him than do his fellow soldiers, we are less impressed by his presumed self-possession than we are by the force of his desires. Still, he persistently wants to find a way to predict his behavior, and more particularly as if in echo of Zola's naturalistic pronouncements about the effects of diverse circumstances—to know how he will act in battlefield conditions:

> He felt that in this crisis his laws of life were useless. Whatever he had learned of himself was here of no avail. He was an unknown quantity. He saw that he would again be obliged to experiment as he had in early youth. He must accumulate information of himself. (7)

Strenuously as he tries "to mathematically prove" that he will not desert, no proof can be had, and all he can do is to settle at last for Jim Conklin's communal rationale: "If a hull lot a' boys started an' run, why, I s'pose I'd start an' run…. But if everybody was a-standin' an' a-fightin', why, I'd stand an' fight. B'jiminy, I would" (9). No law of character emerges or is about to do so in this kind of world, in part because neither deliberation nor resolution forms a warrant for action. Behavior is almost never predictable, at least as Crane conceives Henry Fleming, because his acts are rarely intended. They emerge instead from an impersonal, interdependent nexus of forces—sometimes physical, sometimes psychological, but always finally social—allowing simply what happens to happen to define after the fact the way one is, shaped willy-nilly by the collective behavior of others.

Reinforcing our sense of the ways that the self is excluded from this fictional world is the absence of any scenes of restraint, of instances when Henry refrains from an action he has contemplated. The problem has as much to do with lack of deliberation as with lack of restraint, since so few actions are ever considered beforehand by Henry, who characteristically feels his "mind flew in all directions." On those rare occasions when he does deliberate and does form a resolution, the process fails to enrich our sense of his self-constraining will. Concerned to capture the enemy colors, for instance, "he was resolved it should not escape," as "hard lines of determined purpose" appear on his face accompanied by a "grin of resolution" (102–3). Yet little seems chosen or freely willed about this fit of perseverance, and nothing distinguishes it or other such scenes from sheer desire.

Likewise, when Henry refrains from twitting Wilson about his earlier timid request, the scene is presented ambiguously. He "suddenly" recalls the packet of letters that Wilson gave him for safekeeping, impulsively exclaims aloud at the memory, and then inexplicably "felt impelled to change his purpose" (70). Nothing indicates that he is choosing, like Huck Finn or Isabel Archer, to refrain after due consideration of the merits of the case—or even that he is indeed refraining from a predictable course of action. By the time "he resolved not to deal the little blow," it is clear he is compelled by the grip of pride rather than motivated by compassion. Likewise later, "he made an attempt to restrain himself" from angry outburst, "but the words upon his tongue were too bitter" (75). Even when he does on occasion maintain his resolve—as when he vows, in battle, "not to budge whatever should happen" (100)—no reason for his behavior is adduced, as if to stress his utter lack of responsibility for acting that way.

Deliberation seems shallow at best and at worst cannot be relied upon, but that is not enough in itself to prevent Henry (or us) from tracing a law to his character. The novel more certainly precludes that possibility at a behavioral level by revealing characters so unpredictable as to render identity itself incoherent. Although Henry has known Jim Conklin ever "since childhood" (10), his long-time friend appears enigmatic not only to us but also to him: someone initially loud and boastful, belligerently trading on rumors of war, appears at the same time wise beyond his years in considering the prospect of desertion. With even greater dramatic moment, Wilson's radical change in character occurs literally overnight, from being a "loud soldier" to someone whose "fine reliance" bespeaks "a quiet belief in his purposes and abilities" (68).

These changes challenge some of our deepest assumptions about both constancy and consistency in personal behavior—and this remains so in the face of Bernard Williams' denial that "memory claims and personal characteristics" form necessary conditions for identity. Nothing, according to Williams, requires that we have the same habits, preferences, ideas, and memories today as we had yesterday to be identified as the "same" person. Still, despite his convincing logic, we do ordinarily assume that people act in a consistent fashion, that they maintain from day to day a constant configuration of beliefs, and that their identities therefore involve more or less permanent traits of character.[13] Wilson's sudden about-face may not itself surpass belief but it does contribute to the general process by which identity is brought into question by the novel.

The character who notably lacks a coherent, consistent identity is Henry Fleming, even if the narrative's free indirect discourse occasionally blinds us to this realization. He simply acts as his strongest desires at the moment happen to dictate, and their very unpredictability prevents him from telling the kind of a soldier he will be. Yet the more important question concerns what kind of a person he can be, since even were he predictable, that would not clearly make him a willing agent. Lacking a self, Henry is deprived of the power to alter his behavior, and thereby to choose the kind of person he might in any event *want* to be.[14] He admires Wilson's alteration into a kinder, better man, just as he admires the unseen "cheery soldier" who helps him back to his regiment (61). But he lacks the capacity (much as do they) to transform simple admiration into a larger volition to act like them. For much the same reason that he is unable to order his desires, he cannot direct his actions in accord with an overriding conception of himself.

All Henry can do at first is to justify himself according to a rather complacent sense of his own virtue, attributing motives to himself that are always flattering. And that all too easily becomes a matter of simply rationalizing behavior according to causes he projects back onto experience: "He had proceeded with wisdom and from the most righteous motives" (35). Later, he hopes for the personal vindication that would supposedly ensue from his regiment's defeat, thereby proving "he had fled early because of his superior powers of perception" (52–53). Persistently, he confuses moral judgments with self-justification in a pattern sometimes openly parodied by the narrative voice: "He searched about in his mind then for an adequate malediction for the indefinite cause, the thing upon which men turn the words of final blame. It—whatever it was—was responsible for him, he said. There lay the fault" (50). Disappointed and angry, he flatly denies he can help what he's done, unaware that any resort to determinism argues him out of existence as an autonomous self.

Henry refuses to settle for this paradoxically subversive form of self-justification, having realized how little it addresses the question of what kind of soldier he will be, or otherwise reveals about his "unknown quantity." The advantage of the alternative method he adopts is precisely its greater descriptive accuracy, although in the end it will give him no greater sense of autonomous selfhood: "The only way to prove himself was to go into the blaze and then figuratively to watch his legs to discover their merits and faults" (9). This image ironically matches the pose of the unnamed man in London's story, left "looking at himself in the snow" while he slowly freezes to death. As a process of self-assessment, however, it resembles more closely the response of the garrulous old lady recalled by E. M. Forster, who when accused of being illogical, exclaimed: "Logic! Good gracious! What rubbish! How can I tell what I think till I see what I say?"[15]

Yet Henry's proposal is even more radical than this exclamation implies, corresponding to the concept of "moral luck" in which "how things turn out determines what has been done." The meaning of action, in other words, emerges now only well after the fact, not before, if with the same effect of appearing to remove his actions from Henry's control. His behavior is still apparently governed by something other than a "self," since even without an "indefinite cause" he exists as no more than the things he has done. The major difference in the way he rationalizes his motives is that he begins to stand outside his actions as a means of judging them. This gradual shift in perspective releases him from narrow self-justification ("I acted that way from the best of motives") to a logic that connects his behavior with a set of larger social categories ("I am the way my actions turned out").

Despite his shift in self-appraisal, his logic remains no less circular, leaving Henry still victim of consequences rather than master of dispositions. All he can do, once having adopted an external view of behavior, is to apply fixed categories of cowardice, bravery, duty, and so on to the acts he performs. No more fully now than before does this backward-looking logic structure a self, since his experiences are simply absorbed again into the larger regimental process. As he observes (without understanding), he is a "coward" for no other reason than that his regiment happens to withstand the assault from which he flees. Later, he becomes a "hero" largely because his regiment happens to win: "It was revealed to him that he had been a barbarian, a beast ... Regarding it, he saw that it was fine, wild, and, in some ways, easy. He had been a tremendous figure, no doubt" (80). Having tried a day earlier to assert a law to his character by moral fiat, he ends by accepting the categories imposed on himself by moral luck. The latter method may seem more effective, but it too only reveals how little self he has.

Narrating the Absent Self

The Red Badge of Courage subverts any impulse to view Henry Fleming as a moral agent, establishing through its style itself deep doubts about his claims to being an autonomous actor vested with a capacity for responsibility. It does this by disrupting normal grammatical expectations for a "self" whose emotions, ideas, and actions are integrated, and who stands free of his fictional world."[16] Near the beginning of the novel, Henry overhears Jim Conklin confidently announce that "th' army's goin' t' move":

> He had burned several times to enlist. Tales of great movements shook the land. They might not be distinctly Homeric, but there seemed to be much glory in them. He had read of marches, sieges, conflicts, and he had longed to see it all. His busy mind had drawn for him large pictures, extravagant in color, lurid with breathless deeds. (3)

The effect of this sequence of simple sentences, each of which starts arrestingly afresh, is to lend to Henry a childlike air. As in Jack London's story, the passage relies on an extreme paratactic structure, with the similar effect that time itself seems temporarily forestalled. Because sentences do not progress in a way we have normally been led to expect, our narrative sense of duration and temporal sequence is at least for the moment suspended. As well, however, and more importantly, the syntax here announces the state of its subject by its very lack of causal connectives. Henry seems to consist of a medley of conflicting energies in a world that similarly lacks any pattern, while actions are defined in a way that suggests that agency is something well beyond him.[17] Neither he nor anyone else has the power, so the prose suggests, to coordinate the conflicting desires that go into constituting themselves.

Yet if everyone is struck on first reading by Crane's notoriously eccentric narrative perspective, critics have nonetheless usually slighted its most salient feature: the way in which his descriptions invert our customary assumptions about acting in the world. The madness of war, of course, has always been deemed sufficient to explain altered consciousness, and yet Crane treats the combat setting as little more than a narrative cliché. Neither scene nor plot in themselves, that is, help explain his beguiling transfigurations, which result from a far more violent set of stylistic maneuvers. The effect of that violence is finally to reduce individuals to events, at the same time that a curious semblance of human life is breathed into things. The normal way in which we categorize people and things in the world is disrupted, as characters are made to appear from a thoroughly external and objective point of view, while the natural world conversely appears from a seemingly internal and personal perspective.

Expectations are disrupted, moreover, from the novel's very first lines through rhetorical tropes that have the effect of challenging the syntax of our

thoughts. Consider the famous opening description of the monster army
awakening and trembling, or this brief scene later the next day: "A single rifle
flashed in a thicket before the regiment. In an instant, it was joined by many
others ... The guns in the rear, aroused and enraged by shells that had been
thrown burr-like at them, suddenly involved themselves in a hideous
altercation with another band of guns" (77–78). A skirmish between soldiers
occurs as an "altercation" between weapons, autonomous bands of guns
"aroused and enraged" into "suddenly involv[ing] themselves." Not only is
experience released here as elsewhere from an appearance of human control,
but it manifests a powerful life of its own that reduces individuals to
dependent onlookers. Earlier, a similar description has evoked a similar
sense: "The guns squatted in a row like savage chiefs. They argued with
abrupt violence. It was a grim pow-wow" (29). Unlike Henry's mode of
thought—which invokes the pathetic fallacy in order to justify his actions,
adducing from natural processes a supposed model for his behavior—the
omniscient narrator's style establishes precisely the opposite: that those
capacities we cherish as human hardly need be considered as such.[18]

Conversely, Crane's grammar tends to reduce the human to a
mechanical status, and does so most obviously through forms of repetition
common to naturalist prose. Descriptions are occasionally duplicated word
for word within pages of each other, and accounts of events or of dialogue
are likewise all but exactly repeated.[19] There is, of course, a certain thematic
appropriateness to this stylistic repetition, since the experience of war that
Crane presents is itself endlessly repetitive: "Also, he was drilled and drilled
and reviewed, and drilled and drilled and reviewed."[20] Likewise, battle
scenes repeated over two long days differ little to us, for all the sharp
distinctiveness they appear to have for Henry. The collective impact of these
repetitions is to produce a sense of stasis, as if no progress had been made
and never could be. All that is possible is to repeat what has already been
done many times before, to reiterate again what has been said on countless
other occasions. The novel's conclusion confirms this sense with the news
that the hard-won ground will merely be abandoned by Henry's regiment.
The next day promises only more of the same—of fruitless actions described
in a language incapable of making a difference.[21]

These repetitions and syntactic disruptions have an estranging effect
on the reader, establishing a context within which characters exist not as
agents but as machines. Even prior to that context, the effect is clearly felt in
the earliest reference to Henry as a mere conjunction of parts: "There was a
youthful private who listened with eager ears ... [and then] went to his hut ...
He wished to be alone with some new thoughts that had lately come to him"
(2). The compound sentences themselves, which move an elementary diction

through additive clauses, tend once again to diminish their subject. Here, however, the effect results from something more than a syntactical stutter— from the description's striking reliance on a sequence of prepositions rather than adverbs. By identifying Henry's behavior through a series of separate attributes, rather than the more normal method of modified capacities, the passage transforms his dissociated sensibility into a physical fact. The preposition "with," in other words, links him to "eager ears" and "new thoughts," and by doing so intimates that organs as well as ideas do not cohere in a self.

As the narrative continues, this process becomes increasingly disruptive:

> The youth went along with slipping, uncertain feet. He kept watchful eyes rear-ward. A scowl of mortification and rage was upon his face. He had thought of a fine revenge upon the officer who had referred to him and his fellows as mule-drivers. But he saw that it could not come to pass.... And now the retreat of the mule-drivers was a march of shame to him. (90)

Henry is again shorn of the conventional markings of coherent identity, not only by the characteristic reference to him as "the youth," but by the stilted sequence of simple sentences that reveal his poor self-integration. A paratactic structure once more repeatedly returns to the same subject ("the youth," "he," "he," "but he"), dismissing a complex psychological grammar along with a complex verbal one. Likewise, the syntax of his presentation breaks him again into parts ("with slipping, uncertain feet" rather than "his feet slipped"; "kept watchful eyes" rather than "watched"; "a scowl upon his face" rather than "he scowled"; and so on). Perceptions, behavior, and thoughts seem curiously but profoundly unaligned.

Ironically, the only alignment in the passage is represented by Henry's posture, which is turned to the rear, facing backward, in bodily correspondence to his mental state. Instead of adducing possible motives, no matter how self-justifying—or even simply attempting to identify the physical causes for his present condition—Henry has by now been reduced to the logic of interpreting consequences after the fact. Return, revenge, repetition: the passage is a model of reflexivity. He is compelled bodily, emotionally, and psychologically into accepting the way things turn out as a reading of what has been. All that is left for him to do is to repeat the officer's characterization, rejecting it first only then to accept it quietly as his own interpretation ("the retreat of the mule-drivers was a march of shame").

Even more dramatically elsewhere, the narrative stresses how fully motives actually seem to ensue from behavior instead of the other way around, as we commonly assume.

> Directly he began to speed toward the rear in great leaps. His rifle and cap were gone. His unbuttoned coat bulged in the wind. The flap of his cartridge-box bobbed wildly and his canteen, by its slender cord, swung out behind....
>
> Since he had turned his back upon the fight, his fears had been wondrously magnified. (32)

The description again is disjoining, as Henry metonymically flies apart in the bulging, bobbing, unbuttoning disruption of his apparel. What leads to his reintegration is the interpretive mode into which he falls, insinuated by the final sentence. Or rather, it is the ambivalent opening word of the sentence that offers a key to understanding how self-construction frequently works in the novel ("Since he had turned his back"). The word "since" intimates not just that "fears" occur *following* his flight from battle ("since" here serving in an adverbial capacity, meaning "after"), but that his fears result instead precisely from having run away (serving as a conjunction, and in this case meaning "because"). The suggestion emerges that turning his back and then running generates the fear he feels, in contrast to the more obvious causal pattern that works vice versa. Strange as this inverted process may seem, it perfectly exemplifies the paradox of "moral luck," in which our view of each other depends upon simply what happens to occur.

Even more radically, the novel suggests that the way in which characters tend to view consequences dictates the feelings they initially had, those feelings that led to their behavior in the first place. Of course, any consequence is always viewed through the frames of social convention, but here, characters casually accept a code of behavior that takes no account of motive or even of predisposing emotion. The result of this double process is to rule out the very possibility of an autonomous self, since what one is and what one feels depends on events and codes fully beyond one's control. Much as this double process defies all customary logic, moreover, it corresponds to our sense of how determinism might well work—and does so once again by disrupting our normal projective assumptions.[22]

Compounding this disruptive effect is the problematic status of the narrative voice, which slides back and forth between the free indirect discourse of Henry's atomized perspective and an omniscient third person. Seconds before he receives the gratuitous wound of his "red badge of courage," the narrative evokes his agitated, emotionally fractured state of mind as he stumbles upon a group of fleeing soldiers:

Soon he was in the midst of them. They were leaping and scampering all about him. Their blanched faces shone in the dusk. They seemed, for the most part, to be very burly men. The youth turned from one to another of them as they galloped along. His incoherent questions were lost. They were heedless of his appeals. They did not seem to see him. (58)

The choppy syntax here once again seems to exclude an organizing will, and powerfully evokes the consciousness of someone who lacks a self. Yet some pages later, the same syntactical pattern initially characterizes what is clearly an omniscient voice:

The fire crackled musically. From it swelled light smoke. Overhead, the foliage moved softly. The leaves with their faces turned toward the blaze were colored shifting hues of silver, often edged with red. Far off to the right, through a window in the forest could be seen a handful of stars, like glittering pebbles, on the black level of the night. (64)

The passage brilliantly justifies Conrad's praise of Crane's "impressionist" style, even though that very brilliance raises questions about the narrative voice. After all, both diction and perspective clearly exceed Henry's modest capacities, at the same time that the syntax continues to reflect his limited processes of thought. Only gradually, that is, does the narrator abandon Henry's rudimentary constructions in favor of the compound sentences that attest to a firmer, more confident narrative control.

There are countless other occasions when the narrative voice seems colored by Henry's perspective, although at first no obvious purpose seems to be served by this. Yet the texts of other naturalists reveal similar fractures in narrative voice, sometimes cleft so sharply that the narrator seems to be hectoring characters. These dramatic divisions between alternative points of view has the effect of placing them, ironically, "in perspective," revealing their separate limitations and drawing into question any one's privileged status (as London and Dreiser showed). Conversely, here (as in Norris' novel), the transition between assorted viewpoints and voices is entirely muted, with the result that it is more than occasionally hard to discern which is which. Part of what is achieved, however, by slipping into and out of Henry's consciousness is that he gradually becomes absorbed into the larger discursive world. The very indeterminacy in the pattern of alternating voices contributes to that overall process. Take, for instance, the pathetic fallacy, which characterizes both the narrator's animation of nature and Henry's self-rationalizations. Their separate conceptual habits are linked via a common trope—one that we share as well. What finally distinguishes Henry's usage is not his projective frame of reference, as critics sometimes claim, but rather the fact that he is so complacent about the conclusions to be drawn from his observations.

There is a more troubling aspect, however, to this confused medley of voices, one that becomes particularly apparent at moments of strained syntactical construction. Midway through the novel, Henry is mortified as he recollects his desertion: "Again he thought that he wished he was dead. He believed that he envied a corpse. Thinking of the slain, he achieved a great contempt for some of them as if they were guilty for thus becoming lifeless" (53). Logically, this way of stating the issue tends toward incoherence, since it is hard to see how one might be able to err about one's own feelings, at least as one is feeling them. Either Henry did actually have a wish for something and did in fact envy someone, or else he did not—and at the time he felt these he could not also have "thought" or "believed" he was feeling differently. The principle underlying this assertion is that an emotional state is unlike the world, since we cannot unwittingly misconstrue the contents of our own minds, while we can certainly misrepresent external events (the construction, "he thought he was in pain, but he wasn't," seems nonsensical, while "he thought it was raining, but it wasn't" is both plausible and common).[23] Yet incoherent as such mistaken self-referential claims seem to be, their appearance in the novel attests to something more than narrative incoherence. For by alerting us to a logical conflict, they help to reveal how thoroughly character is constructed through a pattern of conflicting voices. It is as if the very process of foregrounding activities supposedly attributed to oneself were intended to clarify how arbitrary the assumptions we hold about ourselves really are. Once again, the novel reveals that the process of constructing a self consists of certain habitual assumptions we do not (and perhaps cannot) think to question—assumptions we silently impose upon texts that invite quite another way of reading.

The stylistic innovations of *The Red Badge of Courage* breach an assortment of realist conventions—so many that readers have frequently failed to realize their collective philosophical impact. More compellingly than other naturalists, Crane demonstrated how fully our assumptions about what it is like to be in the world help to create the shape of that being. He understood how little proof exists to support the conventional belief in a self able to choose, then to act responsibly. And he quietly withheld from his novel those structures—grammatical, scenic, and narrative—that enable readers to project certain comforting assumptions about agency onto fictional characters. Throughout his career, he imagined quite different kinds of plots and behavior, but he always returned to the problem of how to read ourselves into the world. Henry Fleming, in other words, provides only the most obvious example of a character who exists as little more than a vortex of emotions and desires. Maggie Johnson, the Swede in "The Blue Hotel," the correspondent in "The Open Boat," among others: all are presented as gazing subjects, denied a will by the very narratives that present them as sets of reflexive traits. For us to see them as full personalities, as agents responsible for their acts and their lives, is to submit to a cherished illusion that is everywhere exposed as far in excess of the facts. We need instead, with Crane as with others, to attend to the texture of his idiosyncratic prose. Only then will we come to realize how thoroughly the placement of words on a page can dismantle the otherwise comforting assumptions we bring to bear upon fictional characters, and as well upon ourselves in the world.

NOTES

1. Over thirty years ago, Stanley B. Greenfield perceptively observed: "An examination of the critcism of the novel reveals errors ranging from inadvertent through disturbing misstatements of fact to quotations out of context and gross distortions of sense." "The Unmistakable Stephen Crane," *PMLA* (1958), 73:562. James Nagle provides a good source for Conrad's and other similar comments about Crane, as well as aggressive resistance to the lable of naturalism for Crane, in *Stephen Crane and Literary Impressionism* (University Park: Pennsylvania State UP, 1980).

Richard Chase claimed Crane was a "romancer, and his naturalism remains relatively poetic, abstract, pure, and impressionistic." "Introduction" to *The Red Badge of Courage and Other Writings* (Boston: Houghton Mifflin, 1960), p. x. James Trammell Cox declares Crane was a "symbolist rather than a naturalist" in "Stephen Crane as Symbolic Naturalist: An Analysis of 'The Blue Hotel'," *MFS* (1957), 3:148. Frederick C. Crews asserts: "Where he chiefly differed from the naturalists was in his abrupt metaphorical style and his radical conciseness," in his "Introduction" to *The Red Badge of Courage* (New York: Bobbs-Merrill, 1964), p. xiii. J. C. Levenson calls the novel "realism slightly embellished," in "Introduction" to *The Red Badge of Courage*, CEAA text (Charlottesville: UP of Virginia, 1975), p. xiv.

Donald Gibson claims that only *Maggie* is naturalistic among Crane's works, in *The Fiction of Stephen Crane* (Carbondale: Southern Illinois UP, 1968), p. xvi. And Marston LaFrance asserts that "Crane's irony ... proclaims that he does not believe human irresponsibility is even inevitable or determined by anything other than the wilful dishonesty of human beings." *A Reading of Stephen Crane* (New York: Oxford UP, 1971), p. 40. See also his similar claims in "Stephen Crane Scholarship Today and Tomorrow," *American Literary Realism* (1974), 7:125–35.

2. For discussion of this novel, see in particular Frank Bergon, *Stephen Crane's Artistry* (New York: Columbia UP, 1975), esp. pp. 66–75.

3. For Zola's views, see ch. 2, n. 8.

4. See, e.g., Frederick C. Crews, "Introduction" to *The Red Badge of Courage* (New York: Bobbs-Merrill, 1964), p. xx; Andrew Delbanco, "The American Stephen Crane: The Context of *The Red Badge of Courage*," in *New Essays on "The Red Badge of Courage,"* ed. Lee Clark Mitchell (New York: Cambridge UP, 1986), pp. 64–65; J. C. Levenson,

"Introduction" to CEAA edition of *The Red Badge of Courage* (Charlottesville: UP of Virginia, 1975), esp. pp. xliv–xlvi, lxviii ff.; Donald Pizer, "*The Red Badge of Courage*: Text, Theme, and Form," *South Atlantic Quarterly* (Summer 1985), 84:302–313; Eric Solomon, *Stephen Crane: From Parody to Realism* (Cambridge: Harvard UP, 1967), p. 97; Max Westbrook, "Stephen Crane: The Pattern of Affirmation," *Nineteenth-Century Fiction* (1959), 14:219–29.

5. Georg Lukács' thesis inadvertently bears on Crane's characteristic narrative technique. Posing Scott, Balzac, and Tolstoy against Flaubert and Zola, he claims the former narrate while the latter merely describe: "In Flaubert and Zola the characters are merely spectators, more or less interested in the events. As a result, the events themselves become only a tableau for the reader, or, at best, a series of tableaux. We are merely observers." And later: "Thus every epic relationship disappears in the descriptive style. Lifeless, fetishized objects are whisked about in an amorphous atmosphere.... Description debases characters to the level of inanimate objects." People are transformed "into conditions, into still lives," so he asserts: "Corresponding to the false breadth assigned the external world is a schematic narrowness in characterization. A character appears as a finished 'product' perhaps composed of varied social and natural elements." Lukács' categories privilege the epic, but if what he states is true, Crane's reliance on description has its powerful effect precisely by reducing characters to conditions. See "Narrate or Describe?" in *Writer and Critic and Other Essays*, trans. and ed. Arthur D. Kahn (New York: Grosset & Dunlap, 1970), pp. 116, 133, 139.

6. Thus, Carolyn Porter asserts of American realist texts: "The contemplative stance of the detached observer, by virtue of the extremity to which it is taken, is undermined from within." See *Seeing and Being: The Plight of the Participant Observer in Emerson, James, Adams, and Faulkner* (Middletown, Conn.: Wesleyan UP, 1981), p. 52. Porter defends American writers from the traditional charge that they engaged in ahistoricist celebrations of pure perception so as to escape the implications of their social visions.

From a similarly Marxist perspective, June Howard declares that "enforced spectatorship" and "the paralysis of the observer" are distinguishing features of naturalism, which finally aligns with a reformist movement. See *Form and History in American Literary Naturalism* (Chapel Hill: U of North Carolina P, 1985), esp. pp. 114, 125. Significantly, both Porter and Howard rely upon Georg Lukács' late analyses of reification and narrative technique.

7. *The Red Badge of Courage: An Episode of the American Civil War*, ed. Henry Binder (New York: Avon, 1982), p. 1. All subsequent references to the novel are included in the text. For discussion of reasons for using this edition, see Binder's essay, entitled "The 'Red Badge of Courage' Nobody Knows," in *ibid.*, pp. 111–58. J. C. Levenson provides a close reading of the opening paragraph in his "Introduction" to the CEAA edition of *Red Badge*, p. xiv. See also James Nagel, *Impressionism*, p. 54.

8. See pp. 83, 108, 31, 34, 45, 47. These examples can be multiplied. Sergio Perosa has pointed out that there are "no less than 350" verbs directly indicating perception, "no less than 200" expressions that suggest visual sensation, and numerous other auditory and sensory verbs, in "Naturalism and Impressionism in Stephen Crane's Fiction," *Stephen Crane: A Collection of Critical Essays*, ed. Maurice Bassan (Englewood Cliffs: Prentice-Hall, 1967), pp. 88-89. See also Nagel, *Impressionism*, p. 44.

9. Pp. 97–99. Sergio Perosa has observed that "the rhythm of perception is ceaseless and pressing, continual and almost obsessive" ("Naturalism and Impressionism," p. 89). For an alternative, persuasive reading of this process in the novel, see Amy Kaplan, "The Spectacle of War in Crane's Revision of History," in *New Essays*, esp. pp. 95–98.

10. See, e.g., pp. 21, 38, 47, 71–74, 94, 106.

11. P. 57; also 86. James Trammell Cox has appositely observed that "man's relationship to his universe is paradoxical. He becomes least an animal when most an animal." See "The Imagery of 'The Red Badge of Courage,'" *MFS* (1959), 5:210.

12. James Guetti interprets the connections in *Red Badge* between seeing and knowing, visibility and intelligibility, as evidence of classical realism. See *Word-Music: The Aesthetic Aspect of Narrative Fiction* (New Brunswick: Rutgers UP, 1980), pp. 123, 127–28.

13. See Williams, "Personal Identity and Individuation," and "Bodily Continuity and Personal Identity," in *Problems of the Self: Philosophical Papers, 1936–1972* (New York: Cambridge UP, 1973), pp. 1–18, 19–25.

14. For further development of this idea, see Harry G. Frankfurt's discussion linking free will with "the concept of a person" (ch. 1, n. 18).

15. Cited by E. M. Forster in *Aspects of the* Novel (1927; rev. New York: Harcourt Brace, 1955), p. 101.

16. W. H. Frohock has explored the "modern" effect of Crane's "typical sentence" in "*The Red Badge* and the Limits of Parody," *Southern Review* (1970), 6:137–48. Neil Schmitz makes a more radical claim that "there are no things for Fleming, only words," since for him "reality is a verbal contrivance, simply what one is motivated to articulate." In "Stephen Crane and the Colloquial Self," *Midwest Quarterly* (1972), 14:444–45. Frank Bergon's is the most precise analysis of language in Crane, working from the assumption that Crane's prose is "marked by silences; its essential subject always borders on the inexpressible." As he adds: "Considered only in terms of language and syntax, Crane's style is one which interprets life as fragmented and unpredictable, something about which it is difficult to form express conclusions" (*Artistry*, p. 28).

17. In private correspondence, Douglas Gordon has observed that agency is excluded from this passage stylistically, starting with the first sentence: "he had burned" may technically be an active verb, but our "burnings" are beyond our control. The second sentence then jumps out of Henry's mind, while the "linking verbs" of the third "subvert the sense of Henry actively judging matters for himself." When he does at last act, in the fourth sentence, the actions are "fairly pallid" ("He had read ... he had longed"). The last sentence simply puts him "at the mercy of his mind."

18. Compare the opening description of Henry's bunk: "The sun-light, without, beating upon [the roof], made it glow a light yellow shade. A small window shot an oblique square of whiter light upon the cluttered floor. The smoke from the fire at times neglected the clay-chimney and wreathed into the room. And this flimsy chimney of clay and sticks made endless threats to set a-blaze the whole establishment" (2). Or again: "The little flames of rifles leaped from [the trees]. The song of the bullets was in the air and shells snarled among the tree-tops. One tumbled directly into the middle of a hurrying group ... Other men, punched by bullets, fell in grotesque agonies" (85).

19. Henry Binder and Steven Mailloux agree with Hershel Parker's claim that this is a textual fault. See chapter 6 of Parker's *Flawed Texts and Verbal Icons: Literary Authority in American Fiction* (Evanston: Northwestern UP, 1984), pp. 147–79; and chapter 7 of Mailloux's *Interpretive Conventions: The Reader in the Study of American Fiction* (Ithaca: Cornell UP, 1982), pp. 159–91. For an example of nearly exact repetition of a whole paragraph, see pp. 3, 6.

20. P. 6. Crane invokes a similar stylistic pattern in rendering the repetitive rowing experience of the men in "The Open Boat," as quoted above in the Introduction. See also Bergon, *Artistry*, pp. 86–92.

21. Eric Solomon seems the first to have commented on the duplicated structure of the novel, in *Stephen Crane: From Parody to Realism* (Cambridge: Harvard UP, 1967), esp. pp. 76 ff. But see also Bergon, *Artistry*, pp. 76–81.

22. Donald Pease offers a deconstructive reading of narratives in the novel, which "do not follow battles and provide needed explanation; instead they precede and indeed demand battles as elaborations and justifications of already narrated events." See "Fear, Rage, and the Mistrials of Representation in *The Red Badge of Courage*," in *American Realism: New Essays*, ed. Eric Sundquist (Baltimore: Johns Hopkins UP, 1982), p. 160.

23. Part of what it means to "have" a feeling, in other words, is to have it irrefutably. That is not to deny that feelings sometimes change, or appear less severe from other perspectives, or are often mixed and contradictory. Yet even mixed feelings are so not because they are less certain *as* feelings but because they do not fit the cultural map of our emotional landscape. To enjoy a bitter-sweet taste, for instance, or to feel both guilty and pleased, or to have a "love–hate" relationship, is to be no less certain than we otherwise are about our feelings—although these feelings happen to be expressed oxymoronically simply because of the way our language works. In these cases, as we commonly say, we just don't have the precise words to express what we feel.

The confusion we experience on this issue results from our assumption that supposedly refutable feelings can be lumped together with the category of mixed feelings. We mistakenly treat claims of the former sort ("he believed that he envied a corpse") as if they were the same as the latter ("he felt both guilty and pleased"). Yet the former implies not ambivalence, but uncertainty—that when he was feeling envious he was mistaken *in* the feeling, and was not really feeling it at the time. This is not a state of emotional conflict, of feeling ambivalent because of the sometimes problematic fit between our language and our emotions. Rather, it is a logical problem of self-reference, of the impossibility of being in uncertainty about the feelings we have at any given moment (even, perhaps especially, our feeling of uncertainty about our feelings). Moreover, this has nothing to do with self-correcting references or later revisions to the state of one's earlier feeling (I am assuming through all of this, of course, that no confusion exists about the language itself—that people are not simply ignorant, that is, of the meaning of certain terms, such as "dead" and "corpse").

KEVIN J. HAYES

How Stephen Crane Shaped Henry Fleming

Since its publication by D. Appleton & Co. in 1895, *The Red Badge of Courage* has generated much controversy regarding the personal and moral growth of Private Henry Fleming. For decades, critics, basing their analysis on the Appleton text, have bickered over whether or not Henry Fleming genuinely matures during the course of the novel. More recently, attention toward *Red Badge* has turned away from the first edition text to a reconstruction of the novel based on the final manuscript. Hershel Parker and Henry Binder, the most vocal proponents of the restored *Red Badge*, have persuasively argued that its publication would resolve any critical differences of opinion regarding Fleming's growth, but some remain unconvinced and the controversy naggingly persists.[1] Neither the academic critics nor the textualists, however, has considered the possibility that the controversy could be even more surely resolved by a study of the changes Crane made to Fleming's character during the process of composing the draft and reworking it into the final manuscript.[2] Perhaps the early states of *Red Badge* have been neglected because critics have been reluctant to examine Crane's novel in light of what is now known about the creative process.[3] Or perhaps his development of the novel has been neglected because little historical or biographical evidence survives to identify Crane's intentions for either the story or its protagonist.

From *Studies in the Novel* 22, no. 3 (Fall 1990). © 1990 by the University of North Texas.

R. W. Stallman has gathered the reminiscences about Crane and the few surviving letters written to or by or about him which specifically pertain to *Red Badge*,[4] but the most valuable source for discerning Crane's intentions as he wrote and revised the novel, the extant pages of the draft and final manuscript, has usually been ignored. Although many pages of the draft have been lost, enough of it—58 pages, numbered between 2 and 92—survives to make it possible to understand Crane's early conception of Henry Fleming and to see how he developed his protagonist during composition. In the most important treatment of Crane's revisions to date, Parker has examined several differences between the draft and final manuscript and has concluded that Crane's intentions as he revised "were not inchoate, were not partially confused, were not in a perilous state of flux or reflux. Crane knew what he was doing."[5] Well, the evidence shows that Crane had a basic idea of what to do when he began to write, but as he wrote and then revised the draft into the final manuscript, he achieved a perspective on Fleming's character that allowed him to understand more precisely where to take it. Put simply, as Crane composed *The Red Badge of Courage*, he learned exactly what to do.

Since the continuing critical tug-of-war centers on the issue of Henry Fleming's maturity, I have decided to concentrate on revisions which specifically affect the characterization of Private Fleming. Crane's development of his protagonist falls into three general stages: conception, composition of the first draft, and revision from draft to final manuscript. Before writing anything, Crane, as I will demonstrate below, began mentally developing the character. Then, as he started the draft, he came to understand the role he wanted his protagonist to fill and was able to more fully develop the character. Reworking the novel into the final manuscript, Crane used what he had learned during the composition of the draft to eliminate ambiguity, foreshadow Fleming's conduct in battle, and make the portrayal of him consistent throughout *Red Badge*. From conception to draft to final manuscript, Crane's development of his protagonist was an ongoing one.

When Crane first came up with the idea for Fleming, he spent time mentally developing the character before sitting down to write anything. Willis Fletcher Johnson, in his 1926 reminiscence of Crane's early writing career, recalled what Crane had told him about his protagonist: "At this time he was also greatly engaged with 'The Red Badge of Courage'; not so much on paper as in his own mind. He spoke frequently of its hero as 'growing.' 'He's getting to be quite a character now,' he said one day."[6] In his critical introduction to "Red Badge" in *Stephen Crane: An Omnibus*, R. W. Stallman accepts Johnson's word regarding Crane's mental development of his protagonist, assumes that Johnson meant the winter of 1892 when he wrote "this time," and concludes that when Crane "wrote the first draft of *The Red Badge* in March 1893, he had already worked out the idea for it" since he "had been brooding over his conception for many months before he undertook to write it."[7] But because Johnson really provides no clear antecedent for the demonstrative adjective "this," his time reference cannot conclusively be pinpointed. As I read Johnson, the phrase "this time" seems to refer to the time Hamlin Garland and William Dean Howells were reading *Maggie*, that is, March 1893, the month during which Crane composed his draft of *Red Badge*.[8] If Johnson is referring to March, then Crane had not worked out the idea for the novel after brooding over it for several months. Like any novelist, he undoubtedly spent some time thinking about his protagonist before he sat down to write, but any brooding that had gone on before Crane started writing was still going on during the composition of *Red Badge*. Rather than putting an undue emphasis, as Stallman does, on the indefinite reference, I would prefer to stress exactly what Crane told Johnson about the idea. Crane's use of the present progressives "growing" and "getting" in his statement to Johnson reinforces the ongoing nature of his development of Fleming.

Surviving letters by or about Crane which mention the *Red Badge* generally pertain to the composition of the first draft, reflect Crane's dissatisfaction with the novel, and therefore indicate that he was still honing his approach. For example, in 1900, Louis C. Senger wrote Hamlin Garland: "One day he told me he was going to write a war story and later he showed me some chapters of the *Red Badge*. 'I deliberately started in to do a potboiler,' he told me then, 'something that would take the boarding-school element—you know the kind. Well, I got interested in the thing in spite of myself, and I couldn't, I couldn't. I *had* to do it my own way.'"[9] Although Crane's statement to Senger does not specifically apply to his development of Fleming, it does show that the novel on paper during the composition of the first draft differed from the novel in Crane's head before written composition began. The reminiscences and letters provide hints about the ongoing nature of Crane's development of his war novel and its protagonist, but their contents are neither specific enough nor significant enough to pinpoint Crane's intentions during composition.

The best way to understand how Crane developed his protagonist when he wrote the draft of *Red Badge* in those ten nights in March and recopied and expanded it for the final manuscript during the summer of 1893 is to analyze the alterations he made to the novel. Quite simply, the changes Crane made, predominantly small additions of text, sometimes a phrase or a sentence, usually no more than a few sentences, demonstrate what he learned about his protagonist when he had written the draft and show that he was continuing to learn as he revised the draft into the final manuscript. To demonstrate how Crane's additions to his text reveal his gradual development of Fleming, I would like somewhat arbitrarily to subdivide each manuscript into two parts at the point where Fleming runs from battle, page 49 of the draft, page 56 of the final manuscript. Therefore, throughout my discussion, I will refer to the different parts of the manuscript as the draft before the flight from battle, the draft after the flight, the final manuscript before the flight, and the final manuscript after the flight from battle from battle. It is hard to understand exactly what Crane learned as he wrote the first draft by examining only the draft because he wrote it straight through, making few cross-outs and few substitutions of text. So, to understand what Crane learned about Fleming during the composition of the draft, a careful scrutiny of the first part of the final manuscript is necessary.

In the draft, Fleming's behavior before the flight from battle is somewhat inconsistent with his behavior during and after the flight. Perhaps the dissatisfaction Crane felt with the first version of the novel stemmed from the realization he made during the composition of the draft that he had not properly set up the battle scene and its aftermath. The additions Crane made to the early parts of *Red Badge* as he revised the draft into the final manuscript verify what he learned during the composition of the draft and show where he had decided to take Fleming. Aspects of the character which only appear in later parts of the draft after Fleming runs from battle, Crane incorporated into early sections of the final manuscript before the flight. Crane's alterations emphasize Fleming's discomfort and uncertainty, anticipate his conduct in battle, and, by making his behavior more consistent before and after the flight, negate any possible growth in maturity. Just as Crane learned what to add to the early sections of the novel as he wrote the later parts of the draft, he learned exactly where to take the later sections of the novel as he wrote the early chapters of the final manuscript. Crane inserted more detail to heighten Fleming's feelings of alienation early in the final manuscript and then increasingly isolated him after the flight from battle. Crane's additions to Fleming's thought and behavior progressively distance him from his fellow soldiers, from the front lines, and from reality.

As Crane began his draft in March 1893, he wrote about Jim Conklin's mistaken report of an upcoming battle, Fleming's recollection of home, the confrontation between Wilson and Fleming, and then reached the point where Fleming and the other soldiers in his unit begin marching through field and woods, ostensibly on their way to fight. On draft page 28, Crane wrote, "As he looked, Fleming gripped his out-cry at his throat. He saw that even if they were tottering with fear they would laugh at his oration. They would jeer him and, if practicable, pelt him with missiles. Admitting that he might be wrong, a frenzied declamation of the kind." After he had added the period, however, Crane realized his sentence lacked both predicate and object, crossed out the period and supplied the missing parts of speech, "Would turn him into a worm." Crane then began a new paragraph with "He assumed the demeanor of one who is doomed, a—," paused, put a double-line through "is doomed, a—," and then wrote, "knows that he is doomed, alone, to unwritten responsibilities."[10] Crane made so few deletions during the composition of the first draft that any cross-out longer than one word is noteworthy. By substituting, "knows that he is doomed" for "is doomed," Crane shifted the judgment from that of an omniscient third person observer to one much closer to Fleming's own perception of his condition. As Crane initially wrote the phrase, Fleming was doomed, but after the cross-out and substitution, he only thinks he is doomed. Beyond this point in the draft, Crane would continue to emphasize the differences between what actually happens to Fleming and what Fleming thinks is happening to him.

Revising from draft to final manuscript, Crane tacked on six sentences to the previous passage which greatly affect the character of Fleming. After rewriting the "doomed" sentence onto final manuscript page 34, Crane added: "He lagged, with tragic glances at the sky. He was surprised, presently, by the youthful lieutenant of his company who began to beat him heartily with his sword, and called out in a loud and insolent voice. 'Come Fleming, get up into the ranks there. No skulking will do here.'" He mended his pace, crossed out the capital "P," wrote "with the alcrity [sic]," crossed out "the alcrity," and then finished the sentence so that it reads, "He mended his pace with suitable haste."[11] Next, Crane began a new paragraph, but quickly returned to the previous one to insert two sentences onto the end of it, "And he hated the lieutenant, who had no appreciation of fine things. He was a mere brute." Crane then put a line through "things" to substitute the word "minds." By having him lag behind and skulk, Crane highlighted Fleming's disregard for the others, his selfishness, his unwillingness to face combat, and his difficulty making decisions and acting on his own. On final manuscript page 27, seven pages earlier, Crane had added the sentence, "He was a mental-outcast," a poignant five word statement which signals Crane's decision to completely alienate Fleming from his fellow soldiers. His additions on final manuscript page 34 reinforce and extend that decision. By separating Fleming from the ranks, Crane accentuates the spatial distance between Fleming and the others and therefore makes him physically as well as mentally outcast. Crane's insertion of the two sentences between the paragraphs is particularly important because it links Fleming's physical and mental alienation and clarifies that Fleming feels mental superiority rather than inferiority.

The changes Crane made to the previous passage are indicative of the revisions he made throughout the early chapters of the final manuscript because they reflect what he had learned about his character when he wrote the draft. Several other early additions to the final manuscript have their precedents in later chapters of the draft. As Crane continued the draft beyond the flight from battle, he perceived discrepancies in Fleming's portrayal and consequently developed his personality in the early chapters as he revised from draft to final manuscript to make Fleming's conduct in battle consistent with his behavior before combat and thus negate any maturation on Fleming's part. In chapter 6, draft page 49, for example, Crane had mentioned that immediately prior to the flight from battle, Fleming had been in a trance which was broken only when he began to run. Revising the draft into final manuscript, Crane integrated Fleming's propensity for trances into the first chapter of the novel. When Jim Conklin tells everyone about the upcoming battle, Fleming's reaction to Conklin's report on draft page 4 had been simple disbelief: "He could not convince himself of it. It was too strange," but on final manuscript page 4, Crane revised the passage to read: "Fleming was in a little trance of astonishment. So they were at last going to fight. On the morrow perhaps there would be a battle and he would be in it. For a time, he was obliged to labor to make himself believe." By inserting an earlier trance, Crane foreshadowed Fleming's subsequent behavior when facing combat. Only after writing the scene in the draft where Fleming runs from battle could Crane understand exactly how to portray his early behavior before battle.

Crane made other additions to the early chapters of the final manuscript which reflect what he learned when he had written the later chapters of the draft. When Fleming is faced with a combat situation much different than he had imagined, he is unable to adjust his behavior accordingly; since he cannot accommodate the discrepancy, he has no option but to run from battle. Writing the final manuscript, Crane decided to insert an earlier example of Fleming's characteristic inability to adapt to unexpected situations. Rewriting Fleming's recollection of home, Crane slightly modified a sentence from draft page 6 onto final manuscript page 7 which expresses Fleming's response to his mother's rather dry reaction to his enlistment and reflects his somewhat romantic preconceptions about war: "Still she had disappointed him by saying nothing whatever about returning with his shield or on it."[12] Crane then added three sentences: "He had privately primed himself for a beautiful scene. He had prepared certain sentences which he thought could be used with touching effect. But her words destroyed his plans." When his mother's response is different than he had planned, Fleming, after the revision, cannot readjust to accommodate the disparity between what he had imagined would happen and what really happened. He had fully expected his departure to be a "beautiful scene," and when it is not, he becomes dumbfounded. By adding the "touching effect" sentence, Crane makes Fleming much colder and more self-centered in the final manuscript; instead of pitying his mother, he invents ways to make her feel sad in order to satisfy himself. After the revision, Fleming's behavior at home when he first enlists is representative of his conduct in the later parts of the novel: he imagines what a situation will be like, plots his actions, and then, when things turn out differently than he expected, he cannot alter his behavior.

Besides making Fleming prone to trances and intimating that he might not be able to react in battle, Crane inserted some pretty explicit hints in revision to anticipate Fleming's flight. To pages 12 and 13 of the final manuscript, Crane added the sentence, "It had suddenly appeared to him that perhaps in a battle he might run." On final manuscript page 53, after Fleming had survived the first little skirmish, Crane added: "The supreme trial had been passed. The red, formidable difficulties of war had been vanquished." Since Crane had already written the later scene in the draft where Fleming ran from combat and since he so seldom crossed out or rearranged text once it was written, he knew when he added these two sentences to final manuscript page 53 that the supreme trial had not been passed, and he also knew that when eventually faced with the supreme trial, Fleming would fail. The addition clearly indicates that as Crane developed the character, he decided to undermine Fleming's maturity and thus portray him in an ironic fashion. Overall, Crane's revisions to the first part of the final manuscript make Fleming's behavior more consistent, anticipate his conduct in battle, and consequently undermine any possible growth in maturity on Fleming's part.

Crane's ironic intent is particularly obvious in two additions surrounding the flight from combat. Immediately prior to Fleming's retreat, Crane added text to the novel in the final manuscript to anticipate the flight. To the sentence from draft page 48, "The muscles of his arms felt numb and bloodless," Crane added the clause, "His back was quivering with nervous weakness" on final manuscript page 55. Besides intensifying Fleming's fear, the physical description spotlights the part of his body which Fleming was about to turn toward his enemy. After that addition, Crane decided to highlight the same part of the soldier's body again when Fleming starts to run from battle. On draft page 49 Crane had written: "He felt that death was ever about to thrust him between the shoulder blades," but on final manuscript page 56, he expanded the passage to appreciably clarify his meaning: "Since he had turned his back upon the fight, his fears had been wondrously magnified. Death about to thrust him between the shoulder-blades was far more dreadful than death about to smite him between the eyes."

Revisions Crane made to the final manuscript after Fleming had run from battle reflect changes he had made to the early chapters of the novel in the final manuscript. The text Crane added beyond Fleming's hasty retreat from the front lines primarily serves to heighten both his physical and mental alienation from the other soldiers. After running from battle in both the draft and the final manuscript, Fleming seeks a dark place for refuge, enters a woods, and encounters a squirrel. Crane's description of the incident on draft page 55 is only three sentences long: "He threw a pine-cone at a jovial and pot-valiant squirrel and it ran with chattering fear. There was the law, he thought. Nature had given him a sign." On final manuscript page 63, Crane greatly expanded the episode to provide Fleming's interpretations of the squirrel's behavior. He wrote, "He threw a pine-cone at a jovial squirrel and it ran with chattering fear. High in a treetop, it stopped and, poking h..." Crane wrote the "h" as the first letter of the word "his," but he crossed it out and wrote "it's [sic]" because he realized that he had already used the impersonal pronoun "it" to refer to the squirrel, but then he crossed out "it's," substituted "his" above it, returned to cross out the two previous instances of the word "it," and wrote "he" above both. After the alterations, Crane finished the sentence so that it reads, "High in a tree-top, he stopped and, poking his head cautiously around a branch, looked back with an air of trepidation." He then wrote the next paragraph which consisted of three short sentences: "Fleming felt triumphant at this exhibition. There was the law, he said. Nature had given him a sign." Next, he began a new paragraph with "He wended, feeling that nature," crossed out those five words, returned to the previous line at the end of the three sentence paragraph, and added the following four sentences to it: "The squirrel immediately upon recognizing a danger, took to his legs, without ado. He did not stand stolidly, baring his furry belly to the missile, and die with an upward glance at the sympathetic heavens. On the contrary, he had fled as fast as his legs could carry him. And he was but an ordinary squirrel; doubtless no philosopher of his race."[13]

The revisions Crane made to the squirrel episode as he moved from draft to final manuscript indicate how his additions to the first part of the final manuscript helped him to understand what to include in the second part and therefore serve as evidence to further substantiate the ongoing nature of Crane's development of Fleming's character during the composition of *Red Badge*. The squirrel's "upward glance at the sympathetic heavens" recalls an earlier expansion Crane had made on final manuscript page 34 when

Fleming had dropped back from the ranks and made "tragic glances" toward the sky.[14] Furthermore, the frequent cross-outs show that Crane continued to learn as he worked on the final manuscript. Altering his pronouns from the impersonal "it" to the third person "his," Crane heightened the parallel between the squirrel and Fleming, between animal and man. Fleming perceives the squirrel's flight to be a sign from nature which justifies his own behavior, but at the same time, he considers himself above nature. The squirrel may not be a philosopher of his race, but Fleming certainly sees himself that way. Crane's addition of the "philosopher" sentence is consistent with earlier changes he had made in the final manuscript and consequently serves as an ironic reversal of Fleming's previous rationalizations. Before battle, Fleming "knows" that he is doomed, but here, he perceives himself as one of the most knowledgeable sages ever.

Other additions Crane made to *Red Badge* in the final manuscript verify his decision to increasingly alienate Fleming. When Fleming comes across four or five corpses on draft page 61a, Crane wrote, "As he looked, Fleming felt like an invader and he hastened by." Crane expanded the sentence into the following paragraph on final manuscript page 69: "In this place, Fleming felt that he was an invader. This forgotten part of the battle-ground was owned by the dead men, and he hurried, in the vague apprehension that one of the swollen and ghastly forms would rise and tell him to begone." By changing the simile to a metaphor Crane makes the figure of speech more forceful; Fleming is no longer "like" an invader, he is an invader. He can find neither company nor solace among either the living or the dead. Among the living, Fleming feels like an outcast and among the dead, an invader.

Likewise, he feels out of place in that middle ground between living and dead, among the wounded. When Fleming first discovers the parade of wounded men retreating from battle in both the draft and the final manuscript, he is accosted by the tattered man who asks him where he has been hit. Fleming is "startled" by the question on page 64 of the draft, but on final manuscript page 73, he feels "instant panic." After the tattered man repeats his question, Fleming turns and slides away from him. By changing the diction in the final manuscript, Crane further heightened Fleming's inherent fear, but the addition he made after the tattered man's question affects Fleming's characterization even more significantly. On final manuscript page 73, Crane copied the second to the last sentence from draft page 64, "He turned away suddenly and slid through the crowd," and then added two sentences to describe Fleming's behavior as he escapes the tattered man: "His brow was heavily flushed, and his fingers were picking nervously at one of his buttons. He bent his head and fastened his eyes studiously upon the button as if it were a little problem." Although Fleming shares with the wounded the common factor that both are retreating from the front line, he is not part of their group because his retreat, unlike theirs, cannot be justified. After the revision, Fleming's alienation is nearly complete; he has no choice but to withdraw further into himself. Crane's added description of Fleming's physical behavior demonstrates this inward retreat. With his head tucked, his eyes pointed towards his chest, his arms close to his side, and his fingers at his breast, Fleming is regressing back to an infantile or even a fetal state.

In the draft, Fleming discovers Jim Conklin among the ranks of the wounded and suddenly sees that attaching himself to his friend might be a way to counter his feelings of alienation. Crane retained the scene in the final manuscript, but he clarified the ambiguity to show how Conklin's death completes Fleming's isolation. After Conklin dies, the tattered man, reaching out for help, tells Fleming that he is not feeling too well either. Fleming's response to this is ambiguous on draft page 72: "Fleming groaned. 'Oh Lord!'" Is Fleming groaning because another person might die, or is he groaning because he might have to witness another death? Crane eliminated the ambiguity with the addition of an interrogative on final manuscript page 82: "'Oh, Lord!' Was he to be the tortured witness of another grim encounter?" Fleming's response after the revision affirms that his isolation and his selfishness have reached such a level that even when he is given an opportunity to show some compassion and understanding by providing support for another soldier, he cannot.

In the draft and in the final manuscript, Fleming contemplates returning to his unit after his encounter with Conklin and the tattered man and tries to compare his conduct in battle with that of other soldiers. On page 80 of the draft, Crane wrote: "He was not like those others, he said, in despair. He now conceded it to be impossible that he should ever grow to be one of them."[15] Revising the passage on final manuscript page 93, Crane wrote: "He now conceded it to be impossible that he should ever become a hero. He was a craven loon." As the passage stands in the draft, the antecedent for the pronoun "them" is the rather vague "those others," but Crane's substitution of "hero" for "them" in the final manuscript crystallizes his intent. In the draft, the despair Fleming feels after his un-hero-like behavior might have brought him back to an understanding of the reality of his predicament, but in the final manuscript, Fleming's contrition is fleeting, and his selfish delusions recur with Crane's next addition to the text. After Fleming's humble understanding that he is not a hero on final manuscript page 93, Crane immediately revised the text from draft page 80 as he wrote final manuscript page 94 to further heighten Fleming's selfishness. Crane changed the phrase "his troubles" to "his unprecedented sufferings" and altered the ambiguous "many things" to the slanted "many favourable things." After the revision, the passage reads: "He told himself that despite his unprecedented suffering, he had never lost his greed for a victory, yet, he said, in a half-apologetic manner to his conscience, he could not but know that a defeat for the army this time might mean many favorable things for him." Regardless of the death of Conklin and the injury to the tattered man, Fleming, in the final manuscript, sees his own sufferings as unprecedented. Furthermore, he denies any allegiance to his countrymen as he considers how their defeat might be to his favor.

Beyond final manuscript page 93, Fleming's inflated sense of his own importance reaches a considerably higher level than it had in the draft. As Crane expanded his text from draft page 81 to final manuscript page 94, for example, he made Fleming think that "if he himself could believe in his virtuous perfection, he concieved [sic] that there would be small trouble in convincing all others." After the revision, Fleming has become so deluded that he automatically assumes that the others will understand why he ran from battle and why his flight was the most sagacious action any soldier could have taken. Crane reinforced Fleming's self-centered attitude with an addition on page 95 of the final manuscript, "A serious prophet, upon predicting a flood, should be the first man to climb a tree. This would demonstrate that he was indeed a seer." With the addition, it is clear that Fleming has little conception of the reality of his situation, but it is also apparent by this stage of the final manuscript that Crane had fully developed his protagonist.

The composition of *Red Badge* was a learning process for Stephen Crane. He used what he learned from writing the draft to revise the early sections of the final manuscript; he then built on the additions and alterations he had made in the early parts of the final manuscript to revise later sections of it. When Crane first began his novel, he did not realize exactly how Fleming would turn out, but as he expanded the 92 pages of the draft to the first 107 pages of the final manuscript, Crane emphasized that Fleming's rationalization of his intellectual superiority as well as his isolation would lead to an extreme selfishness and completely remove him from the reality of his predicament. Crane's revisions show that he shaped his protagonist to undercut his subsequent heroics at the end of the novel. Reworking the draft into final manuscript, Crane never planted hints that Fleming might have the potential to become a genuine hero in the end. The only addition to the novel in the final manuscript which might serve to anticipate Fleming's presence at the front lines at the end of the novel is his ironic realization that facing the enemy is less frightening than exposing his back to them.

Readers who have previously concentrated on Crane's revisions of *Red*

Badge have not been able to come to a consensus regarding his ironic portrayal of Henry Fleming because they have focused their attention on the differences between the Appleton text and the final manuscript rather than looking at the differences between the draft and the final manuscript. The problem with drawing inferences from the revisions Crane made to his novel immediately prior to its publication by Appleton's in 1895 arises from the fact that those changes were neither part of his creative process nor part of his gradual development of Fleming; in the light of the evidence presented by Parker, Binder, and Wertheim and Sorrentino,[16] those alterations seem more and more like simple publishing house expurgations rather than coherent, purposeful changes made by an author during the creation of a novel. Sometime during the summer of 1893, Crane wrote the last sentence of *The Red Badge of Courage* on final manuscript page 192 and followed it with the words, "The End" in big letters. Crane had meticulously worked through his novel, learning throughout its composition, but when he wrote those final words, he signaled that both the learning process and the creative process had been brought to a close. Fleming had become exactly the way Crane wanted him.

NOTES

1. For the best discussion of the controversy inherent in arguments based on the Appleton text, see Henry Binder, "*The Red Badge of Courage* Nobody Knows," in *Studies in the Novel* 10 (1978): 9–47, reprinted in an expanded version with his edition of *The Red Badge of Courage* (New York: Avon, 1983), pp. 123–75. I am indebted to my teacher, Dr. Hershel Parker for suggesting the idea for this paper and for his helpful advice throughout its composition. I would also like to thank my colleague Meoghan Byrne for proofreading the paper.

2. Only William L. Howarth and Hershel Parker have looked seriously at the revisions from draft to final manuscript. Howarth, in "The Badge of Courage Manuscript: New Evidence for a Critical Edition," *Studies in Bibliography* 18 (1965): 232, suggests that a study of Crane's early revisions would clarify his "developing sense of theme and method." See also, Parker, "Getting Used to the 'Original Form' of *The Red Badge of Courage*," *New Essays on The Red Badge of Courage*, ed. Lee Clark Mitchell (New York: Cambridge Univ. Press, 1986), pp. 25–37.

3. Albert Rothenberg, in *The Emerging Goddess* (Chicago: Univ. of Chicago Press, 1979), provides the most thorough treatment of the creative process available. Hershel Parker in *Flawed Texts and Verbal Icons* (Evanston: Northwestern Univ. Press, 1984), p. 23, synthesizing the work of Rothenberg, shows that "authorial intentionality is built into the words of a literary work during the process of composition, not before and not afterwards."

4. Robert Wooster Stallman's *Stephen Crane: An Omnibus* (New York: Knopf, 1957), pp. 175–224, contains a thorough discussion of contemporary documents pertaining to the composition of *Red Badge*. Crane's letters are most accessible in Stanley Wertheim and Paul Sorrentino, eds., *The Correspondence of Stephen Crane*, 2 vols. (New York: Columbia Univ. Press, 1988).

5. "Getting Used to the 'Original Form,'" p. 32.

6. "The Launching of Stephen Crane," *The Literary Digest International Book Review* 4 (1926): 289.

7. *Omnibus*, p. 2 10.

8. Responding to a letter from Crane dated March 28, 1893, Howells wrote that he had only glanced at *Maggie*. See *Correspondence* 1:52.

9. *Stephen Crane. Letters*, ed. R. W. Stallman and Lillian Gilkes (New York: New York Univ. Press, 1960), p. 319.

10. Fredson Bowers, ed., *The Red Badge of Courage, A Facsimile Edition of the Manuscript*, 2 vols. (Washington: NCR/Microcard Editions, 1973). All pages numbers cited in the text refer to Crane's original holograph numbers, not those of the facsimile.

11. Crane also made a few other stylistic changes to the passage as he composed the final manuscript, none of which affect the meaning of the additional text. He crossed out "began to" and "heartily" to substitute "began heartily to," substituted "a" for "his" and "calling" for "and called," and contracted "No skulking will" to "No skulking'll."

12. The sentence on draft page 6 reads, "Still she had disappointed him by saying nothing about returning with his shield or on it." When Crane rewrote the sentence in the final manuscript, he began it with the word, "She," but then returned to rewrite "Still" at the beginning of it. Since he restored the word "Still," the only difference between the sentence in draft and final manuscript is the Crane's addition of the word, "whatever."

13. For the sake of clarity, I have omitted the capital "H" Crane wrote and then crossed out after the word "sympathetic." He obviously intended it as the first letter of "Heaven," but he crossed the "H" out in favor of an uncapitalized "heaven." During this stage of composition, Crane also substituted "had taken" for "took" in the first of the four additional sentences.

14. Parker has already noted this revision. See "Getting Used to the 'Original Form,'" p. 31.

15. On draft page 80, Crane had ended one paragraph with "He was not like those others," began the next with "A desire for news kept him in the vicinity of the battle-ground," but then crossed out that sentence to return to the previous paragraph and finish the earlier sentence with "he said, in despair."

16. In a footnote to a letter from Crane to Nellie Crouse in which Crane derisively mentions Ripley Hitchcock, the editor the 1895 Appleton text, Wertheim and Sorrentino, *Correspondence* 1:173, mention a copy of an 1896 issue of *Red Badge* inscribed by Hitchcock's second wife, Helen Sargent Hitchcock: "'Two versions of this book written, Mr Hitchcock made Crane rewrite it and this was the first published version.'" Mrs. Hitchcock's note further substantiates that Crane's pre-publication changes were not part of his compositional process.

JAMES M. COX

The Red Badge of Courage:
The Purity of War

As I write this essay on *The Red Badge of Courage*,[1] we are once again at war. It is the fourth war in my lifetime in which this country has engaged in major conflict. I do not of course count the Spanish Civil War in which Americans sent significant volunteer units; nor do I count such recent paltry rehearsals for the present war in Iraq—Grenada, Libya, Panama—in which instant success was inevitable. Our last major war was in Viet Nam—the longest though far from bloodiest war we have ever fought—and the reaction to it was so negative that one would have thought we would never fight a war again. Yet only a bit more than fifteen years later we are again at war, and many who opposed the Viet Nam war almost to the death now find themselves dusting off theories of just wars by way of explaining their approval of what in their youth appalled them. To review this history with a slight detachment (even I was in World War II) is to know how great a title Hemingway had for his first collection of short stories. *In Our Time* he named it, quoting from the Book of Common Prayer, yet with an irony that must strike any reader as little short of savage when considered in relation to the contents of those remarkable chapters that lie between the stories forming the interchapters. The irony is even greater when the title is considered in relation to this now dying century, which seems to have given us more war than peace in our time. Not only that. We might as well realize

From *Southern Humanities Review* 25, no. 4 (Fall 1991). © 1991 by Auburn University.

that war, if it is not necessary, is nonetheless inevitable—that we can't do without it, that we need it, that somewhere and somehow as human beings we want it. Like hate and love, killing and birthing, living and dying, peace and war are a binary axis in the mind and heart of humanity as well as in its language. Hard pressed as we might be to define war, we know what it is. We know that far from being merely savage, it is nothing if not civilized, the civilized form of at once channeling and releasing the instincts of aggression that reside in the heart and soul—yes, the soul—of humanity. Milton was well on target when he put his pure war not on earth but in heaven. Seeing war as the process of civilizing aggression is as essential as seeing the family as the civilizing form for the control and release of sexual energy. No wonder the craft of war—the discipline, the codes of conduct, the making of arms— is as much art as science. Any visitor to West Point has to be struck by the evidence on every hand that the institution wants to think of military art as much as it wishes to emphasize military science.

Being both civilized and instinctual, both science and art, war is at once dynamic and inertial. It carries with it all the acceleration at the command of civilization to discover new and more powerful forms of weaponry just as it forever retains the possibility of hand-to-hand combat. The very word "arms" evokes the development from club through gunpowder to rifle to bomb at the same time that it refers to the aggressive upper limbs of the body. The combination of acceleration and inertia works through the emotions attending war. War is after all a hastening toward death; it is for the young, who, whether eager for it or forced into it, whether reckless or afraid, whether angry or appalled, find themselves both rushing and rushed toward an end that by the logic of peace ought to be further in their future. Given such acceleration, wonder that the emotions of fear and anger, the twin expressions of helplessness, are forever at play beneath the soldier's burden of facing death in the form of an enemy.

Given this form, a science and art at the heart and soul of civilization, we should not be surprised at the fierce reality it holds for our imagination. Since its essence is mortal conflict, it fatally attracts narration. We may deplore the narration we get—the censored presentations from the Pentagon, the lies and shameless exaggerations, the bureaucratic masking of violence, the banal human interest stories, the gamelike accounts of missiles hitting their targets—yet we are both galvanized and magnetized by these reports and wish to read and hear and see more and more of them. Indeed, the technology of communication is equal in its acceleration to the technology of weaponry, as if the processes of war and narration were one vast symbiosis. Here if ever is proof that the technology of language itself is equal to the technology of war—so much so, that we well could wonder whether the technology of language may have preceded the technology of war, whether the origin of language may have been a curse, whether the mouth itself were the prefiguration of the caves our ancestors once occupied. We always come out to such an uncertainty between the primacy of word or world.

There is a reason that the acceleration of both communication and weaponry have brought us increasingly disappointing accounts. Even with reporters near the front to relay stories and images *instantly* to us of soldiers in their trenches, or planes roaring off a runway, or antiaircraft explosions making a thousand points of light over Baghdad, we seem as far as ever from what we know is the truth of war, and so we settle for the observation, now proverbial, that truth is the first casualty of war. Thinking of that truth, we know that it must have at its heart fear, excitement, recklessness, hate, rage, horror, and death. Melville's lines are apt here. In a poem, "The Coming Storm," after claiming that Sanford Gifford's painting of that name served as a prefiguration of the Civil War, be concluded by relating both picture and war to the primary language of Shakespeare:

> No utter surprise can come to him
>   Who reaches Shakespeare's core;
> That which we seek and shun is there—
>   Man's final lore.

Surely, reflecting on the dynamic and inertial nature of war, we might well brood, in this last decade before the millennium, on the fact that the United States, claiming that it possesses the most advanced civilization and the accelerating technological weapons that accompany it, is bombing Baghdad, located at the confluence of the Tigris and Euphrates rivers—the very place that we learned in our earliest schooling was the Cradle of Civilization. Beyond that, there is the first great image of the war disclosing the incinerated bodies being pulled from the rubble of an air raid shelter in Baghdad—a building that the Pentagon insists was a command and communications center. Such reflections could lead us to a larger fact: that the Middle East, which sustained the birth of three of the world's great religions, has held beneath its surface the richest oil wells in the world. Facing such a fact we know that the burning bush did indeed burn. As the dynamic force of religion has faded, or been converted, into the secular force of science, the inertial force of oil has been discovered to fuel the "advanced" nations.

All of which brings us to the Civil War—the one war that, for all its horror, has come down to us as a just war. Even Bob Dylan in his antiwar song of the Viet Nam era significantly omitted it from the list of wars which were brutally conducted with "God on our side." That war, far more than any of our others, was surely fought with God on our side. Beside every other war, even World War II, it has to seem to the majority of Americans a just war. At the same time it was the most total and bloody war in our history; its 700,000 dead would be in relation to our current population fifteen million. It was also a modern war, replete with great advances in weaponry and communications. If railroads, ironclads, submarines, and breechloading carbines came into use, so did the telegraph, observation balloons, and hordes of reporters to file their stories. Both during and after the war it was the most *written* war that had ever been fought anywhere. There were the day-to-day accounts in hundreds of newspapers, there were the letters home; then came the endless postwar accounts by participants, the 128 volumes of Official Records published by the United States Government, the countless histories of the war that continue to be written, and finally the innumerable fictive efforts to capture the "reality" of the war.

Of all the fictions, *The Red Badge of Courage* is without question preeminent. In the almost one hundred years since its publication in 1895 it has incontrovertibly established itself as the greatest Civil War novel and one of the great war novels of world literature. It still seems miraculous that the novel could have been written by a twenty-four-year-old author who had not even been born until six years after Appomattox. From almost the moment of its publication, its striking power seemed to be grounded on two contradictory categories of life: experience and youth. Since it immediately brought Crane both popularity and notoriety, the compressed authority of its representation of battle experience was belied by the youth and art of its author. If the book brought Crane forward in this country as a Bohemian writer, it brought him recognition, particularly in England (when it was published there in 1896), from the literary establishment. A writer as strong as the young Conrad and a critic as acute as Edward Garnett immediately recognized that the element that resolved the contradiction between experience and youth was nothing less than the remarkable art of Crane's narrative. The art, in a word, was what made the book new, or we could say young, at the same time that it reorganized the vision of war, one of the oldest subjects to attract the narrative efforts of humanity. After all, what we consider Homer's oldest epic was *The Iliad*.

Those who focussed on the youth of the author found themselves at pains to provide a literary precursor from whom Crane had descended, an effort that has continued down the years. Was it Tolstoy, or Zola, or Stendhal? Was it, among American authors, J. W. DeForest (*Miss Ravenal's Conversion*) or Wilbur Hinman (*Corporal Si Klegg and His Pard*)? Or was it

Battles and Leaders of the Civil War, a series of articles by former commanders published in the *Century* magazine? Or could it have been the monumental *Official Records*? Although these questions, in the form of scholarly claims and contention, have been put forth throughout the century, the stark originality of *The Red Badge* continues to remain by far the most striking aspect of the book. The originality is, after all, at once the experience of the narrative. Small wonder that it would be classed as a work of realism, since it seemed true to what we now imagine is the reality of war. Or that it would be seen as naturalistic, since that classification places it in an up-to-date relationship with the sequence of literary movements that followed realism. Or that it would be called impressionistic, since that designation places it in graphic relation to the art of its time.

These efforts to locate the book either in relation to its author or in relation to its literary origins or to literary history are but an index to the manner of its originality. What no one would or could doubt is its identity; as a war novel—and a war novel not just about any war but about the Civil War. We feel that we would know that much even if its subtitle were not *An Episode of the American Civil War*. As a matter of fact, the subtitle is usually absent in most editions of the novel. Yet here again, the hunger for more specific references has led to many speculations as to what particular battle of the war is being represented. Of the many interpretive forays in this direction, the battle of Chancellorsville has been the leading candidate, yet the book itself is utterly mute in the matter of naming either battle or state where the action takes place.

To see, in what we never doubt is a Civil War novel, just how little there is of what we traditionally associate with the historical Civil War, may not tell us what the novel is, but will at least impress us with what it is not. Not only are there no actual place names; there are no fictive place names. If there is topography in the form of a small river or an open field or a forest, it remains utterly generalized. There is exactly one mention of Richmond and Washington. There is no Grant or Lee or Hooker or Jackson or Meade or A. P. Hill. There is not even a North or a South. Even the terms "Yankee" and "Rebel" appear only once or twice as "yank" and "reb." There is no fight for the union or against slavery. There is not a mention of Abraham Lincoln or Jefferson Davis. There is not a hint of states' rights or the protective tariff. Even the characters themselves are barely named; they are a tall soldier, a loud soldier, and a youth before they are Jim Conklin or George Wilson or Henry Fleming. A tattered soldier and a cheery soldier, although they play significant roles in the book, have no names at all. Beyond all this absence, there is no real sense of the technology of war. We know that Henry Fleming has a rifle, that he moves through a world of bullets and exploding artillery shells, that there are horses and wagons and gun carriages, but we get no particular or detailed identity of any of the machinery. We get no mention of supply depots or howitzers. Finally, there is no romance in the book—no real girl left behind or met—no letters from home, no sense of a society behind or outside the society of the battlefield. True there is Henry's mother and a girl schoolmate Henry believes is looking at him as he readies for departure (this all stated in a few paragraphs in the first chapter), but they are left behind as completely as Aunt Charity in *Moby Dick* when the *Pequod* makes its plunge into the lone Atlantic.

To see what is left out—or better, cut away—is to see how Crane achieved both reduction and concentration of his vision to the field of battle and to the single consciousness of a *private* soldier. He emerged with an incredibly short novel—shorter even than *The Scarlet Letter*—whose twenty-four short chapters stand at once as reminders of the twenty-four books of *The Iliad* and as a line of sentinels marking the violently abrupt sequence of war. The very first paragraph of the book sets the scene:

> The cold passed reluctantly from the earth, and the retiring fogs revealed an army stretched out on the hills, resting. As the landscape changed from brown to green, the army awakened, and began to tremble with eagerness at the noise of rumors. It cast its eyes upon the roads, which were growing from long troughs of liquid mud to proper thoroughfares. A river, amber-tinted in the shadow of its banks, purled at the army's feet; and at night, when the stream had become of a sorrowful blackness, one could see across it the red, eyelike gleam of hostile camp-fires set in the low brows of distant hills.

So much is done here. First there is the pathetic fallacy hard at work throughout the passage: the cold *reluctantly* passing, the fogs *retiring*, the river *purling* by day and *sorrowful* at night. Nature itself is being personified as if it had a human will, and at the end of the paragraph it has become an animated form containing the eyelike gleam of hostile campfires set in the *brows* of distant hills. Even more important, the natural process *reveals* the army stretched out and resting, awakening, and trembling at the noise of rumors. Yet if nature is sufficiently animated by the repertorial narration to reveal the scene, it nonetheless must be invested with the power. In such an exchange we can see at the very outset that the book is neither fully naturalistic nor impressionistic, neither deterministic nor subjective but involved in both worlds even as it is subjected to a repertorial narration that implicates both forces, glaringly mixing them together.

Naturalism and impressionism are not the only literary registers brought into focus in the text. There is also realism. No wonder W. D. Howells saw in Crane's early work—he was less enthusiastic about *The Red Badge*—a writer who was extending the range of realism into the urban streets. In *The Red Badge*, Crane extends realism down into the society of soldiers. They are invariably middle class soldiers, speaking an American vernacular that could be either urban or rural. The narration is clearly committed to erasing any distinction that could be made between the two. Crane, who had written *Maggie, a Girl of the Streets*, could clearly have made such a distinction, but here he wants merely to mime an informal language characterized by its deviation from formally "correct" speech yet not individuated to city or region. More important, the language is not discriminated in terms of character. The youth, the tall soldier, the loud soldier all speak alike. If they are privates they nonetheless speak a "general" vernacular—a representative language of their society—an ungrammatical, slightly deviant, and unschooled language, yet not one to evoke sympathy so much as to express a unity, directness, and informal simplicity of background. Just as their designation as tall soldier, loud soldier, and youth takes precedence over their individual names, their language designates their identity as soldiers rather than individuals.

For all that they are soldiers, their world is not in any strict sense military. True, they are subject to orders from the officers, but there is nothing in this beginning that stresses the abuse, repression, and rigorous discipline so familiar in narratives of military life. Indeed these private soldiers seem wonderfully free in their informality. Instead of being called to attention or suffering under highhanded officers, they are subject to the vanity, skepticism, and restiveness that come from the boredom of waiting for action. When the tall soldier, whose name is later revealed to be Jim Conklin, brings a new rumor of a military action, he "swells" with the importance of his narration but is greeted with such scoffing disbelief by a loud soldier that their exchange threatens to descend into anger. Then a corporal begins to swear at the thought of moving from the comfortable quarters he has constructed for himself. Finally the company joins in a "spirited debate" replete with arguments about strategy. The entire discussion resembles nothing so much as a small town cracker barrel discussion. What is uppermost in the representation is the *ordinariness* of the participants. They have no real distinction, yet if their foolishness and pretensions are exposed by the narration, they are not belittled. The informal, unschooled ordinariness of these soldiers is the very stamp of Crane's realism.

From this introductory scene and action, accomplished in less than two pages, the narration moves to a "youthful private" who is listening to the "words of the tall soldier," and we are brought abruptly in relation to the consciousness of the central figure of the book. The relation between the narration and Henry Fleming's consciousness is not so much one of invasion as it is of concentrated attachment. The consciousness of Henry Fleming is, after all, his *private* thoughts. The thoughts of the privates we first see are their public thoughts—what they can say to each other.

Upon hearing them, Private Fleming retires through an "intricate hole" into the privacy of his hut—it is not a tent—"to be alone with some new thoughts that had lately come to him." The narrative rarely leaves that consciousness but reports it in such a way that there is always detachment in its attachment. Thus there is always a gap between the report and the thoughts, sensations, and responses of this youth. The essential nature of the gap is one of irony, an irony that results in exposure as much as disclosure. If we see what Henry is thinking and feeling, we also see the illusory nature of his thoughts in relation to the field of battle in which he finds himself. The great force of the narrative rests in its capacity to render the reality of his experience as well as the external nature of battle. His experience of course colors the battle, but the battle colors his experience. His thoughts always at war with each other, he is himself embattled; at the same time, he is in a battle. To see so much is to see both the nature and violence of civil war.

The best way to see that violence is to sketch the action from the moment the narrative attaches itself to the consciousness of this youth. First of all there is the fact that Henry had "of course dreamed of battles all his life" and had enlisted in the army. If he had dreamed of war, his waking consciousness had feared that wars, the "crimson splotches on the pages of the past," were the vividly red moments of history that were now as bygone as crowns and castles. "Secular and religious education had effaced the throat-grappling instinct or else firm finance held in check the passions." Disappointed at his mother's objections to, rather than her support of his enlistment, he had nonetheless volunteered, had then felt a pang at his mother's helpless assent to his departure and her gift of blackberry jam, and had even felt shame at looking back at her tear-stained face as she knelt among the potato parings; but he had felt a thrill of self-importance in the village as he thought he saw a feminine schoolmate looking upon him as he and his company assembled.

The narrative gives but the briefest moment to this recapitulation of his boyish fantasies of Homeric battles—as an inner life they are every bit as ordinary as the public language of the soldiers—before launching its report of the move into battle. Throughout the brief march toward the conflict, replete with the soldiers' inveterate complaints and their continuing arguments about strategy, Henry remains silent with his own continuing doubts. Afraid to reveal them, he is astonished when, at the threshold of battle, Wilson, the outwardly brave and loud soldier, sobbingly announces his belief that he is to die and gives Henry a packet of letters to be sent home. In the ensuing battle, Henry manages to stand his ground against the first attack, forgetting himself in the rage of action; but while he is in the very throes of luxuriating in his accomplishment the enemy attacks again. Seeing men beside him waver and run, Henry joins in a flight as blind as his battle stand had been. His flight brings him to a point behind the lines from which, watching artillerymen mechanically serve their battery, he discovers that the blue line has held. Afflicted with this new knowledge, he feels like a criminal and, rationalizing his behavior, begins to justify his flight as an instinctive effort at self-preservation. This line of thought results in his full retirement from the field, and he finds himself in the isolated depths of a forest where "the high, arching boughs made a chapel." Pushing the boughs aside and entering, he confronts the eyes of a rotting corpse.

Recoiling from this ultimate reach of his retreat, he stumbles into a column of wounded soldiers making their way to the rear amid the rush of horse teams bringing reinforcements to the front. Two figures, a spectral soldier and a tattered soldier, galvanize his attention, and, in a true shock of recognition, he realizes the spectral soldier to be Jim Conklin. Stricken with anguish, he listens to Jim's supplications for protection and then watches him spectacularly die. When the wounded tattered soldier, who has reappeared to watch Conklin die, renews his queries about where Henry is wounded (queries which had made Henry try to escape him), Henry feels his questions like knife thrusts. Fearing that he is about to witness another death and distraught at the tattered soldier's delirium, he tears himself away from such a gruesome possibility.

He then finds himself rounding a little hillock, from which he can see retreating soldiers coming from the front in disarray and being met by another column advancing toward the front. That scene, an objective correlative of his conflicted state of mind, mirrors his wish that the army will be defeated so as to hide his cowardice as well as his shame at his own flight. When the advancing column suddenly bursts upon him in full retreat, he accosts a fleeing soldier with the all but inarticulate question of "Why— why—" only to be smashed in the head with the impetuous soldier's gun. Stunned and bloodied, he struggles through the littered battlefield in confusion until a cheery soldier, whose face he never sees, miraculously leads him back to his regiment.

Reunited with his company, he is treated with great solicitation by Wilson, who, after a time, sheepishly asks for his bundle of letters. If

Wilson's kindness lacerates the inner sore beneath Henry's wound, his shamed request for the letters gives Henry a privileged stance of superiority. The battle continuing on the following day, he and Wilson—both goaded to rage at an officer's referring to the company as mule drivers—perform with distinction not only in a first but also in a second engagement. So the battle ends on a successful note for Henry Fleming, and he once again indulgently luxuriates in his achievements.

This brief summary of the action provides what we might call a dead line along which to chart the sequence of Henry's emotions. Out of the most basic adolescent fantasies that bring him to the ground of battle, there are first the private doubts that isolate him, then the helpless rage of battle, then the pride of having survived without fleeing, then abject fear and flight, then a shame that produces defensive rationalizing, then the recoil from the ultimate horror of death (the images of the rotting dead soldier and the dying Jim Conklin), then more rationalization combining fear, shame, doubt; then the blow, the wound—both false and true—reducing him to a hopeless, helpless, and lost wanderer whose one instinct is to keep on his feet; then the reunion with his company bringing with it a mixture of relief and guilt; then Wilson's shamefaced request for a return of the letters, producing a triumphant superiority and aggression; then the rage of battle once more and a fuller sense of triumph when his actions receive praise, and finally a self-satisfied pride in accomplishment resting yet uneasily on the lie of his wound, his red badge of courage.

This abrupt sequence of emotions forms the ground of Henry's action, determining his behavior more than the orders of his officers. Crane's achievement is to displace the technology of war, its accelerating machinery, with an acceleration of emotions running between the poles of fear and rage. Fear is flight from death, rage the assault upon it. Death is, of course, the enemy, at once the feared and fated end of the natural process of living, and, in battle, the hated and feared living enemy determined to kill. It is no accident that the word "courage"—designating the chief virtue of the soldier—contains within it the word "rage," the aggression of the heart and mind. Both fear and rage are all but blind, instinctual, and both generate the lines of energy that society—in this instance civilian society at war with itself—transforms into shame and honor, cowardice and courage, with all the feelings that attend them. Henry Fleming's inner civil war is his violent experience of these emotions at war within himself. Crowded together in the closest proximity, they are always at the point of conflict and collision.

But there is the outer war, whose external reality we never doubt. If it is an expression of Henry's inner conflicts, he is equally an expression of its intensity. It is, as I have noted, the objective correlative of his inner turbulence, but the point is that it is objective. Its essential nature is violent civil disorder—a melee of discordant sounds, as if civil society and speech were themselves dissolving into roars and curses even as the machinery of war assumes the role of civil discussion. Thus artillery opens with a "furious debate," musketry "sputters," cannons "enter the dispute," guns "argue with abrupt violence," shells hurtle overhead in "long wild screams," cannon are engaged in a "stupendous wrangle," artillery "assembles as if for a conference." At the same time the speech of soldiers increasingly descends into incoherence, emanating in curses, oaths, screams, bellowing, yells, roars. Chapter XI concludes with this description of Henry Fleming: "He was a slang phrase." Battle utterances are characterized by incompleteness. A good example—one among many—occurs late in the book when the lieutenant rallies his men:

> As they halted thus the lieutenant again began to bellow profanely. Regardless of the vindictive threats of the bullets, he went about coaxing, berating, and bedamning. His lips, that were habitually in a soft and childlike curve, were now writhed into unholy contortions. He swore by all possible deities.
>
> Once he grabbed the youth by the arm. "Come on, yeh lunkhead!" he roared. "Come on! We'll all git killed if we stay here. We've on'y got t' go across that lot. An' then"—the remainder of his idea disappeared in a blue haze of curses.

That blue haze of curses brings us to the matter of color. Just as Crane's sounds of war veer always between curses and roars, his colors are boldly primary. The brown and green of the opening paragraph set the tone. There we see the process of nature revealed not in gradual but bold change. And we see that process again startlingly shown in the description of the dead soldier in the green forest chapel:

> He was being looked at by a dead man who was seated with his back against a columnlike tree. The corpse was dressed in a uniform that once had been blue, but was now faded to a melancholy shade of green. The eyes, staring at the youth, had changed to the dull hue to be seen on the side of a dead fish. The mouth was open. Its red had changed to an appalling yellow. Over the gray skin of the face ran little ants. One was trundling some sort of a bundle along the upper lip.

The strength of the passage gives the corpse a life of its own, which indeed it has, since it is still in the process of nature's change; the youth is the one who is arrested in the face of those staring eyes.

But the more memorable presence of color comes about when Crane seems to have almost violently asserted it by abruptly and visibly thrusting it on objects. A sort of index to the process is disclosed in the final battle sequence when Henry, resting on the laurels he feels he has won, recalls "bits of color that in the flurry had stamped themselves unawares upon his engaged senses." This stamping of color is evident in the very title of the book. Even more telling are the "crimson splotches" that, in Henry's mind, constitute the wars on the pages of history. Then there is the red god of battle. Rage, like new blood, is red, though like old blood it can also be black. Flames of musketry are seen as yellow tongues. This flash and splash of color is seen in the red badge itself that Henry wishes for when he enters the column of wounded men; and later, angry at being called a mule driver, he pictures "red letters of revenge" to be written to the insulting officer. Though a search for color will disclose that sound is actually much more present in the prose, the instances of color have a vivid force. The title of the book has its own finality, reminding us almost helplessly of those other American titles, *The Scarlet Letter* and "The Masque of the Red Death," and reminding us too that Poe and Hawthorne are deeply inscribed in this book. Given other Crane titles—"The Blue Hotel," "The Bride Comes to Yellow Sky," *Black Riders*, and *The Third Violet*—possibilities of color begin to haunt the mind. It is possible, of course, to pursue these colors into patterns of meaning and symbolism, yet such pursuits inevitably evade the much more important fact that the violent presence of color abruptly converts meaning into vivid images that annihilate prior symbolic reference. Henry Fleming is both enacting and fulfilling this instantaneous process of conversion when, in his triumphant red rage of charging the enemy lines, he becomes the color bearer of his company.

Finally there is the primary quality of form itself. The images in *The Red Badge* violently assert deformity. Corpses are twisted, bodies writhe, faces are contorted, dead soldiers lie upon the field as if they have been dumped from the sky, a dying soldier is seen "thrashing about in the grass, twisting his shuddering body into many strange postures," soldiers in battle are stretched on the ground or on their knees "as if they had been stricken by bolts from the sky." All the qualities of sound, color, and deformity are concentrated, at almost the exact center of the book, in the description of Jim Conklin's death:

> His spare figure was erect; his bloody hands were quietly at his
> side. He was waiting with patience for something that he had

come, to meet. He was at the rendezvous. They [Henry and the tattered soldier] paused and stood, expectant.

There was a silence.

Finally, the chest of the doomed soldier began to heave with a strained motion. It increased in violence until it was as if an animal was within and was kicking and tumbling furiously to be free.

This spectacle of gradual strangulation made the youth writhe, and once as his friend rolled his eyes, he saw something in them that made him sink wailing to the ground. He raised his voice in a last supreme call.

"Jim—Jim—Jim——"

The tall soldier opened his lips and spoke. He made a gesture. "Leave me be—don't tech me—leave me be—"

There was another silence while he waited.

Suddenly, his form stiffened and straightened. Then it was shaken by a prolonged ague. He stared into space. To the two watchers there was a curious and profound dignity in the firm lines of his awful face.

He was invaded by a creeping strangeness that slowly enveloped him. For a moment the tremor of his legs caused him to dance a sort of hideous hornpipe. His arms beat wildly about his head in expression of implike enthusiasm.

His tall figure stretched itself to its full height. There was a slight rending sound. Then it began to swing forward, slow and straight, in the manner of a falling tree. A swift muscular contortion made the left shoulder strike the ground first.

The body seemed to bounce a little way from the earth. "God!" said the tattered soldier.

The youth had watched, spellbound, this ceremony at the place of meeting. His face had been twisted into an expression of every agony he had imagined for his friend.

He now sprang to his feet and, going closer, gazed upon the pastelike face. The mouth was open and the teeth showed in a laugh.

As the flap of the blue jacket fell away from the body, he could see that the side looked as if it had been chewed by wolves.

The youth turned, with sudden, livid rage, toward the battlefield. He shook his fist. He seemed about to deliver a philippic.

"Hell——"

The red sun was pasted in the sky like a wafer.

There it all is. The violent heaving, the strained motion, the animal action, Henry's sinking wail and unfinished supreme call, the muscular contortion, the pastelike face fixed in a frozen laugh, the wolf-like wound, the truncated philippic, and the final sentence sealing the passage in the color of the red sun.

It is hardly surprising that the striking final sentence of this passage has arrested critics in search of meaning. Robert Wooster Stallman took the wafer to refer to communion and Jim Conklin—with his initials, his wound in the side, and the tattered soldier's accompanying passionate cry, "God"— to be the Christ. Stallman has been sufficiently flogged for his interpretation, so I shall not join the host of his detractors other than to note that he, like those seeking for literary precursors, actual battle sites, and color symbolism as literary, historical and symbolic subtexts of the narrative, was yearning for a religious subtext. The point is that all these subtexts have been blown away by the violence of battle. Henry's philippic breaks off with but one word— "hell." Hell in this text has utterly lost its theological sense; it, like all the other curses, is but the expression of present rage springing from the annihilation of traditional religious meaning. The wafer of the final sentence is, as others have seen, like the molten wafer of wax used to seal a letter. Whether it comes from Kipling's *The Light that Failed*, which Crane had surely read, is beside the point. Just as a wax wafer is pasted on a letter to seal it, so is the sun, as if it had been passed over Conklin's pastelike dead face, pasted in the sky.

The force that pastes the sun in the sky is of course the sentence itself. The entire passage shows just how, even as Henry's voice is unable to complete sentences, the narrative does nothing but complete them. Sentences in this book are the units of force effacing and displacing the author behind them with their own authority. They both report and execute the action. They literally sentence Henry Fleming to the war he has dreamed of all his life. They boldly and visibly stand forth, in the manner that Emerson spoke of his own sentences, as infinitely repellent particles. They all but annihilate paragraphs in their determination to stand alone. Of course they are in sequence, but they expose the discontinuity as much as the continuity of sequence. Their conclusiveness has sufficient finality to transform the silence between them into an abrupt gap of stillness as astonishing as the grotesque images they assert. That astonishment is really the ultimate emotion of battle more violent than mere surprise. It is an emotion that *excessively* fulfills the anxiety and curiosity of suspense, those emotions on which novelistic narration so much depends.

That is why these sentences not only threaten to annihilate paragraphs, they threaten the plot and suspense of traditional novelistic narrative. They are as determined to conclude action as they are to continue it. All but equal to each other in their declarative brevity, they have a genuinely democratic order, transforming turning points and climaxes of narrative into a continuum of violent intensity and at the same time annihilating the distinctions of military hierarchy and rank. The officers speak the same informal, ordinary, and violent language as the privates; Henry and the lieutenant are utterly equal in their united bellowing appeals for the men to charge. Higher battle strategy, like the battle lines that dissolve in the violence of battle, disintegrates into the soldiers' arguments about strategy.

Still, this book is a narrative, and the conventions of narrative, like all the traditional meaning and symbols of history and religion are, like the enemy, threatening a counterattack. That threat, indicating that there is also a civil war in the very form of the book, is very much evident in the concluding movement of the novel. In the midst of Henry's heroic charge when men, "punched by bullets, fell in grotesque agonies," and the regiment "left a coherent trail of bodies," we are given this passage:

> It seemed to the youth that he saw everything. Each blade of the green grass was bold and clear. He thought that he was aware of every change in the thin, transparent vapor that floated idly in sheets. The brown or gray trunks of the trees showed each roughness of their surfaces. And the men of the regiment, with their starting eyes and sweating faces, running madly, or falling, as if thrown headlong, to queer, heaped-up corpses—all were comprehended. His mind took a mechanical but firm impression, so that afterward everything was pictured and explained to him, save why he himself was there.
>
> But there was a frenzy made from this furious rush. The men, pitching forward insanely, had burst into cheerings, moblike and barbaric, but tuned in strange keys that can arouse the dullard and the stoic. It made a mad enthusiasm that, it seemed, would be incapable of checking itself before granite and brass. There was the delirium that encounters despair and death, and is heedless and blind to the odds. It is a temporary but sublime absence of selfishness. And because it was of this order was the reason, perhaps, why the youth wondered, afterward, what reasons he could have had for being there.

The delirium that encounters despair and death is, then, the sublime absence of selfishness. Here the novel hovers at the threshold of ennobling Henry's "heroism" and we might well be lulled into seeing the narrative, which is so much in the convention of the *bildungsroman*, as a register of Henry Fleming's moral growth toward maturity. The book's conclusion, with the regiment retiring from the battlefield and Henry once more luxuriating in a feeling of accomplishment, can be seen to reinforce such a vision of growth. Nearing its end, the narrative boldly asserts, "He was a man."

Yet to conclude moral growth and maturity from this sentence is to displace the iron irony of the narrative with blatant sentimentality. Although Crane cut some passages from the concluding chapter which expose the same complacent self-satisfaction, there is sufficient irony remaining to indicate that his asserted manhood is no more secured than it was after his first battle when the narrative asserted the same thing. He is really no better or worse than he was then nor is there evidence that he is better or worse than all the men who were killed or who survived. He could just as well have been killed, but that end would truly have made the book sentimental. Crane did better to keep him alive, letting all that selfishness, which had been for a moment sublimely absent, return in the form of pride.

This does not mean that there was nothing to Henry's bravery. He did fight as blindly as he ran, and presumably he killed some of the enemy when he kept blindly firing after his company had retreated, though we are spared actually seeing him in the act of killing. His distinction in battle comes from the excessive rage that is within him if it comes from anything. He had *of course* dreamed of battles all his life, and he just as arbitrarily of course fought out of the rage and dream that was in him. If war is an expression of death and grotesque disorder, it is nonetheless the sentence of existence, as near as the rage and dream that are always in us. The sentence of war was always in Crane, evident in the violence of *Maggie* with its opening on a street fight and in *George's Mother* opening with a woman battling with pots and pans in a kitchen. In *The Red Badge* he made it fully and exclusively *present*, so present that he could do little afterward except pursue it over the world as a reporter.

Grotesque and terrible as war may be, Crane does not write *against* war; he writes through it. His sentences, flattening perspective in their bold and visible presence, have the strength of line and form that we see in a Cezanne painting. They possess the "curious and profound dignity in the firm lines of [Jim Conklin's] awful face." If George Wyndham, who reviewed the book when it appeared in England and who had himself been a soldier, felt that it perfectly expressed his past experience of battle action, Ford Madox Ford, who fought in World War I, felt that it perfectly foretold the experience of that war, too. It retains to this day a remarkable modernity.

Joseph Conrad was good, in his memoir of Crane, to leave us his remembered image of Crane sitting at a table with a half-empty glass of beer gone flat, writing by hand in steady deliberation. No one who reads *The Red Badge* can doubt that that hand—the inertial hand that writes writing about the hand that fights—was possessed of true courage.

NOTE

1. Stephen Crane, *The Red Badge of Courage: An Annotated Text, Backgrounds and Sources, Essays in Criticism*. Edited by Sculley Bradley et al. New York: W. W. Norton and Company, 1962.

JOHN E. CURRAN, JR.

"Nobody seems to know where we go": Uncertainty, History, and Irony in The Red Badge of Courage

In his essay concerning Stephen Crane's *The Red Badge of Courage*, Thomas Kent treats the issue of "epistemological uncertainty" in the novel, concluding that it succeeds in casting the reader in the same predicament as its bewildered characters, and thus the reader is "confronted with the disturbing possibility that a knowable, interpretable universe may well be nonexistent."[1] Another scholar, Harold R. Hungerford, approaches the novel from a historical angle, arguing that although Crane never outwardly designates which Civil War battle is being depicted in the novel, the author "consistently used the time, the place, and the actions of Chancellorsville as a factual framework within which to represent the perplexities of his young hero."[2] These two critics seem to address entirely different concerns; the former treats the epistemological questions the author forces upon his reader, while the latter discusses the degree to which Crane was preoccupied with historical accuracy. But when considered together, the two theses point to an important tension in the novel. Kent indicates that Henry and the reader share a struggle to know and understand the events of the novel, while Hungerford suggests that, if we look carefully enough, we might be able to come to an understanding of those events by relating them to historical ones. It is as if Crane manipulates the novel such that we are confounded and oppressed by lack of knowledge, even as we gain the possibility for uncovering knowledge. The appropriate question then becomes: How does

From *American Literary Realism 1870–1910* 26, no. 1 (Fall 1993). © 1993 by McFarland & Company, Inc.

the strategy of withholding information while simultaneously building the story upon a "factual framework" function in *The Red Badge*?

The answer is that this scheme forces the reader to face the unpleasantness of ignorance and to ask certain questions, while it subtly and ironically provides ugly revelations. The result is a negative impression of Henry Fleming's situation as a soldier in the Civil War. Since the reader is allowed only into the consciousness of this single lad, the reader's conception of the happenings in this novel is based entirely upon what Henry thinks about and observes, and what he fails to think about and observe. An examination of the soldier's consciousness proves Kent's notion that we share Henry's "epistemological uncertainty," as we discover that his thoughts are characterized by narrowness, and his interactions with other characters reveal a pervading, collective ignorance. Henry's mental processes, or the lack of them, become even more disturbing when we realize that they comprise part of the historicity of the novel. Real soldiers existed in such a state of unawareness, and Crane lets us sample this limitedness of perspective for ourselves. Placed in this uncomfortable position, we reach a state where, like Henry, we crave answers. The irony is, however, that if we were enlightened, if we were permitted to comprehend that which is going on around Henry, our repulsion to Henry's predicament would only be greater. As Hungerford argues, Crane designs the story to conform to real historic details. The particular episode Crane chooses to represent, however, is pregnant with meaning: he selects Chancellorsville, one of the most disillusioning battles of the war. Crane not only places his character is one of the war's most humiliating debacles, but also in the section of that battle which was the cause of Chancellorsville's disastrous outcome. Thus Crane creates in this novel an epistemological system in which the reader is, through the unawareness of the protagonist, kept from the truth, but in which that truth, which we can discover through the "factual framework," justifies our worst fears.

As we follow the narrative, we notice the shallow quality of Henry's thinking. Dominating his consciousness is his prolonged, childish attempt to convince himself of his own heroism. When he departs from his mother, "ashamed of his purposes," we feel that his shame derives from his lack of any sensible or ethical motivations.[3] Henry never develops any real sense of purpose. He is so engrossed in egotism that he fails to evaluate in any meaningful way the events around him. Words like "slavery" and "union" are conspicuously absent from *The Red Badge*; concepts of why the war is happening, and why it might be a legitimate thing for him to participate in, do not enter Henry's mind. That mind, the only lens we possess to see into the world of the novel, is inadequate.

While Henry's private thoughts provide little elucidation about his "purposes," his interactions with his comrades provide just as little-about the overall situation. We should be able to learn something from what he sees and hears, but we do not. The introverted Henry is merely a microcosm of the entire army, as it shares with him a crisis of insecurity and blindness. Throughout the novel the soldiers demonstrate anxiety about their own ability to fight, as they fluctuate between self-deluded assurances of success and dismay at incessant failure. We learn that Henry remembers, "Almost every day the newspapers printed accounts of a decisive victory" (8), while he is soon to hear Wilson lament, "If th' truth was known ... *they've* licked *us* about every clip up to now" (18). Later, during the second day of battle in Chapter XVI, Henry and his comrades "were bewildered by the alleged news and could not fully comprehend a defeat" (76). They debate about where the blame for this defeat belongs, with themselves or with their generals. The youth condemns his leaders and avers that the men "fight like the devil" (77), but the hypocrisy of his statement only compounds our suspicion that they do not. Finally, Crane closes the novel with the soldiers arguing about "the accomplishment of the late battle" (109). Did they win or lose? Can they fight or are they weaklings? From the novel's start to its finish, such questions plague Henry, his fellows, and the reader.

This lack of confidence is coupled with a lack of knowledge about the soldiers' environment. Crane opens *The Red Badge* with Henry listening to Jim Conklin's rumor-mongering. But we realize almost immediately that when Jim refers to the battle plans, his grasp of them will never go beyond that they are "some dodge like that" (12). At one point, Henry is moved to cry,

> Good Gawd ... we're always being chased around like rats. It makes me sick. Nobody seems to know where we go or why we go. We just get fired around from pillar to post and get licked here and get licked there, and nobody knows what it's done for.... Now, I'd like to know what the eternal thunders we was marched into these here woods for anyhow. (78)

Our insights into where and why they go come only sporadically and mysteriously from lesser officers. For example, we are to understand that "Th' enemy's formin' over there for another charge.... an' I fear they'll break through there unless we work like thunder t' stop them" (84), which Henry happens to overhear from someone "whom the boys knew as the commander of their division" (84). This man is the highest ranking officer Crane allows us to see, but he is only a division commander, and even he seems like an obscure, remote presence to "the boys."[4] Moreover, his statement gives us one of the most informed accounts of what is actually transpiring, but it does not tell us very much. The generals of the higher command remain as a nameless, faceless, and menacing group of "lunkheads" (76) manipulating the hapless soldiers. We share Henry and his comrades' desire to know where and why they go, and we probably would prefer to know who the "lunkheads" in command might be, but Crane denies us.

Thus exposed exclusively to Henry's thoughts and observations, the reader finds himself trapped in a world the prevailing features of which are self-doubt and ignorance, and so the prospect that Henry's world is an authentic portrayal becomes distressing. Crane's soldiers are realistic, argues Stanley Wertheim, because several personal chronicles of the war were available to the author, and were probably a fundamental resource for what he truly wanted to know—how the men of the Civil War *felt*.[5] Historical knowledge of their state of mind substantiates Wertheim's claim, for somehow Crane gained such an understanding. The "purposes" of most Union soldiers were no more advanced than those of Henry. The historian Bell Irvin Wiley, who derives much of his information from personal accounts, tells us that few men who enlisted in the army went with much consideration for patriotism or for emancipation.[6] Moreover, real Northern soldiers of the time around and before Chancellorsville had reason to suspect their own battle-worthiness, for Wilson's confession of their poor combat record was true. Before the Chancellorsville Campaign in the spring of 1863, they had lost eleven of the thirteen major engagements in which they had fought, and had seen four demoralized commanders come and go.[7] Because of repeated defeat, they were vexed by what Wiley calls "the lingering fear of rebel invincibility."[8] Soldiers were also commonly kept in the dark about their own activities. Wiley notes, "A battle was ... a chaotic event and especially so to the man in the ranks."[9] Hungerford suggests that Crane refuses to reveal the truth of where and why Henry goes because, in all probability, a real soldier would not have known.[10] Here, then, we begin to see how Kent's ideas and Hungerford's can be related—Crane pays careful attention to history, and the frustration we begin to feel as we step into Henry's world of blindness is an integral part of that attention.

The critic David Halliburton eloquently describes Crane's epistemological pattern:

> Time after time the youth and his comrades hear without knowing, see without knowing, think without knowing.... Uncertainty and apprehension are endemic, lack of knowledge chronic ... Crane implies that a man is what he knows, but he knows little.[11]

Why are they fighting? Can they fight? Have they won? What is their strategy? What role do they have in the battle? Who is directing the battle? What battle is it? The reader, like the soldiers, does not know. But Crane has certainly inculcated a desire to know—in them and in us. He has also covertly planted enough clues that we may find out.

The actual battle which corresponds to *The Red Badge of Courage* must be Chancellorsville, contrary to what some scholars have contended. Hungerford, in his exhaustively researched article, successfully manages to refute arguments by critics like Syndon U. Pratt and Thomas F. O'Donnell that "the novel may rather be regarded as a synthesis of more than one battle than a historical portrayal of a single engagement."[12] Pratt finds elements of Antietam in the novel, while O'Donnell agrees and adds Winchester to the "synthesis" theory.[13] Pratt, however, admits that Chancellorsville is the "traditional" setting ascribed to *The Red Badge*, as the novel refers to the "plank road" (60), "the Rappahannok" (75), "pontoon bridges" (20), and various other features peculiar to that battle.[14] Hungerford points out many additional features, and also notes that Crane himself indicates that Henry's battle is Chancellorsville in the short story "The Veteran."[15] Furthermore, Hungerford states that the evidence that Crane was interested in historic details, and that he knew quite a lot about Chancellorsville in particular, is considerable.[16]

But Hungerford's assertions that Crane was dedicated to historic accuracy, and that he deliberately and strictly used Chancellorsville as a "factual framework," are sensible for artistic reason as well. If Crane took such pains to replicate authentically the state of mind of Union soldiers, why would he then place his characters in a fictitious situation? Why would the author want to conflate scenes from several battles into an imaginary "Episode of the Civil War"? It is hard to believe that he would consider time, place, and actions to be such dispensable or uninteresting factors, particularly when he leaves so many hints about them. Rather, it seems more likely that Crane be cryptic, and yet revealing, about his novel's setting because the setting is deeply symbolic. Hungerford states that Chancellorsville most likely appealed to Crane's "sense of the ironic and colorful," and to his sense of "tragic futility," but the battle is much more thematically significant than this.[17] Not merely a losing cause, Chancellorsville is an embarrassment, the epitome of everything distasteful and ridiculous about the Union army. Crane gratifies our demand for answers by providing a decidedly bleak context for Henry's experiences.

For example, the "when" and "where" of the battle contribute effectively to Crane's irony. The Union army in the Eastern Theater had been continuously demoralized up to the spring of 1863, so Chancellorsville culminates two years of Northern military bungling. The "months of monotonous life in a camp" (10) Henry whiles away would be the winter of 1862–1863, which found Northern spirits at their nadir.[18] The place of Crane's novel is even more dismal than the time. It occurs to Henry, as he runs into "trees and branches," and "constantly" gets "entangled in briars," that "It looked to be a wrong place for a battle field" (22). Chancellorsville is located in the area near the town of Fredericksburg known as the Wilderness, "a tangled maze of second growth woodland."[19] This jungle made a terrible battlefield, but it was nevertheless a common one. Over 100,000 men died there in four bloody engagements.[20] Crane's character is in a "wrong" place—a dark, tainted forest conducive not to heroism, but only to death.

The dynamics of the battle of Chancellorsville itself are just as grim (from a Union perspective, at least) as its time and place. It was Confederate General Lee's greatest and boldest victory over vastly superior Union forces: historian Peter J. Parish comments, "Seldom if ever can an army have so thoroughly bemused and humiliated an adversary twice its size."[21] Even as Crane's soldiers wonder whether they have won or lost, they exist in the midst of the North's most stunning defeat. Ironically, their confusion and lack of knowledge reflect that of the actual Union command. The generals "could not find out where the Confederates were," making them "worried and somewhat bewildered"; just as ignorance permeates *The Red Badge*, ignorance is responsible for the Chancellorsville disaster.[22] Crane seems to be aware of this connection. Among Jim Conklin's initial theories of the army's movements, the only one which his fellows do not dispute is the cavalry's departure (12). The bulk of Union cavalry was dispatched from the army about a week before Chancellorsville occurred, a foolish manoeuvre which effectively "deprived the army of its eyes," since the cavalry in the Civil War was used primarily to determine enemy position.[23] It is as if Crane carefully and selectively injects particular events of the Chancellorsville Campaign into the novel. Just as he lets us hear about the cavalry movement, he allows us to see the "dark waves of men come sweeping out of the woods," attesting to Henry that "the fight was lost" (59), a description which must allude to the rout of the Eleventh Corps at Chancellorsville. The battle was won on May 2 by Confederate General "Stonewall" Jackson's audacious flanking movement around and to the right of the Federal army, a position held by the Eleventh Corps, which was demolished.[24] Hungerford notes that the men of Crane's fleeing mob resemble the German-American soldiers of the ill-fated Corps.[25] Crane's protagonist might have run anywhere, but he happens to run straight into a stampede of panicked, "burly men" who talk strangely (59–60); Crane has Henry stumble upon the battle's most climactic, and most disheartening, event. It seems to be the author's strategy to expose his reader to the most egregious features of Chancellorsville.

One question that remains unanswered throughout the novel is who is the general responsible for the defeat. Appropriately enough, the anonymous commander is actually Joseph "Fighting Joe" Hooker, an alcoholic, an "egoist and intriguer," and a braggart.[26] Moreover, there seems to exist a parallel between Hooker's conduct at Chancellorsville and Henry's. Before the battle, Henry is scolded for talking as if he thought he "was Napoleon Bonaparte" (19). Hooker certainly talked in this manner before Chancellorsville, with famous claims such as "May God have mercy on General Lee, for I will have none." But during the execution of the battle, the General, as he himself later said, "Just lost confidence in Joe Hooker," balking on his well-laid plans and handing the initiative, and thus the victory, over to an inferior force.[27] Similarly, Henry's courage fails him at the critical moment, as he runs away from a skirmish at which he should have stayed and fought, as his comrades did. "Fighting Joe" shares with "wildcat" (81) Henry a loss of nerve on the pivotal day which cost the Union the battle. If the battle of Chancellorsville has its presence in *The Red Badge*, so too does the general who lost it.

But the link between Chancellorsville and *The Red Badge* runs deeper still. Our questions can be answered more specifically. It would be pointless to attempt to determine which factual Union regiment Crane's 304th New York is supposed to represent, as the 304th itself is fictitious, and while its actions "loosely parallel the movements of many regiments at Chancellorsville—they directly parallel the movements of none."[28] Crane creates fictional soldiers, like Henry and Wilson, in a fictional regiment, the 304th, but places them within a real battle which remains nameless, suggesting that the story is imaginary as far as the names it permits us to hear and the faces it permits us to see. There were not, for example, general officers in the Union army at Chancellorsville by the names of "Perry" (26) or "Whiterside" (84).[29] Nor do we have any indication that Crane's aforementioned division commander has any relationship to a real person. Perhaps this particular level of command serves as the break between fiction and reality; since Crane lets us view Henry's division leader, Henry's division is most likely imaginary, but since this general's superiors remain faceless and nameless, Henry's corps, as well as his army, could well be based on fact.

Hungerford believes that the movements of Henry's regiment can be traced to those of a particular corps, and designates that corps as the Second. His own findings, however, might suggest that the corps which actually corresponds to Henry's is the Third Corps. First, Hungerford notes that the Second Corps crossed the Rappahannock River on two pontoon bridges on the evening of April 30, much as Crane describes in *The Red Badge*.[30] The Third Corps crossed on two pontoon bridges as well, and was ordered to begin that crossing in the evening of April 30 and finish by early morning on May 1.[31] Hungerford goes on to state that the next day was an intervening day between crossing and fighting for Henry, just as May 1 was at Chancellorsville, but the scholar never accounts for Henry's regiment's "rapid march" of a number of "miles" (20) which began early on that intervening day.[32] The Third Corps early on May 1 "rapidly marched to Chancellorsville" from its crossing point, a distance of several miles.[33] Furthermore, upon meticulously reviewing the 304th's movements on the next day, Hungerford concludes that Henry's group marched southeast of Chancellorsville and engaged the enemy early in the afternoon, much as some regiments from the Second Corps did.[34] The Third Corps, on the other hand, sent an entire division on an expedition to Hazel Grove, South of Chancellorsville proper, and then to Catherine Furnace, further south, where the division met with heavy fighting early in the afternoon with the rear guard of Jackson's flanking column and with a separate rebel brigade, requiring reinforcements to hold out and overcome the rebels.[35] This skirmish in the Furnace resembles adequately the skirmish from which Henry flees. Moreover, from what can be deduced about Henry's location, Hungerford determines that Fleming's regiment must be situated near the center of the Federal line but not far from the right, as it is clear from the text that Henry during his flight was "over on th' right" (65).[36] The Second Corps, however, on May 2 was in position at the left of the line, while much of the Third was placed in the center, adjoining the Eleventh Corps, which held the right flank.[37] Finally, Hungerford points to the 124th New York regiment, which represented Crane's home town, as a possible source for Crane's 304th, because the charge of the latter on the second day of battle is much like the actual charge of the former.[38] The 124th New York was a member of the Third Corps.[39] Hence, if it is possible to associate a corps with *The Red Badge*, the Third Corps could probably qualify.

If Crane did have this Corps in mind, perhaps he chose it because of its potential for irony. The Third Corps played a pivotal role at Chancellorsville, as it was constantly involved in the worst mistakes of the battle. For example, the crossing of the river and the "rapid march" both resulted from a misjudgment by Hooker. Before the battle, the general changed his mind about where to place the Third Corps. First deploying it across the river, he had to wait at Chancellorsville for its arrival, a waste of precious time.[40] There is also an allegation that the Third Corps was more directly responsible for the defeat. Many historians, Augustus Choate Hamlin among them, feel that the expedition to the Furnace was the fatal error of the battle. The commander of the Third Corps, upon hearing news that a large Confederate force was moving through the woods in front of him, quite wrongly deduced that the rebel column, which was actually Jackson's flanking column, was in retreat. By moving first one division, and then a second, southward into the Furnace in pursuit, the Third Corps left the adjacent Eleventh Corps without support, and thus vulnerable to Jackson's attack.[41] That the displacement of the Third Corps led to the disaster is by no means indisputable, as commentary like that of John Bigelow, Jr., testifies.[42] More recent accounts than Bigelow's, however, such as the narratives of Bruce Catton and Bruce Palmer, accept the assumption that the gap between the Eleventh Corps and the Third caused the defeat, suggesting that in modern analysis the notion is not far from conventional wisdom.[43] Also, Bigelow, writing in the early 1900s, acknowledges that the Third Corps had often been criticized for losing the battle.[44] Probably, then, a student of the war like Crane, writing in the 1890s, would have at least been aware of such criticism, if he did not himself subscribe to it. Hungerford tells us that Crane learned much of his Civil War history by reading *Battles and Leaders of the Civil War*, which includes the personal accounts of many generals.[45] If Crane happened to examine the journals dealing with Chancellorsville, particularly those of General Howard, commander of the Eleventh Corps, General Couch, and General Pleasonton, he might well have concluded that the reconnaissance of the Third Corps to the Furnace was a critical mistake.[46] It is plausible that Crane, like so many others, viewed this movement as "reckless," "stupid and ridiculous."[47] The Third Corps also figures prominently in the next day's difficulties. Its position at the Furnace, so disastrous initially, suddenly became strategically desirable. Hooker foolishly relinquished this position by withdrawing the Corps, abandoning all hope of salvaging victory.[48] So, the Third Corps has the distinction of being the instrumental unit of a devastating loss.

That these movements would enlighten Henry about where and why he goes during the battle seems fitting to Crane's ironic scheme. If the actions of the Third Corps can be applied to *The Red Badge*, we have the following scenario: what Henry feels is a "supreme trial" (34), an "onslaught of redoubtable dragons" (36) so furious that it compels him to flee, is really a minor skirmish which diverted the attentions of the Federals from the real threat; the next day, his heroism goes toward nothing but an ill-advised and cowardly retreat. As a member of the Third Corps, when Henry perceives that he is "marched from place to place with apparent aimlessness" (24), he is not far from the truth. The Third Corps did redeem itself somewhat the night of May 2, helping to cover for the Eleventh Corps' retreat, but Crane affords Henry no part in this action.[49] At this time he is contemplating his own "wound" and following the soldier with the "cheery voice" (62–64). Where there exists heroism, Henry is absent, and thus we do not see it.

Furthermore, the commander of the Third Corps, the man in charge of this "aimlessness," is as unattractive as his superior, Hooker. His name was Daniel Sickles, and he embodies much of the "fears of stupidity and incompetence" (25) which assail Henry. Described as an "impulsive" general, Sickles was one of the "Northern Political Generals," men who had earned rank through political connections and contributions to the cause, instead of military qualification. Often, as Catton notes, their troops paid dearly for their lack of military skill; Sickles himself "was the target of criticism both military and political, public and personal."[50] He was also the only amateur corps commander at Chancellorsville, and he was a politician from Crane's home state of New York.[51] Crane makes in the novel what well might be a reference to the political Union generals: "The officers labored like politicians to beat the mass into a proper circle to face the menaces" (93). Crane permits us to observe officers who act like politicians, but not officers who act like generals; we see rallying and admonishing, but no strategy or cunning, and thus we witness defeat. In the case of Sickles, as in the case of Hooker, Henry's recurring suspicion that "The generals were idiots" (23) is born out.

Crane makes a poignant statement about the Civil War by figuring both "epistemological uncertainty" and precise historical detail into his novel, and by using these two effects in accord with one another for the purpose of irony. Part of the realism behind the fiction is the woeful state of the soldiers' minds. Ironically, we gain an awareness of the condition of real Civil War soldiers by partaking in the blindness of Crane's fictitious soldiers. The other part of the realism is the truth surrounding the blindness. The event which Crane's characters—and his reader—fail to understand is the battle of Chancellorsville, and the activities we fail to understand are those of the Third Corps. Thus, we are made to seek a cure for our blindness, and we receive an ironically bitter one. It is as if Crane's message is that American men muddled through a wretchedly conducted and pointless war, and they knew not what they did.

NOTES

1. Thomas Kent, "Epistemological Uncertainty in *The Red Badge of Courage*," *Modern Fiction Studies* 27 (1982), 628.

2. Harold R. Hungerford, "'That was Chancellorsville': The Factual Framework of *The Red Badge of Courage*," *American Literature* 34 (1963), 520.

3. Stephen Crane, *The Red Badge of Courage*, ed. Sculley Bradley, Richmond Croom Beatty, and Hudson Long (New York: W. W. Norton and Company, 1962). Subsequent

references to *The Red Badge of Courage* will be to this edition and will be noted parenthetically.

4. Civil War forces were organized, in descending order of importance, into armies, corps, divisions, brigades and regiments. See Peter J. Parish, *The American Civil War* (New York: Holmes and Meier, 1975), p. 152.

5. Stanley Wertheim, "*The Red Badge of Courage* and Personal Narratives of the Civil War," *American Literary Realism* 6 (1973), 61–65.

6. Bell Irvin Wiley, *The Life of Billy Yank* (Indianapolis: The Bobbs-Merrill Company, 1951), pp. 38, 40.

7. Bruce Palmer, *Chancellorsville: Disaster in Victory* (New York: The Macmillan Company, 1967), pp. 16, 11.

8. Wiley, p. 283.

9. Wiley, p. 77.

10. Hungerford, p. 530.

11. David Halliburton, *The Color of the Sky* (Cambridge: Cambridge University Press, 1989), p. 110.

12. Syndon U. Pratt, "A Possible Source for *The Red Badge of Courage*," *American Literature* 2 (1939), 9.

13. Pratt, p. 8; Thomas F. O'Donnell, "John B. Van Petton: Stephen Crane's History Teacher," *American Literature* 27 (1955), 196.

14. Pratt, p. 8.

15. Hungerford, p. 520.

16. Hungerford, pp. 529–530.

17. Hungerford, pp. 530–531.

18. Wiley, p. 282.

19. Bruce Catton, *The American Heritage Picture History of the Civil War* (New York: American Heritage, 1960), p. 297.

20. Joseph P. Cullen, *Where a Hundred Thousand Fell* (Washington, D. C.: National Park and Handbook Series, 1966), p. 5.

21. Parish, p. 278.

22. Catton, p. 292.

23. See Parish (p. 276) for a description of this cavalry movement, and Parish (p. 158) for the role of cavalry.

24. Parish, pp. 277–278.

25. Hungerford, p. 526.

26. Parish, p. 276; Catton, p. 296; Palmer, p. 13.

27. See Catton, pp. 297, 299, for Hooker's quotes; see Palmer, p. 35, for the loss of the general's initiative.

28. See Pratt, p. 8, on the 304th being fictional; see Hungerford, p. 524, for the description of his detailed study comparing the movements of the 304th to those of actual regiments in the battle.

29. These two names do not appear in the listings of general officers at the battle of Chancellorsville in J. H. Stine's *The History of the Army of the Potomac* (Washington D. C.: Gibson Brothers, 1893).

30. Hungerford, p. 523.

31. John Bigelow, Jr., *The Campaign of Chancellorsville: A Strategic and Tactical Study* (New Haven: Yale Univ. Press, 1910), p. 229.

32. Hungerford, p. 524.

33. Stine, p. 333.

34. Hungerford, p. 524.

35. Bigelow, pp. 279–283.

36. Hungerford, p. 525.

37. Augustus Choate Hamlin, *The Battle of Chancellorsville* (Bangor, Maine: Published by the author, 1896). p. 19, map 1.

38. Hungerford, p. 528.

39. Stine, p. 402.

40. Bigelow, p. 235.

41. Hamlin, p. 48–50.

42. Bigelow feels that General Sickles, the commander of the Third Corps, was right to pursue Jackson, that a more active pursuit would have "sent Jackson's column flying toward Richmond," and that the responsibility for the gap between the Third Corps and the Eleventh lies with the commander who remained behind and did not pursue, General Howard of the Eleventh Corps. Thus, contrary to Hamlin's opinion, Bigelow thinks the disaster was caused not by the expedition to the Furnace, but by the lack of a more extensive expedition, and that the destroyed corps, the Eleventh, was at fault for its own destruction. See Bigelow, p. 338.

43. Catton, p. 304; Palmer, pp. 49–52.

44. Bigelow, p. 338.

45. Hungerford, p. 529. For an account of Crane's readings of *Battles and Leaders*, see Corwin Knapp Linson, *My Stephen Crane* (Syracuse, NY: Syracuse University Press, 1968), pp. 37–38.

46. This claim warrants demonstration. For the following statements, see Robert Underwood Johnson and Clarence Clough Buel, eds., *Battles and Leaders of the Civil War*, 4 vols. (New York: Thomas Yoseloff, 1956), vol. 3.

Howard relates how he was told that Sickles was planning a "grand attack" (197), and how the entire reserves of the Eleventh Corps, consisting of Barlow's Brigade, were taken from the Corps to assist Sickles. Howard notes that he discerned "no real battle" in the direction of Sickles' "promised attack" (197), and that soon the Confederates were bearing down on the Union right. Howard gives the following reasons for the rout of his Corps: First, the woods were too dense to ascertain Jackson's position; second, the panic that arose from the surprise confused his men; and third, his only reserve, Barlow's Brigade, was gone (202). Thus, Howard tells us that he was led to believe in Sickles' expedition, but that the expedition accomplished nothing while it left Howard defenseless.

Of the faulty notion that Jackson's column was retreating, and of Sickles' movement to harass it, General Couch says, "I thought, without speaking, if [that] conception [of retreat] is correct, it is very strange that only the Third Corps should be sent in pursuit" (163). Couch intimates here that the judgment of Hooker and Sickles was probably incorrect, and that Sickles' movement was decided on rashly. Couch also states flatly that Sickles' attack did nothing to inhibit Jackson, and that "no corps in the army, surprised as the Eleventh was at this time, could have held its ground under similar circumstances" (163).

General Pleasonton notes that "the moving out to the Furnace of the two divisions of the Third Corps left a gap of about a mile from Hazel Grove to the right of the Twelfth Corps" (197), which implies a large gap in the Union line between the Eleventh Corps and any other corps, as the Third Corps joined the Eleventh and the Twelfth. Pleasonton says that Sickles, preoccupied at the Furnace with Jackson's rear guard, thought that "the enemy were giving way" and that cavalry could be useful in pursuit (179). Pleasonton quickly realized that cavalry was useless there, and when he began to hear "spattering shots going more and more to the north-west," the direction of the Union right flank, he became "satisfied that the enemy were not retreating" (179). The next thing Pleasonton describes is the rout of the Eleventh Corps. He has told us, then, that Sickles' movement caused a gap which isolated the Eleventh Corps, that the movement was conducted under inaccurate conceptions, and that it diverted Pleasonton's attention from the true threat.

So, it seems that all three Generals feel that the Third Corps, under a false presumption, was in the wrong place, and that its placement was related to, if not responsible for, the debacle.

47. Catton, p. 304; Hamlin, p. 50.

48. Parish, p. 278.

49. Palmer, p. 56.

50. See Palmer, p. 48, on Sickles' impulsiveness; see Catton, p. 82, on Sickles' reputation and on the Northern Political Generals.

51. Stine, p. 390.

JOSEPH URBAS

The Emblematics of Invulnerability in
The Red Badge of Courage

Perhaps the greatest ambiguity in *The Red Badge of Courage* lies in its emblems—among them, those the main character would proudly bear and those he would prefer to hide. There is no doubt, for example, that Private Henry Fleming feels "psychological anguish at being alone and unscarred among a community of the wounded" (Tanner 140), as this well-known passage in chapter IX shows:

> *At times* he regarded the wounded soldiers in an envious way. He conceived persons with torn bodies to be peculiarly happy. He wished that he, too, had a wound, a red badge of courage.[1]

Overpowering though this feeling may be, it is no less ambivalent and fleeting than the other feelings Henry has (in chapter XI he envies by turns the living and the dead, the "chosen" heroes rushing off to battle and the corpses littering the fields and forest [47, 48, 50]). If there is one thing the reader learns in this novel, with its dizzying onrush of disparate moods, it is that Henry's impressions and desires are neither simple nor unvarying. His guilt at being unharmed is matched by an equally strong, if often less explicit, desire to remain that way (a desire that should not always be confused with mere faint-heartedness, as we shall see). The deceptively simple opposition

From *Q/W/E/R/T/Y* 4 (October 1994). © 1994 by Publications de L'Université de Pau.

between the symbolics of heroism emblazoned in the title of the work itself and the various stigmata of cowardice we encounter along the way ("letters of guilt", "marks of his flight", "the sore badge of his dishonor" [41, 49, 50]) is in the end supplanted by a third and no less ambiguous emblematics of invulnerability.

To chart this evolution, we shall first examine two contrasting depictions of what may at first blush seem a rather surprising emotion to find in a war novel—love—in order to see what they reveal about Henry's attitude toward vulnerability, Then we shall consider the import of Henry's overriding preoccupation on the eve of battle: control, and its diametrical opposite, contingency. Third, we shall analyze two kinds of vulnerability that haunt the main character: outward and inward, physical and moral vulnerability. Finally, we shall argue that at the end of *The Red Badge* the imagination projects a lasting triumph over human weakness with the creation of a new, invulnerable, disembodied self.

Love

There are two revealing images of love in this novel. The first concerns the tattered man Henry Fleming meets while marching in a procession of wounded soldiers on his way back to the regiment:

> There was a tattered man, fouled with dust, blood and powder stain from hair to shoes, who trudged quietly at the youth's side. He was listening with eagerness and much humility to the lurid descriptions of a bearded sergeant. His lean features wore an expression of awe and admiration. He was like a listener in a country store to wondrous tales told among the sugar barrels. He eyed the story-teller with unspeakable wonder. His mouth was agape in yokel fashion (39);

> His homely face was suffused with a light of love for the army which was to him all things beautiful and powerful. (40)

The second involves Henry Fleming at a crucial, epiphanic moment of the second day of battle:

> Within him, as he hurled himself forward, was born a love, a despairing fondness for this flag which was near him. It was a creation of beauty and invulnerability. It was a goddess, radiant that bended its form with an imperious gesture to him. It was a woman, red and white, hating and loving, that called him with the

voice of his hopes. Because no harm could come to it he endowed
it with power. (80)

In both cases love is bestowed on something associated with power and
beauty. But there the similarity ends.

The tattered man loves the army, that is to say a group of his fellow
men. All his faith and admiration are reserved for them. Like him, they are
wounded soldiers. They are thus embodiments of human vulnerability to
contingency, as their presence in the procession of battle victims makes clear.
The tattered man is also the very pattern of Christian meekness. He is
described as "diffident," "gentle," "pleading," "humble," "lamblike," and
"brotherly." Unlike most of the soldiers in *The Red Badge*, when he speaks it
is "timidly," "in a small voice," with "an air of apology." He has to "muster
up sufficient courage" or "achieve the fortitude" to strike up and maintain a
conversation with Henry (39–40). In sum, despite his two "red badges" ("two
wounds, one in the head, bound with a blood-soaked rag, and the other in
the arm, making that member dangle like a broken bough" [39]), the tattered
man is depicted as someone naturally unendowed with courage. What is
more, his very name figures forth human frailty, a body subject to wear and
tear. Not only does the tattered man love creatures that are themselves
vulnerable, this love, together with his country naiveté, also renders him
vulnerable to ridicule ("sardonic comment" [39]) at the hands of the very
man he admires in the passage quoted above, the bearded sergeant. Love,
like trust (as we shall see in section 4), is one of the relational virtues that
leaves us at the mercy of chance.[2]

Henry Fleming's love, on the other hand, is directed toward an
inanimate object. The flag is beautiful and powerful precisely because it is
neither human nor vulnerable.[3] in other words, Henry invests it with power
because of its indestructibility (*Because no harm could come to it he endowed it
with power*). He worships the flag as a deity of invulnerability, but he also
confers upon it a talismanic power to protect him from harm ("He kept near,
as if it could be a saver of lives..." [80]). Thus it is fitting that he should
appropriate this emblem of immortality for himself, but that to do so he must
first snatch it from the jaws of Death (the corpse of the fallen flagbearer [80])
and later from Wilson, who has come to embody values similar to those of
the tattered man (61–62). It is obvious, then, that Henry, unlike this man,
wants a love safe from human vulnerability to contingency, a love that is
proof against "the thousand natural shocks that flesh is heir to."

For Henry, the flag represents a mythologized femininity that is
indestructible because abstract and immortal, hence eminently worthy of
love and admiration. This goddess unites the extremes of passion (hate and

love, despair and hope)—the better, as we shall argue in our analysis of chapter XXIV, to cancel them out. And unlike Henry's mother (5), she appears to command unconditional obedience (*imperious*), thereby relieving the youth of one of his biggest burdens—that of responsibility for individual choice in action. Finally, we should emphasize that this highly prized emblem is also referred to in specific terms as a creation. As we learn in the very first chapter of the novel, Henry Fleming has a fertile imagination (a "busy mind" [5]). As signifier, the flag is a product of the mythopoeic power of an imagination that creates things, and then in turn identifies wholly with them. It is a mirror of Henry's soul. Which is why the deity he sees reflected there speaks directly to his individual aspirations (*that called him with the voice of his hopes*).[4] It is a pure projection of what is "within him". Through this mythmaking process, Henry at the same time fashions a new self. In our view, it is no mere accident that Crane rings an ironic change on the book of *Genesis* at the end of *The Red Badge*, when Henry Fleming stands back like a "spectator" to admire his *oeuvre*, the new identity he has forged for himself ("He saw that he was good" [96]).

Control

For Henry Fleming, then, love in its most exalted form is synonymous with invulnerability. Consistent with this ideal, we shall examine, in sections three and four, two types of human weakness that Henry longs to transcend. But beforehand we should consider a corresponding goal that eludes him from the outset.

The "great problem" (11) that nags Henry at the beginning of *The Red Badge* can be seen as a struggle against contingency. Simply put, it is one of control, especially self-control. Will he run or not? Unfortunately for the youth, no mental answer is forthcoming; no argument, no "proof" or "demonstration," nor yet any past experience (since he is "untested" [19])—nothing can guarantee Henry's reactions under fire:

> For days he made ceaseless calculations. but they were all wondrously unsatisfactory. He found that he could establish nothing.... He reluctantly admitted that he could not sit still and with a mental slate and pencil derive an answer. To gain it, he must have blaze, blood, and danger, even as a chemist requires this, that, and the other (10–11).

Still worse, none of Henry's actual preparations, plans or schemes work out (6, 22, 48–49, 51, 56); all are either deliberately abandoned or thwarted by circumstances. Indeed, before the second day of battle, Henry gives up planning altogether (65). Perhaps one of the most disturbing aspects of *The Red Badge of Courage* is this utter failure of "intelligent deliberation" (34) to influence the course of events in a positive manner.[5] In short, rational thought seems to offer no sure way to escape vulnerability to contingency.

We should note that in this problem of self-control the accent may also be placed on the first term. That is to say, Henry's inability to predict his future actions raises questions about the very nature of his individual identity:

> It had suddenly appeared to him that perhaps in a battle he might run. He was forced to admit that as far as war was concerned he knew nothing of himself....
> He felt that in this crisis his laws of life were useless, Whatever he had learned of himself was here of no avail. He was an unknown quantity. (8)

The ultimate challenge for Henry is to create a new self; war is of course seen as the means to achieve that end:

> The youth had been taught that a man became another thing in a battle. He saw his salvation in such a change. (20)
> He would have liked to have used a tremendous force, he said, throw off himself and become a better. (48)

But, we should add, Henry wants a self that is safe from accident and circumstance, a self he controls completely.

In a sense this problem is also very concrete. Just as his regiment struggles for possession of the physical terrain of battle, so Henry must secure command over his own corporeal being. After observing a regiment in flight, this is the way Henry imagines the immediate challenge he faces:

> The battle reflection that shone for an instant in the faces on the mad current made the youth feel that forceful hands from heaven would not have been able to have held him in place if he could have got intelligent control of his legs. (24–25)

It is a question of mind over body, of retaining mastery (*intelligent control*) over one's own recalcitrant limbs whatever the circumstances (of having, in Henry's own words, "master's legs" [34]), but also over one's ungovernable instincts and passions—all of this in a life-and-death situation.

Outer Vulnerability

The status of the human body—in particular body *parts* (Henry's head and legs, the lieutenant's hand, Bill Smithers's fingers, to name just a few), to which Crane devotes an exceptional amount of descriptive attention—is indeed quite singular in *The Red Badge of Courage*. It is perhaps to be expected that in a war novel the author should lay stress on the body, its vulnerability (think of the soldiers' obsessive fear of being trampled upon), the likelihood of having an arm or leg ground up or blown off by the "awful machinery" (39) of war. Still, one also gets the strange impression here that bodily members acquire, as it were, a life of their own; they are often eerily separate, unfamiliar ("His fingers were dabbled with blood. He regarded them with a fixed stare" [53]), unruly. Henry sometimes looks upon his own limbs (his legs especially) as he would upon some foreign object, as if they did not truly count as parts of himself (which, we would argue, is in a sense the conclusion he finally draws at the end of the novel) but were rather things he could disavow because capable of treason. Indeed, parts of the body also seem to take on an ethical life of their own, appearing at times to be credited with distinct moral or intellectual qualities. Legs are the object of praise and blame alike ("merits and faults" [11]); knee joints and feet are "uncertain" (31, 45, 81).[6] Finally, bodies present a double risk: on the one hand, there is the danger of absorption of the self by a larger corps, of its becoming a mere part or member of a larger entity; on the other hand, with limbs there is always the risk of dismemberment. Either way, individual integrity is threatened. These two threats are clearly illustrated in a key passage in chapter V:

> He suddenly lost concern for himself, and forgot to look at a menacing fate. He became not a man but a member. He felt that something of which he was a part—a regiment, an army, a cause, or a country—was in a crisis. He was welded into a common personality which was dominated by a single desire. For some moments he could not flee no more than a little finger can commit a revolution from a hand.
>
> If he had thought the regiment was about to be annihilated perhaps he could have amputated himself from it. (26)

Unlike his injured comrade Bill Smithers, who is still sufficiently attached to his three crushed fingers to oppose adamantly any talk of amputation (23), Henry imagines such a figurative operation as a life-saving measure in an emergency. In a sense, this is the measure he takes when he breaks away from his regiment in chapter VI. To jump ahead for a moment: one could even argue that at the end of the novel Henry performs a double amputation on himself, mentally cutting himself off at one and the same time from his regimental corps and from his corporeal self, with all its burdensome characteristics. The apartness and abstract self-sufficiency that characterize him in chapter XXIV lend credence to this argument.

Added to the "otherness" of the body there is the threat posed by its chronic debility, which we have already mentioned. One of the more interesting variants on this idea can be found in the images of babies in this novel, babies being of course the epitome of human helplessness. And helpless is precisely how Henry feels just prior to the first battle:

> The youth perceived that the time had come. He was about to be measured. For a moment he felt in the face of his great trial like a babe, and the flesh over his heart seemed very thin. (17)

What in a sense could be more natural in a novel of initiation like *The Red Badge of Courage*? Henry's war experience takes him from infancy to true adulthood ("He was a man" [98]). On this view, reaching manhood would mean overcoming physical and moral weakness. But this is to ignore what adult and infant have in common: their *shared* fragility (In *Moby-Dick* Melville yokes the two together in the apt expression "baby man" [298]). Imperceptibly, through a kind of hubris we shall analyze more fully in our conclusion, a difference of degree becomes a difference in kind. Elsewhere, however, Crane uses baby imagery to stress this common vulnerability. The dying Conklin, for instance, hangs "babelike" (42) to the arm of his friend. The dazed and reeling Henry is himself "like a babe trying to walk" (53). The cheery-voiced man manipulates him as if he had "the mind of a child" (55). Finally, a captured rebel soldier nurses his wound "baby-wise" (94).

We should emphasize that in Henry's view corporeal weakness is what hinders his spiritual quest for courage. His feebleness keeps him from being a hero:

> various ailments had begun to cry out. In their presence he could not persist in flying high with the wings of war; they rendered it almost impossible for him to see himself in a heroic light. (49)
> While he had been tossed by many emotions, he had not been aware of ailments. Now they beset him and made clamor. As he was at last compelled to pay attention to them, his capacity for self-hate was multiplied. In despair, he declared that he was not

like those others. He now conceded it to be impossible that he should ever become a hero. (49)

Courage thus calls for the repression of bodily instincts. (As we shall see, extraordinary indifference to physical pain—as when Henry holds a rifle "so hot that ordinarily he could not have borne it upon his palms" [71]— leads ultimately to the illusion of its permanent suppression.) In other words, as a soldier Henry also has to fight *against his own body*:

> Suddenly his legs seemed to die. He sank writhing to the ground. He tried to arise. In his efforts against the numbing pain he was like a man wrestling with a creature of the air.
> There was a sinister struggle. (53)
> He fought an intense battle with his body. His dulled senses wished him to swoon and he opposed them stubbornly, his mind portraying unknown dangers and mutilations if he should fall upon the field. He went tall soldier fashion. He imagined secluded spots where he could fall and be unmolested. To search for one he strove against the tide of his pain. (53)
> his body persisted in rebellion and his senses nagged at him like pampered babies. (54)

The "enemy" here is Henry's own pusillanimous physical being; the civil war, one between indomitable spirit and cowardly flesh.[7] Is the "union" symbolized in the flag that Henry bears at the end of *The Red Badge* to be achieved only by the defeat and unconditional surrender of this "rebel" side? Or is it merely another kind of secession, as we have already suggested? We shall have to address these questions more fully in our conclusion.

Stranger, baby, or rebel force—the body is also what Delmore Schwartz called in one of his poems "That inescapable animal."[8] *The Red Badge of Courage* is rife with animal imagery, which provides us with another key to Henry's development. Our bestial nature, our brute animality is synonymous with the uncontrollable within. If true courage requires tight control over the biological base of our being, its opposite—fear—is a primitive passion that puts us on essentially the same level as animals. In chapter VII, after his flight, Henry's rebellious feelings against "his fellows, war in the abstract, and fate" are described as "animal-like" (35). Then follows the famous passage where the protagonist compares his flight with that of a frightened squirrel (35–36). It is no accident that chapter VII, with its revelation of the power of baser instincts and the reality of bodily putrefaction (36), is one of the low points in Henry's spiritual quest. Nor is it a coincidence in our view that with the approach of death, the animal imagery recurs, such as in the following description of Jim Conklin going into convulsions:

> Finally, the chest of the doomed soldier began to heave with a strained motion. It increased in violence until it was as if an animal was within and was kicking and tumbling furiously to be free. (43)

Likewise, nearing his end, the tattered man reverts to a sub-human state:

> The youth looking at him, could see that he, too, like that other one, was beginning to act dumb and animal-like. (46)

As we know, Henry turns his back on the second dying man, leaving him "bleating plaintively" in the field (46). He is reluctant to undergo another "grim encounter" (45). It is this *intimate* otherness of Death, this deep familiarity with man's animalistic side that Henry would now vigorously deny. Which may be why, to return to Jim Conklin's death for a moment, Henry calls his childhood friend (the man of whom he has "intimate knowledge" [11])[9] by name, repeatedly, as though to call him *back* to life. Unfortunately, by this time the tall man is already unrecognizable. A "creeping strangeness" (44) has overcome him. He is fast becoming like the "thing" (36) that Henry recoils from in the woods—a corpse.

Perhaps it is this forced recognition of a common biological fate with the dead ("The dead man and the living man exchanged a long look"), this unwilling acknowledgment of his corporeal unity with the animal world, that strikes fear into the heart of the protagonist:

> He was pursued by a sight of the black ants swarming greedily upon the gray face and venturing horribly near to the eyes. (36)

Ultimately, not even "the windows of the soul" are safe from the scavengers that feed on man and beast alike. At the heart of the forest "chapel" that Henry has entered—more one of the architectural supports of this "religious" edifice ("with his back against a columnlike tree" [36])—is a rotting corpse. This temple would seem to rest on a very unsure base indeed.

In *The Red Badge of Courage* religion and religious enthusiasm (5) are most often associated with the savage (92), the barbarian, the pagan, the beastlike (72) in man, with our primitive, violent and animalistic nature. Like that other highly ritual activity—war (the "red animal" [52])—with which it appears to share common roots in our primal urges, religion savors of madness and destruction, as in Conklin's *danse macabre*, which Henry and the tattered man are compelled to witness:

> They began to have thoughts of a solemn ceremony. There was something ritelike in these movements of the doomed soldier. And there was resemblance in him to a devotee of a mad religion, blood-sucking. muscle-wrenching, bone-crunching. (43)

As we shall see in section 5, this is not the sort of religion Henry identifies with at the end of the novel when he rejects his "earlier gospels" (97). Quite the contrary.

In any case, we would argue that in the overarching structure of the narrative it is highly significant that Henry's return to the regiment involves abandoning these embodiments of feebleness, animality, and Death.

Inner Vulnerability
> "The human body is the best picture of the human soul"
> (Wittgenstein 178-e)

In *The Red Badge of Courage* vulnerability is not only physical. The battlefields are of course bristling with all manner of lethal weapons, but Henry Fleming needs to remain "close upon his guard" (8) against another type of threat: the verbal weapon. In the war of words waged among themselves, the soldiers appear to observe no truce; sarcasm and ridicule are turned against comrades as often as rifles and canons against the enemy.

Such being the case, Henry's first reflex is to seek safety in isolation, by keeping from "intercourse with his companions as much as circumstances would allow him" (14). Whether he will or no, Henry withdraws both physically (into his tent in chapter 1, into the gloom in chapter 11) and mentally; he is "alone in space" but also "a mental outcast" (16). As defensive strategies go, however, seclusion is no more successful than the other plans the youth makes in this novel. Henry's relative tranquility is always disturbed by the return of his fellow soldiers (9, 14); and as we have seen, even when he goes "to bury himself" (35) in the solitude of a figurative grave in the forest, he encounters a comrade-in-arms in the dead man. *The Red Badge of Courage* shows that, whatever the circumstances, one can never truly be alone.

Even so, the feeling of solitude is painful for Henry. He longs to confide his secret fears to someone, but he knows full well that this will leave him vulnerable to ridicule:

> He was afraid to make an open declaration of his concern, because he dreaded to place some unscrupulous confidant upon the high plane of the unconfessed from which elevation he could be derided. (11)

Like love, as we saw with the tattered man, trust leaves one exposed to the risk of betrayal. This is the inward danger. This is why, later on, Henry prefers to be in the more advantageous position of confidant to Wilson. In "a weak hour", the loud soldier "had delivered himself into the hands of the youth." The tables have been turned: now Henry is in control; he is the "master":

> He now rejoiced in the possession of a small weapon with which he could prostrate his comrade at the first signs of a cross-examination. He was master. It would now be he who could laugh and shoot the shafts of derision. (64)[10]

As we have already observed, in the metaphorical universe of *The Red Badge*, words too are weapons: "shafts," "arrows" (51), and "missiles" (56, 57). Against these, Henry is a "soft target" (56), his "tender flesh" (85) easily pierced. To counter these threats he "mortally" fears, Henry's only defenses are also verbal: namely, the "protecting tale." The problem is, this story is "vulnerable" (51) as well. Consequently, a certain fear of being discovered persists almost to the end (97). Henry is convinced that, with such armor-piercing weapons darkening the sky, the truth will out:

> The simple questions of the tattered man had been knife thrusts to him. They asserted a society that probes pitilessly at secrets until all is apparent. His late companion's chance persistency made him feel that he could not keep his crime concealed in his bosom. It was sure to be brought plain by one of those arrows which cloud the air and are constantly pricking discovering proclaiming those things which are willed to be forever hidden. He admitted that he could not defend himself against this agency. It was not within the power of vigilance (47, italics added)

Once again, foresight and planning are useless; Henry is vulnerable to chance, "hateful circumstances" (35), dumb luck. A stray "bullet" can lay him low at any moment. Shortly after his return to the regiment, for example, Henry's overweening pride leads him to imagine himself safe:

> His self-pride was now entirely restored. In the shade of its flourishing growth he stood with braced and self-confident legs, and since nothing could now be discovered he did not shrink from an encounter with the eyes of judges, and allowed no thoughts of his own to keep him from an attitude of manfulness. He had performed mistakes in the dark, so he was still a man. (64)[11]

But it is not long before his vulnerability to contingency is reasserted by a casual remark from a sarcastic comrade:

> The speech pierced the youth. Inwardly he was reduced to an abject pulp by these chance words. His legs quaked privately, He cast a frightened glance at the sarcastic man. (68; italics added)

The metaphorical logic of *The Red Badge* insists on a common vocabulary for the inward and the outward, for the spiritual and the physical realms. Legs are obviously symbolic of fortitude and manliness (31, 53, 64), whether of the body or the soul. "Physicalist" description in this novel militates against the Platonic vision of the soul as touchstone of invulnerability[12] and—notwithstanding Henry's notions to the contrary—against a vision of the body as the sole impediment to higher virtues such as courage. It re-establishes the body as a basic, unavoidable category in subjective experience.

Cathartic disembodiment: from "animal" to lover"

"being in the utmost isolation, dismissing the body, and, as far as she is able, having no communion and no contact with it, [the soul] reaches after true reality"

(Plato 121)[13]

As we have already suggested, Henry fashions a new self at the end of *The Red Badge of Courage*. This is accomplished by a thoroughgoing break with the past. Henry now clears his mind of the harrowing encounters in the "chapel" and in the killing fields.[14] He undergoes a radical conversion-experience involving on the one hand an act of self-absolution, a sort of Hegelian negation of the negation whereby "reproach," "error," and "sin" (97) are simultaneously canceled out and transcended. On the other hand, this "new condition" (96) entails a repudiation of the "mad religion" that springs from our baser being, for the sin that is remitted is ultimately one of the flesh; the scourge to be lifted, that of embodiment itself. The "new ways" (97) that open up before the protagonist lead away from the snares of corporeity.[15]

Henry's salvation (20) or rebirth has a strong epistemological element:

> At last [his acts] marched before him clearly. From this present view point he was enabled to look upon them in *spectator* fashion and to *criticize* them with some *correctness*, for his new condition had already defeated certain *sympathies*. (96; brackets and emphasis added)[16]

The youth's eyes "seemed to open to some new ways" (97); he sees "truly" (98) now. The phrase "certain sympathies" is, admittedly, rather cryptic. But etymology may help here. Henry can see clearly *because* certain feelings and emotions have been vanquished. With regard to the suffering (or "passion" [41]) of others, he is no longer *sumpathès* (i.e., moved by similar feelings).[17] He has achieved a *dispassionate* appraisal of his actions.

The outcome of Henry's "Greeklike struggle" (5)[18] thus appears as a kind of cognitive purgation or *katharsis*[19]—a false catharsis in our opinion. His mind has "cast off its battleful ways"; his brain has "emerged from the clogged clouds" (96). But what militates against this self-image is that this is hardly the first time Henry's pride has led him to a similar conclusion. Before going into battle on the first day he thought that "There was but one pair of eyes in the corps" (19)—his own. He was the one with "superior perceptions and knowledge" (35, 50); his, one of the "fine minds" (20). Nor is it the first time that a dialectical reversal of perspectives has afforded Henry a sudden view of himself as he shifts roles, moving from actor to spectator, from participant to observer (29, 72, 74, 85). Nevertheless, Henry deems this standpoint to be totalizing. In a sense, his desire to get an unobstructed, undistorted view beyond the limitations of individual perception is the epistemological equivalent of invulnerability—namely, perceptual infallibility. Henry would transcend the ordinary human perspective (as when he and Wilson, searching for water, are able to look "over their own troops" [74]) and the limits it imposes on understanding. He would like to see himself, to be the spectator *ab extra* of his own actions, to fuse the first- and third-person points of view (or to alternate them at will), to overcome the blind spots resulting from his finite nature.[20]

The internal distancing that this privileged viewpoint implies is rendered not only spatially but temporally as well. Simply put, Henry acquires hindsight; he looks back (97) on his actions. The beginning of his final "enlightened" self-appraisal sets the tone here, which, as we shall see in a moment, is carried to a rhapsodic extreme in the penultimate paragraph of the novel:

> He understood then that the existence of shot and counter-shot was in the past. He had dwelt in a land of strange, squalling upheavals and had come forth. He had been where there was red of blood and black of passion, and he was escaped. His first thoughts were given to rejoicings at this fact. (96)

Henry appears to be leaving strife behind him once and for all in his move towards a post-conflictual existence no longer subject to the paroxysms of passion. Although the remark may appear trivial, it is clear at the end of the novel that the most important change in Henry is not physical or external; it is not the "red badge" on his head. Rather, it is the transformation his soul has undergone:

> So it came to pass that as he trudged from the place of blood and wrath his soul changed. He came from hot plowshares to prospects of clover tranquility, and it was as if hot plowshares were not. Scars faded as flowers. (98)

Significantly, the emergence described in this passage assumes the form of a negation of physical discomfort and the signs of bodily injury. It is also a negation of the past (*as if hot ploughshares were not*). Like unobserved actions, the past does not exist and can therefore be safely denied. Which allows Henry to transcend his corporeal, animal nature, with everything that implies in the way of fragility:

> He had rid himself of the red sickness of battle. The sultry nightmare was in the past. He had been an animal blistered and sweating in the heat and pain of war. He turned now with a lover's thirst to images of tranquil skies, fresh meadows, cool brooks— an existence of soft and eternal peace. (98)

Apparently Henry is never again to be driven by fear or racked with pain.[21] If the terms of the final image are ostensibly those of bodily desire (*thirst*) and comfort (*cool, soft*), this ideal existence of pure and everlasting repose is tantamount to a form of disembodiment—the only means to a truly eternal peace. This is precisely the conclusion drawn by Socrates in the *Phaedo*:

Yes, it is the body and its desires, nought else, that brings on wars, dissensions, and fighting. (Plato 122)[22]

The experience of war has purged Henry—or so he imagines—of the "all too human" side of himself.[23] "Weakness is a thing of the past. He will no longer be among the "animals tossed for a death struggle into a dark pit" (71). Suffering, be it physical or moral, is at an end. Here again, though, this is not the first time Henry has considered himself free and clear. The parallel with chapter XV, where Henry looked at his experiences of the first day "from a distance", is striking: "His panting agonies of the past he put out of his sight" (64). For the youth, in any event, the outcome of this second day of battle resembles a victory over "the ultimate contingency" (Nussbaum 1986, 73)—death:

> He had been to touch the great death, and found that, after all, it was but the great death. (98)

Such clarity of vision places Henry in splendid isolation at the end of the novel. His feeling of invulnerability stems in part from an impression of self-sufficiency. He is aloof, not mixing with "his prattling companions":

> He took no share in the chatter of his comrades, nor did he look at them or know them. (97)

Henry stands out from the crowd, in a world apart:

> It rained. The procession of weary soldiers became a bedraggled train, despondent and muttering, marching with churning effort in a trough of liquid brown mud under a low, wretched sky. Yet the youth smiled, for he saw that the world was a world for him, through many discovered it to be made of oaths and walking sticks. (98)

His attitude is markedly different from the weakness and bodily exhaustion of the "many," the youth's "ragged" (97)—a word strangely close to "tattered"—comrades.[24] Not for Henry the sullen outbursts of swearing against fate and human frailty. This too harks back to chapter XV, where we find the youth dissociating himself from "the doomed and the damned who roared with sincerity at circumstance" (64).

Yet Henry Fleming has emerged from war virtually unscathed. He appears to have successfully eluded "his tireless fate" (49) by sloughing off his former self, body and all but unlike the main character, the reader of *The Red Badge of Courage* has not forgotten that to a large extent Henry's invulnerability is the combined result of sheer luck and a fertile imagination. This is arguably one of the finer ironies of the novel.

WORKS CITED

CRANE, Stephen. *Prose and Poetry*. Ed. J. C. Levenson. New York Library of America, 1984.

———. *The Correspondence of Stephen Crane*. Eds. Stanley Wertheim, Paul Sorrentino. 2 vols. New York: Columbia UP, 1988.

———. *The Red Badge of Courage*. Ed. Donald Pizer. 3rd ed. New York: Norton, 1994.

DOOLEY, Patrick K. *The Pluralistic Philosophy of Stephen Crane*. Urbana: U of Illinois P, 1993.

HORSFORD, Howard C. "'He Was a Man.'" *New Essays on "The Red Badge of Courage"*. Ed. Lee Clark Mitchell. Cambridge: Cambridge UP, 1986. 109–127.

JANKÉLÉVITCH, Vladimir. *Les verfus et l'amour*. Vol. 1. Paris: Flammarion, 1986. 2 vols.

MELVILLE, Herman. *Moby-Dick or, The Whale*. New York Penguin, 1992.

NUSSBAUM, Martha C. *The Fragility of Goodness: Luck and Ethics in Greek Tragedy and Philosophy*. London: Cambridge UP, 1986.

———. *The Therapy of Desire: Theory and Practice in Hellenistic Ethics*. Princeton: Princeton UP, 1994.

PLATO. *Plato on the Trial and Death of Socrates: Euthyphro, Apology, Crito, Phaedo*. Trans. Lane Cooper. Ithaca: Cornell UP, 1967.

SCHWARTZ, Delmore. *Selected Poems (1938–1958)*. New York: New Directions, 1967.

TANNER, Tony. *Scenes of Nature, Signs of Men*. Cambridge: Cambridge UP, 1987.

WITTGENSTEIN, Ludwig. *Philosophical Investigations*. Trans. G. E. M. Anscombe. 3rd ed. New York: Macmillan, 1958.

NOTES

1. Crane (41); italics added. All further page references will appear between parentheses in the text. Typographical errors in the Pizer edition have been silently corrected.

2. On "the sheer contingency of love, and our vulnerability to contingency through love," see the outstanding analysis in Nussbaum 1986 (174).

3. We should mention, however, that during the first day of action the flag appears to stand for the very opposite of invulnerability in Henry's mind as he observes it from afar: "The battle flag in the distance jerked about madly. it seemed to be struggling to free itself from an agony"; "The flag suddenly sank down as if dying. Its motion as it fell was a gesture of despair" (24). This reversal points not only to the radical convertibility of signifiers in general but also to the shift in Henry's view of himself. The emblem in question is obviously a *mirror*.

4. Whether born of despair or hope, the creatures of Henry's imagination—even the ones that have "originals" in reality—are often endowed with extra- or non-human powers. At several points, Henry imagines that the rebel army, for example, is indestructible: "They must be machines of steel" (31; cf. also 71, 81).

5. In our view Howard Horsford is quite right to emphasize the "mindless" character both of Henry's flight and of his heroic stand at the end of the novel, and to speak of "the world of human irrationality that Crane conceives, of action not consciously volitional" (Horsford 110). See also Dooley 1993 (70, 86). One of the most striking things in the descriptions of the second day of battle is the plethora of terms signifying the negation of conscious awareness ("not conscious", "not aware", "absorbed", "engrossed", "not to know", "to forget", "to cease to remember", "to lose sense of everything" [see especially 71, 90]).

6. The merits and faults in question would be discovered "figuratively" as Crane points out (11), and the word "uncertain" can of course be applied to things, in which case it simply means "unsteady". Still, we would maintain that Crane's diction is intentionally ambiguous. Perhaps we have here, with this confusion of realms, a variation on Crane's marked taste for the pathetic fallacy, which is obvious from the very first paragraph of the novel. In any case, the next section will provide examples of the reverse—that is, where the descriptive categories of the body are applied to the spirit.

7. To give another instance of this conflict: at the end of *Moby-Dick* Captain Ahab "disowns" his body, railing against it as an impediment to heroic action. "—But even with a broken bone, old Ahab is untouched; and I account no living bone of mine one jot more me, than this dead one that's lost. Nor white whale, nor man, nor fiend, can so much as graze old Ahab in his own proper and inaccessible being"; "Accursed fate! that the unconquerable captain of the soul should have such a craven mate!" (Melville 610). Like Ahab, Henry is loath to acknowledge that his unwieldy frame is also what enables courage. In other words, the body is both means and impediment, both enabling and disenabling, as Vladimir Jankélévitch observes: "*cet obstacle qui empêche le courage est aussi l'aliment qui le fait vivre; ce poids est un lest, cette lourdeur une légèreté. Sur le tremplin de la frayeur et de la chair pesante la volonti prend son élan pour rebondir vers les hauteurs; ou, si ton préfère, elle recule pour mieux avancer; la fuite vers le bas ou vers l'arrière, c'est-à-dire la constante retombée et la constante déroute de la chair craintive, est le contre-poids qui développe sa force ascensionnelle et sa force progressive. Cette force est le courage*" (96).

8. The phrase is from "The Heavy Bear Who Goes with Me" (1.20), which affords some brilliant poetic insights into the burdens of embodiment (Schwartz 74).

9. Conklin also embodies hedonistic pleasures: "During his meals he always wore an air of blissful contemplation of the food he had swallowed. His spirit seemed then to be communing with the viands" (21).

10. This is an especially blatant example of the incoherence of Henry's thinking. To suspect his friend as he does, Henry obviously still misunderstands the extent of the change Wilson has undergone—even after remarking the same change himself (61–62)!

11. Henry's "Berkeleyan" ethical claim—crudely put: "No one witnessed it, so it did not happen"—should be interpreted in light of poem 50 from *The Black Riders*, dealing with the appraisal of seemingly unobserved actions: "You say you are holy, / And that / Because I have not seen you sin / Ay, but there are those / Who see you sin, my friend" (Crane 1984, 1317).

12. Quoting Alcibiades in Plato's *Symposium*—"All and only body is vulnerable to happenings in the world. I am inwardly bitten, pierced. Therefore this whatever-you-call-it is bodily (or very like body)")"—Martha Nussbaum observes: "it is an argument that appeals to subjective experience, indeed to subjective suffering, to deny a 'Platonic' view of the soul as a thing that is at one and the same time the seat of personality and immortal/invulnerable" (1986 192). Taking this cue from Nussbaum, we would argue that the physicalism of *The Red Badge of Courage* is one of the main sources of the novel's power to convey subjective experience. But of course it also renders all the more implausible Henry's final vision of eternal peace.

13. The passage quoted is from the *Phaedo*; the words between brackets have been added for clarity.

14. When the repressed memory of the tattered man does return in "spectral" guise, it is paradoxically his damaged, debilitated body that is highlighted ("gored by bullets and faint for blood," "blind with weariness and pain" [97]). We should also point out that Crane emphasizes the fleeting nature of this "pursuing recollection" ("For a moment," "For an Instant," "For a time" [97]).

15. "The branches, pushing against him, threatened to throw him over upon it. His unguided feet, too, caught aggravatingly in brambles; and with it all he received a subtle suggestion to touch the corpse. As he thought of his hand upon it he shuddered profoundly" (36).

16. Lest too much be made of the accuracy of Henry's perception, the reader of *The Red Badge* would do well to recall Maggie and the deep irony created by Maggie's first impression of Jimmie, the Bowery tough who is soon to become her seducer: "His mannerisms stamped him as a man who had a correct sense of his personal superiority. There were valor and contempt for circumstances in the glance of his eye," (Crane 1984 25). "Correctness," we might say, is in the eye of the beholder.

17. See Nussbaum 1994 (especially chapter 10) for an excellent discussion on the Stoic ideal of an extirpation of the passions (as distinct from their moderation). The comparative reading Nussbaum gives of the Epicurean and Stoic approaches to anger (chapters 7, 10, and 11) through her analysis of Lucretius's *De Rerum Natura* and Seneca's *De Ira* is particularly pertinent to *The Red Badge of Courage*. Unfortunately, space forbids.

18. On the second day of battle, one of Crane's ironic vignettes transforms Henry's heroic stance into the stuff of mock epic: "The awkward bandage was still about his head, and upon it, over his wound, was a spot of dry blood. His hair was wondrously tousled, and some straggling, moving locks hung over the cloth of the bandage down toward his forehead. His jacket and shirt were open at the throat, and exposed his young bronzed neck. There could be seen spasmodic gulpings at his throat" (70).

19. For Plato, true catharsis means severance of the soul from the body. As he has Socrates say in the *Phaedo*: "But does not purgation [*catharsis*] mean the utmost separation of the spirit from the body? And to collect and rally herself at all points from the body, and to dwell, as far as possible, both here and now and in the time to come, alone and by herself, released from the body as from chains?" (123). But of course the name for this ultimate release, as Socrates is quick to point out, is death. See also note 22 below.

20. Spectatorship, as Amy Kaplan observes in "The Spectacle of War in Crane's Revision of History" (see our edition of *The Red Badge*), also means control: "Henry's obsession with seeing suggests that he runs away, in part, to trade the role of actor for spectator, to gain both a sense of control and a vicarious thrill from observing the battle at a safe enough distance not to be crushed by it" (287). For Kaplan, being a flag-bearer allows Henry to be both actor and spectator at the same time: "He can, for the first time, safely see and be seen" (288).

21. This image should be contrasted with a passage earlier in the novel where excruciating bodily pain elicits a nostalgic image of home, with its security and creature comforts (54). With his rejection of the past, Henry can only turn to the future.

22. Just as the only person explicitly referred to as invulnerable in *The Red Badge* is, like the flag, "inanimate" (an "invulnerable dead man" [181]), so the only way to attain a true state of ataraxia seems to be through death, as Crane himself implies in a letter to Nellie Crouse (March 1, 1896): "Dear me, how much I am getting to admire graveyards— the calm, unfretting, unhopeing end of things—serene absence of passion..." (Crane 1988, 1:207).

23. "If part of our humanness is our susceptibility to certain sorts of pain, then the task of curing pain may involve putting an end to humanness" (Nussbaum 1986 120). This sentence appears in a brilliant reading of the *Protagoras* and the stark choice it imposes between fragility and control.

24. Again, the example of Maggie is instructive for what it reveals about the widespread illusion of exceptionality. This illusion (summed up in the line "Maggie was diff'ent") explains why none of the characters can understand Maggie's fate. Thus Pete: "He was trying to formulate a theory that he had always unconsciously held, that all sisters, excepting his own, could advisedly be ruined" (Crane 1984 44; see also 57).

DANIEL SHANAHAN

The Army Motif in The Red Badge of Courage *as a Response to Industrial Capitalism*

In 1904, four years after the death of his friend Stephen Crane, Henry James returned to the United States for the first time in twenty-one years. He describes his approach to New York City this way:

> ... the monster grows and grows ... becoming ... some colossal set of clockworks, some steel-souled machine room of brandished arms and hammering fists and opening and closing jaws. The immeasurable bridges are but as the horizontal sheaths of pistons working at high pressure, day and night ... (75)

This was the New York which, in the two short decades of James's absence, had replaced the prosaic city of James's youth; this new city of motion and machines was the New York Crane had lived in as he wrote *The Red Badge of Courage*. It was a city that, like the country it represented, had been "seized by change" (Martin 361).

Indeed, probably nothing could better characterize the period of James's absence than the overwhelming transformation and retransformation that America underwent from 1880 to 1900.[1] And the forces behind the changes which took place in those years were largely those which underlie James's description of New York: the impetus of capitalism and

From *Papers on Language & Literature* 32, no. 4 (Fall 1996). © 1996 by the Board of Trustees of Southern Illinois University.

industrialization, of the competitive drive to succeed and the machine which helped make success possible. As Larzer Ziff points out, the early literary response to the social upheaval created in America by capitalism and industrialization was ambiguous—and weak. The problem was not lack of talent: it was lack of vision. As Ziff suggests of the architectural establishment of the time, writers who had grown up in pre-Civil War America "yearned to impose upon the whirl of late-nineteenth-century America the dream of stasis, an ideal and all-covering beauty ... Static idealization of the human condition seemed to be the answer to the impossibly unaesthetic whirl of social conditions" (22). But what was needed was a vision which would unify the "unaesthetic whirl" without confining it, and to achieve that vision a writer would have to be willing to allow the whirl to emerge without bending it to his own purposes. Didacticism, ideal or apocalyptic, could easily betray the integrity of any attempt to distill the temper of the times into a literary work.

"Static idealization" was not, however, the only response to the turmoil and confusion. There had been one fairly recent instance in which an overriding national spirit had been forged into a purposive and intensely satisfying—at least for some—*raison d'etre*: the American Civil War. In the face of the rapid transformation of American social, political and even moral life, what had been to some a national tragedy of overwhelming proportions became for others a touchstone upon which they tried to base a new sense of national character, a national pride, and, above all, national direction. By the 1880s, the Civil War was close enough in time to have been the most formative national experience in the lives of men of letters, and far enough distant to have become ripe for mythologizing. As John L. Thomas says, it was common in the 1880s for

> social observers, many of them New Englanders, to prescribe martial virtue as a cure for the ills of society or to recommend the lessons of the Civil War as a means of renewing national vigor ... In the years after 1880 Francis A. Walker, Thomas Wentworth Higginson, and Oliver Wendell Holmes Jr.—all veterans of the Civil War and sons of New England acutely conscious of its heritage of nationalism—elaborated new concepts of the "useful citizen" and the "soldier's faith" derived from experiences on Civil War battlefields. (61)

Two of the more popularly successful attempts to draw on aspects of the "martial" experience of the Civil War as a way of addressing the social convulsions of a society hurtling into capitalism and industrialization did not actually portray the War itself, but both rely on an army motif to evoke the social climates of nascent competition and mechanization in the fictional worlds they create. Edward Bellamy's utopian *Looking Backward: 2000–1887* envisions a future society in which mechanization has been tamed and competition transformed into cooperation, largely through the aegis of a huge "industrial army" into which society, now harmonious and productive, has been organized. *Looking Backward* was the third most popular novel of its time; it produced a wave of nationalism in the country, and thus became a social event in its own right.[2] But it also spawned a series of responses and rebuttals, one of the more apocalyptic of which was Ignatius Donnelly's anti-utopian *Caesar's Column*. In Donnelly's dystopian work, an oligarchical dictatorship which has harnessed the miracles of modern mechanization to perpetuate an Orwellian-style slave state is overthrown by an underground army of loosely organized rebels; but because the rebel chiefs cannot harness the fury of the subjugated masses that erupts once the insurrection begins, civilization as we know it is destroyed.

Despite the contrasting nature of their respective visions, both Bellamy and Donnelly seem to use the army motif because it evoked for them the importance of social organization in an age beset by the "unaesthetic whirl" of social transformation. As Thomas puts it,

> The time in Bellamy's own experience when Americans had massed and marched as armies was the Civil War, and to that "grand object-lesson in solidarity," as he called it, he instinctively returned for the organizational principle of his utopia. (2)

However, their didactic purposes—Bellamy's determination to show how American society could transform itself into a humanistic utopia, and Donnelly's equally determined attempt to prove Bellamy wrong—kept either man from using the army motif as powerfully as they might have. Neither of their novels captures the unsettling vibrancy of the 1880s and 90s, and neither is a work of lasting fictional importance.

While there is no direct evidence that Stephen Crane read either Bellamy or Donnelly, it is hard to imagine that anyone who lived and traveled, as Crane did, in the literary circles of the 1890s could have avoided reading *Looking Backward*. Indeed, the novel's popularity was such that almost any college student of the late eighties or early nineties is likely to have read and discussed both Bellamy and Donnelly. But whether or not Crane read either, it can hardly be mere coincidence that he, like the others, chose the army as one of the overriding images with which he develops his most important work. More importantly, because *The Red Badge of Courage* brings the themes of capitalistic competition and technological advancement into play without subordinating them to a didactic purpose such as Bellamy's or Donnelly's, Crane was able to use a motif similar to theirs to create one of the major literary works of his time.

Crane wrote *The Red Badge of Courage* immediately after *Maggie: A Girl of the Streets*, a novel which presents a vision of contemporary society as a ruthlessly competitive domain in which all men—and women—are reduced to their predatory instincts and all of their distinguishing characteristics are effaced by the brutality to which they themselves become subject. The effects of emergent capitalism on American society are never far from view in *Maggie*, and given the novel's highly competitive social environment, it comes as no surprise that the theme of competition so thoroughly informs *Red Badge*. From the opening moments of the book, in which Crane portrays two soldiers arguing over rumors about troop movements, to the near-brawl that erupts before the first chapter closes—this time about how well the regiment will fight—contention is the dominant mode of social interaction. In the world Crane creates, the army is rife with internal contention even before it enters into the grand competition by which, Marx had argued only a few years before, industrial capitalism sustains itself

But throughout the first half of the novel, the main character, Henry Fleming, is an exception to the rule of contention and competition as the dominant mode of behavior, and while it is common to see Henry as a character taken from romantic idealism about war to a tempered bravery, it is less common to see how Henry's reluctance to compete, and his later willingness to do so, punctuate his change in character.

Because he seems to lack the innate competitive instincts of the other men in the regiment, Henry never takes part in any of the arguing, sparring or contending that goes on between his fellows. In short, he fails to communicate with them on the terms in which they most frequently seem to communicate with one another, so he remains an outsider, and only nominally a member of the army. Only after he witnesses the death of his friend, Jim Conklin, does Henry begin to show signs of adopting the aggressiveness he will need to face the realities of war. Moments after Jim's violent death, Henry makes "a furious motion" in response to the tattered soldier's questions about Henry's non-existent wound; Henry became "as one at bay" (55) and he feels "the quiver of war desire." This is the first competitive flicker in Henry's character, and its appearance marks his readiness for the "red badge" which will initiate him into the fellowship of his social environment.

Surprisingly little has been made of the fact that Henry's "wound," the red badge of "courage" which marks the turning point in his character development, comes neither from the enemy nor even from a random unidentifiable bullet: it comes from one of his own men, a soldier fleeing wildly, as Henry did, and who perceives Henry as merely another opposing force, another competitor. In this pivotal moment, Henry is attempting to communicate; however, he cannot see that his attempt has only one meaning in the lexicon of men each battling for his own survival: he is a threat to the soldier. And as a consequence, Henry receives the one response which makes sense: the man floors him with a single, vicious blow from his rifle—used by a man in his most primitively competitive frame of mind, as a club.

Ironically, but not surprisingly, given that from the outset of the novel contention has been the currency of social communication, it is this blow from a comrade that punctuates the end of Henry's isolation from his fellows and initiates him into their ranks. Henceforth he is truly a member of the army, and as time goes on he reveals the effect of that initiation by becoming supremely competitive. Markedly contentious on several occasions during the night and morning after his return to the regiment, Henry enters battle with "his teeth set in a curlike snarl" (80); "he lost everything but his hate, his desire to smash into pulp the glittering smile of victory which he could feel upon the faces of his enemies." Not surprisingly, Henry shines in battle, possessed by "the spirit of a savage religion-mad," engulfed in "wild battle madness," and awaiting "the crushing blow that would prostrate the resistance."

In short, by the end of the novel Henry has reached the apotheosis of competition: he has become a true predator, and as such he demonstrates William Graham Sumner's belief "that the struggle for existence and the competition of life ... draw out the highest achievements" (85). Congratulated by his fellows for his performance and complemented by his superiors, Henry ultimately finds himself a deeply different person for his experience. "He was," Crane tells us, "a man" (109) and, of course, he has also become "one of the men" in a way he could not previously. He has joined the army—that motif which seemed to carry such potency for writers trying to deal with the "unaesthetic whirl" of the late 19th century—he has found membership in society, and the catalyst of that discovery has been his acquiescence to the competitive spirit shared by his fellows.

There is another way in which *The Red Badge of Courage* echoes *Looking Backward* and *Caesar's Column*, but here again Crane's achievement is one of lasting importance, where those of Bellamy and Donnelly are of rather passing interest. Like the other two, Crane uses mechanical imagery to position his novel on the pivot of the change wrought by the technological transformation of America wrought by industrialization, but because he does so without any overt didactic purposes, he comes much closer to making of the "unaesthetic whirl" what Tolstoy had made of national pride in *War and Peace* and what Kafka would make of faceless bureaucracy in *The Trial*: a vibrant undercurrent which transforms social realities into a lasting vision of the human condition.

Early on, in the first battle scene, machine imagery begins to appear after Henry has fired his first wild shot: "Directly," Crane says, "he was working at his weapon like an automatic affair" (31); soon the entire regiment "wheezed and banged with a mighty power" (31). Before long both Henry and the regiment are described in assembly-line images: clanking and clanging become the dominant sounds of the battle. This imagery pervades the novel. In the battle in which Henry flees, he imagines that the enemy "must be machines of steel" (36); the men who fail to run Henry calls "methodical idiots! Machine-like fools!" (37). As he wanders aimlessly, Henry finds the battle "like the grinding of an immense and terrible machine" (43), the purpose of which is to "produce corpses," and when he joins the wounded column he reflects how the "torn bodies expressed the awful machinery in which the men had been entangled" (45). Even the death of his friend, Jim Conklin, takes on a machine-like quality: as it goes into its final death spasms, Conklin's body is like some engine wheezing and sputtering jerkily to a final halt, its broken gears causing the grotesque and halting dance of death. Indeed, in a later battle in which the regiment seems near its own death, Crane calls it "a machine run down" (91).

Machine imagery does not, however, account for the powerful evocation of turmoil Crane achieves. As R. W. Stallman long ago pointed out, "motion and change [are] ... the dominant leitmotif of the book and a miniature form of its structure" (xxiv). Henry's initiation into the regiment's competitive, contentious mode of life is the consequence of having plunged himself into the motion of the battle; joining in the surging "blue demonstration," he becomes part of it and thereby achieves coglike membership in his social environment. Similarly, when the flux of battle begins to dominate the novel, the battlefield itself takes on the appearance of a giant engine in which the armies are like pistons crashing to and fro in a wild orgy of mechanical power.

For example, late in the novel, as Henry and his comrades watch the battle from a distance, Crane describes the sound of the artillery as "the whirring and thumping of giant machinery"; then

> On an incline over which a road wound he saw wild and desperate rushes of men perpetually backward and forward in riotous surges. These parts of the opposing armies pitched upon each other madly at dictated points. To and fro they swelled. (100)

While overtly the natural image of the sea, the to and fro motion coupled with the "whirring and thumping of machinery" and the pitching of armies upon each other at "dictated points" make this passage strongly suggestive of piston motion. Unlike Henry Adams, who finds the steam engine and its mechanics too spiritless when compared to the dynamo, Crane finds in them the essence of the world of his time, plunging his readers headlong into the piston-like fury of the mechanical age—as his friend Henry James would when he returned to America four years after Crane's death.

This riot of motion continues as Henry and his regiment enter the final engagement of the battle. Twice Crane describes them as moving "to and fro" (100, 101); they begin to fire automatically, "without waiting for word of command." And as they approach the climactic confrontation with the enemy, Henry anticipates the moment this way:

> As he ran a thought of the shock of contact gleamed in his mind. He expected a great concussion when the two bodies of troops crashed together. This became a part of his wild battle madness. He could feel the onwards swing of the regiment about him and he conceived of a thunderous, crushing blow that would prostrate the resistance and spread consternation and amazement for miles. The flying regiment was going to have a catapultian effect. (103)

Here Crane reaches his crescendo: Henry has immersed himself in the regiment, the regiment plunges itself piston-like into the fray, and as they become caught up in the furious motion of battle, both Henry and his regiment, as we have seen, take on the attributes of predatory animals as Crane brings together the two churning forces which have created his world's "unaesthetic whirl": competition and technological change.

The question of whether Crane's vision of Henry is ironic has elicited a great deal of discussion among readers of the novel.[3] But perhaps a passage Crane deleted from the final paragraphs of the novel's final version holds the key to understanding both Crane's attitude towards Henry and the world he creates for him and his comrades to inhabit. In the deleted passage, Crane says of Henry:

> He was emerged from his struggles, with a large sympathy for the machinery of the universe. It was a deity laying about him with the bludgeon of correction ... He would no more stand upon places high and false, and denounce the distant planets. He beheld that he was tiny but not inconsequent to the sun. In the space-wide whirl of events no grain like him would be lost. (116)

To look for Crane to approve or disapprove of Henry, or of the society of which he becomes a part, would be to attribute to Crane a didactic purpose which he did not have. His aim was to distill the essence of his time, not to show its potential, like Bellamy, or warn of its horror, like Donnelly. As an artist, Crane set out to capture the "unaesthetic whirl" in an aesthetic rendering that would preserve the dark tension of its beauty, and *Red Badge* is entirely consistent with that aim.

Unquestionably, Henry has changed by the novel's end; unquestionably, he has become more courageous and more selfless. He has even become more humble. But he has done so within a context that deals bludgeoning blows to its creatures. He has reacted involuntarily to those blows where one might prefer measured response; he has even learned to deal them himself, where one might hope he would refuse to do so; and he has given up the one thing which might have allowed him responsible refusal: his individuality. Yet at the same time he has matured over the course of the novel, he has become broader and more tested than he was at the novel's outset, and he no longer lives life as an alienated onlooker: he has jumped with both feet into his social context. In other words, by the end of the novel not only has Henry become, as Crane tells us, "a man" (109), he has become a man of his time.

In that sense, Crane is much closer to Kafka than to Tolstoy. Just as Kafka takes one aspect of his own experience of contemporary life and uses the underlying purposelessness he finds there to portray the larger vacuity to which we may all be susceptible, Crane takes one aspect of his contemporary experience and uses it to develop a broader picture of the human condition. Crane uses the army and the war to portray the mass mentality which has begun to replace individualism in his time, to evoke the spirit of predatory competition which has begun to dominate the American landscape, and, at the same time, it affords him the opportunity to expose the powerful engines of change and motion which underlie this new, predatory mass society. And by avoiding the didacticism of a Bellamy or Donnelly, Crane creates for his readers a novel which is both of its time and at a distance from it, a vision which confronts the "unaesthetic whirl" and makes of it a truthful symmetry.

NOTES

1. The titles of some of the works which deal with the period reflect its temper very aptly: Martin's *Harvest of Change*; "The Shock of Change," Chapter 2 of Samuel Hays's *Response to Industrialism*; *The Big Change*, by Frederick Lewis Allen—to name but three.

2. See also Eric Fromm's introduction to the Signet edition of *Looking Backward* (New York, 1960).

3. Milne Holton's *Cylinder of Vision* still contains the best summary of the positions taken in this discussion. See 114–15.

Works Cited

Allen, Frederick Lewis. *The Big Change*. New York: Harper, 1952.

Crane, Stephen. *The Red Badge of Courage*. Eds. Bradley, Beatty, Long and Pizer. New York: Norton, 1976.

Fromm, Erich. Introduction. *Looking Backward*. By Edward Bellamy. New York: Signet, 1960.

Hays, Samuel. *Response to Industrialism*. Chicago: U of Chicago P, 1957.

Holton, Milne. *Cylinder of Vision*, Baton Rouge: Louisiana UP, 1972.

James, Henry. *The American Scene*. Bloomington: Indiana UP, 1968.

Martin, Jay. *Harvests of Change*. Englewood Cliffs: Prentice, 1967.

Sumner, William Graham. "Sociology." *American Thought: Civil War to World War I*. Ed. Perry Miller. New York: Holt, 1954.

Stallman, R. W. Introduction. *The Red Badge of Courage*. By Stephen Crane. New York: Random, 1951.

Thomas, John L. Introduction. *Looking Backward*. By Edward Bellamy. Cambridge: Harvard UP, 1967.

Ziff, Larzer. *The American 1890s*. New York: Viking, 1966.

Chronology

1871	Stephen Crane is born on November 1 in Newark, New Jersey. He is the youngest child of the Reverend Jonathan Towley Crane, a Methodist minister, and Mary Helen Peck Crane.
1878–82	Reverend Crane moves his family to Port Jervis, New York, where Stephen first attends school. After the Reverend's death in 1880, Stephen's mother moves the family to Asbury Park, New Jersey.
1891	Stephen Crane attends Syracuse University, where he meets Hamlin Garland. He leaves after his first year and moves the family to Asbury Park, New Jersey.
1892	Crane fails at several newspaper jobs but publishes six "Sullivan County Sketches."
1893–94	*Maggie: A Girl of the Streets* is printed privately. Crane meets W.D. Howells. He begins work on *The Red Badge of Courage*, *George's Mother*, and a collection of poems.
1895–96	Crane travels to Mexico. The publication of *The Red Badge of Courage* and *The Black Riders* wins him instant fame. He publishes a revision of *Maggie* with *George's Mother*. En route to Cuba, Crane meets Cora Taylor, proprietress of a house of prostitution in Florida.
1897	Crane is shipwrecked off the coast of Florida. He bases "The Open Boat" upon the incident. He travels to Greece

with Cora Taylor to cover the Greco-Turkish War. Crane writes "The Monster" and "The Bride Comes to Yellow Sky" and becomes acquainted with Joseph Conrad.

1898   *The Open Boat and Other Tales of Adventure* is published. Crane becomes a correspondent in the Spanish-American War.

1899   Crane publishes *War Is Kind*. He resides with Cora in extravagance at Brede Place in England. He suffers a massive tubercular hemorrhage.

1900   Stephen Crane dies of tuberculosis in Badenweiler, Germany, on June 5. *Whilomville Stories*, *Great Battles of the World*, and *Last Words* appear posthumously. A novel, *The O'Ruddy*, is completed by Robert Barr.

Contributors

HAROLD BLOOM is Sterling Professor of the Humanities at Yale University and Henry W. and Albert A. Berg Professor of English at the New York University Graduate School. He is the author of over 20 books, including *Shelley's Mythmaking* (1959), *The Visionary Company* (1961), *Blake's Apocalypse* (1963), *Yeats* (1970), *A Map of Misreading* (1975), *Kabbalah and Criticism* (1975), *Agon: Toward a Theory of Revisionism* (1982), *The American Religion* (1992), *The Western Canon* (1994), and *Omens of Millennium: The Gnosis of Angels, Dreams, and Resurrection* (1996). *The Anxiety of Influence* (1973) sets forth Professor Bloom's provocative theory of the literary relationships between the great writers and their predecessors. His most recent books include *Shakespeare: The Invention of the Human* (1998), a 1998 National Book Award finalist, *How to Read and Why* (2000), and *Genius: A Mosaic of One Hundred Exemplary Creative Minds* (2002). In 1999, Professor Bloom received the prestigious American Academy of Arts and Letters Gold Medal for Criticism, and in 2002 he received the Catalonia International Prize.

DONALD PEASE teaches English at Dartmouth College. He is the editor or co-editor of several books, including *Revisionary Interventions into the Americanist Canon*.

FREDERICK NEWBERRY teaches at Duquesne University. He is the author of a book on Hawthorne.

CHESTER L. WOLFORD teaches at Penn State Erie, The Behrend College. He is the author of *The Anger of Stephen Crane* and *Fiction and the Epic Tradition*.

MICHAEL FRIED is Professor of Humanities, Professor of the History of Art, and Director of the Humanities Center at Johns Hopkins University. He is the author of *Realism, Writing, Disfiguration: On Thomas Eakins & Stephen Crane*, as well as the author or co-author of numerous other titles, including a book of poems.

DONALD PIZER was Professor of English at Tulane University. The author of numerous books, he has written much about realism, naturalism, and Dreiser.

DONALD B. GIBSON is Distinguished Professor of American literature at Rutgers University, New Brunswick, NJ. He is the author of several books, two covering Stephen Crane. He has written extensively on black American writers.

LEE CLARK MITCHELL teaches English at Princeton University. He is the editor of *New Essays on The Red Badge of Courage*. He is also the editor or author of a number of titles covering authors such as Twain and Dreiser.

KEVIN J. HAYES teaches at the University of Central Oklahoma. He has written or edited numerous books, covering authors such as Henry James, Poe, and Melville.

JAMES M. COX is Professor Emeritus of English at Dartmouth College. One of his more recent books is *Recovering Literature's Lost Ground: Essays in American Autobiography*. He is the editor of a collection of Robert Frost's poetry and has written on Frost, Twain, Hawthorne, and Poe.

JOHN E. CURRAN JR. has taught at Pennsylvania State University. He is the author of a book on Roman invasions.

JOSEPH URBAS teaches at Université Paris X-Nanterre. He is the author of a book on Huckleberry Finn.

DANIEL SHANAHAN has taught English at the École Hautes Études Commerciales in Paris. He is the author of *Toward a Genealogy of Individualism*.

Bibliography

Allred, Randall W. "'The Gilded Images of Memory': *The Red Badge of Courage* and 'The Veteran.'" A special issue of *War, Literature and the Art: An International Journal of the Humanities* (1999).

Beaver, Harold. "Stephen Crane: The Hero as Victim." *Yearbook of English Studies* 12 (1982).

Beidler, Philip D. "Stephen Crane's *The Red Badge of Courage:* Henry Fleming's Courage in Its Contexts." *CLIO* 20, no. 3 (Spring 1991).

Benfy, Christropher. "Two Cranes, Two Henrys." A special issue of *War, Literature and the Arts: An International Journal of the Humanities* (1999).

Binder, Henry. The Red Badge of Courage: *An Episode of the American Civil War*. New York: Norton, 1979.

Clendenning, John. "Visions of War and Versions of Manhood." A special issue of *War, Literature and the Arts: An International Journal of the Humanities* (1999).

Colvert, James B. "Unreal War in *The Red Badge of Courage*." A special issue of *War, Literature and the Arts: An International Journal of the Humanities* (1999).

Conder, John. "*The Red Badge of Courage:* Form and Function." Young, Thomas Daniel, ed. *Modern American Fiction: Form and Function*. Baton Rouge: Louisiana State University Press, 1989.

Dooley, Patrick K. *Stephen Crane: An Annotated Bibliography of Secondary Scholarship*. New York: G. K. Hall, 1992.

Dunn, N. E. "The Common Man's *Iliad*." *Comparative Literature Studies* 21, no. 3 (Fall 1984).

Egri, Péter. "The Genetic and Generic Aspects of Stephen Crane's *The Red Badge of Courage.*" *Acta Litteraria Academiae Scientiarum Hungaricae* 22, nos. 3–4 (1980).

Fisher, Benjamin F. "*The Red Badge of Courage under* British Spotlights Again." *War, Literature and the Arts: An International Journal of the Humanities* 12, no. 2 (Fall-Winter 2000).

González Groba, Constante. "*The Red Badge of Courage*: Henry Fleming's Battles with Readers and Literary Critics." *Revista Canaria de Estudios Ingleses* 22–3 (Apr.–Nov. 1991).

Green, Melissa. "Fleming's 'Escape' in *The Red Badge of Courage*: A Jungian Analysis." *American Literary Realism* 28, no. 1 (Fall 1995).

Habegger, Alfred. "Fighting Words: The Talk of Men at War in *The Red Badge of Courage.*" Murphy, Peter F, ed. *Fictions of Masculinity: Crossing Cultures, Crossing Sexualities.* New York: New York University Press, 1994.

Halladay, Jean R. "Sartor Resartus Revisited: Carlylean Echoes in Crane's *The Red Badge of Courage.*" *Nineteenth-Century Prose* 16, no. 1 (Winter 1988–89).

Harkins, William E. "Battle Scenes in the Writing of Tolstoy and Stephen Crane." Belknap, Robert L, ed. *Russianness: Studies on a Nation's Identity.* Ann Arbor: Ardis, 1990.

Kalaga, Wojciech. "Courage, Cowardice, and Maturity: *The Red Badge of Courage* and *Catch-22.*" Lobzowskiej, Marii, ed. *The Image of War in the Anglo-American Literature of the Twentieth Century.* Katowice, Poland: University of Slaski, 1983.

Kent, Thomas L. "Epistemological Uncertainty in *The Red Badge of Courage.*" *Modern Fiction Studies* 27, no. 4 (Winter 1981–82).

Kotani, Koji. "Stephen Crane's Strategy of Irony in *The Red Badge of Courage.*" *Studies in English Language and Literature* 40 (February 1990).

Lee, Robert A. "Stephen Crane's *The Red Badge of Courage*: The Novella as 'Moving Box.'" Lee, A. Robert, ed. *The Modern American Novella.* New York: St. Martin's Press, 1989.

Levenson, J. C. "*The Red Badge of Courage* and *McTeague:* Passage to Modernity." *The Cambridge Companion to American Realism and Naturalism: Howells to London.* Cambridge: Cambridge University Press, 1995.

McIlvaine, Robert. "Henry Fleming Wrestles with an Angel." *Pennsylvania English* 12, no. 1 (Fall 1985).

Mitchell, Lee Clark. *New Essays on* The Red Badge of Courage. Cambridge: Cambridge University Press, 1986.

Mitchell, Verner D. "Reading 'Race' and 'Gender' in Crane's *The Red Badge of Courage*." *College Language Association Journal* 40, no. 1 (Sept. 1996).

Monteiro, George. "John Hersey's Guadalcanal Report: Drawing on Crane's War." A special issue of *War, Literature and the Arts: An International Journal of the Humanties* (1999).

———. "The Mule-Drivers' Charge in *The Red Badge of Courage*." *Stephen Crane Studies* 1, no. 1 (Spring 1992).

———. *Stephen Crane's Blue Badge of Courage*. Baton Rouge: Louisiana State University Press, 2000.

Myers, Robert M. "'The Subtle Battle Brotherhood': The Construction of Military Discipline in *The Red Badge of Courage*." A special issue of *War, Literature and the Arts: An International Journal of the Humanties* (1999).

Nichols, Prescott S. "*The Red Badge of Courage*: What Is Fleming Fleeing?" *Literature and History* 12, no. 1 (Spring 1986).

Orr, John C. "A Red Badge Signifying Nothing: Henry Fleming's Corporate Self." A special issue of *War, Literature and the Arts: An International Journal of the Humanties* (1999).

Parker, Hershel. *Flawed Texts and Verbal Icons: Literary Authority in American Fiction*. Evanston: Northwestern University Press, 1984.

Pizer, Donald. *Critical Essays on Stephen Crane's* The Red Badge of Courage. Boston: Hall, 1990.

———. "Henry behind the Lines and the Concept of Manhood in *The Red Badge of Courage* ." *Stephen Crane Studies* 10, no. 1 (Spring 2001).

Reynolds, Kirk M. "*The Red Badge of Courage*: Private Henry's Mind as Sole Point of View." *South Atlantic Review* 52, no. 1 (January 1987).

Rao, B. Gopal. "The Demythologization of War: A Study in Stephen Crane's *The Red Badge of Courage*." Rao, E. Nageswara, ed. *Mark Twain and Nineteenth Century American Literature*. Hyderabad: American Studies Research Centre, 1993.

Satterfield, Ben. "From Romance to Reality: The Accomplishment of Private Fleming." *College Language Association Journal* 24, no. 4 (June 1981).

Scacchi, Anna. "Engendering the Male Subject: *The Red Badge of Courage* as a Sexual Battlefield." Pisapia, Biancamaria, Ugo Rubeo, and Anna Scacchi, eds. *Red Badges of Courage: Wars and Conflicts in American Culture*. Rome, Italy: Bulzoni, 1998.

Schneider, Michael. "Monomyth Structure in *The Red Badge of Courage*." *American Literary Realism* 20, no. 1 (Fall 1987).

Shulman, Robert. "*The Red Badge of Courage* and Social Violence: Crane's

Myth of His America." *Canadian Review of American Studies* 12, no. 1 (Spring 1981).

Shaw, Mary Neff. "Henry Fleming's Heroics in *The Red Badge of Courage*: A Satiric Search for a 'Kinder, Gentler' Heroism." *Studies in the Novel* 22, no. 4 (Winter 1990).

Tavernier-Courbin, Jacqueline. "Humor and Insight through Fallacy in Stephen Crane's *The Red Badge of Courage*." A special issue of *War, Literature and the Arts: An International Journal of the Humanities* (1999).

Vanouse, Donald. "Catastrophe Theory and Character Transformation in *The Red Badge of Courage*." A special issue of *War, Literature and the Arts: An International Journal of the Humanities* (1999).

Wolford, Chester L. "*The Red Badge of Courage* Mocks the Greek Epic." Szumski, Bonnie, ed. *Readings on Stephen Crane*. San Diego: Greenhaven, 1998.

Zhu, Weihong Julia. "The Absurdity of Henry's Courage." *Stephen Crane Studies* 10, 2 (Fall 2001).

Acknowledgments

"Fear, Rage, and the Mistrials of Representation in *The Red Badge of Courage*" by Donald Pease. Sundquist, Eric J., ed. *American Realism: New Essays:* 155–75. © 1982 by The Johns Hopkins University Press. Reprinted by permission of The Johns Hopkins University Press.

"*The Red Badge of Courage* and *The Scarlet Letter*" by Frederick Newberry. Reprinted from *Arizona Quarterly* 38, no. 2 (1982) by permission of the Regents of the University of Arizona.

"The Anger of Henry Fleming: The Epic of Consciousness & *The Red Badge of Courage*" by Chester L. Wolford. From *The Anger of Stephen Crane: Fiction and the Epic Tradition:* 37–75. © 1983 by the University of Nebraska Press. Reprinted by permission.

"Postscript: Stephen Crane's Upturned Faces" by Michael Fried. From "Realism, Writing, and Disfiguration in Thomas Eakins's *Gross Clinic*" in *Representations* 9 (Winter 1985): 89–95. © 1985 by The Regents of the University of California. Reprinted by permission.

"*The Red Badge of Courage*: Text, Theme, and Form" by Donald Pizer. From *The South Atlantic Quarterly* 84, no. 3 (Summer 1985): 302–313. © 1985 by Duke University Press. All rights reserved. Used by permission of the publisher.

"Nature" by Donald B. Gibson. From *The Red Badge of Courage: Redefining the Hero:* 66–81. © 1988 by Twayne Publishers. Reprinted by permission of The Gale Group.

"The Spectacle of Character in Crane's *Red Badge of Courage*" by Lee Clark Mitchell. From *Determined Fictions: American Literary Naturalism*: 96–116. © 1989 by Columbia University Press. Reprinted by permission of the publisher.

"How Stephen Crane Shaped Henry Fleming" by Kevin J. Hayes. From *Studies in the Novel* 22, no. 3 (Fall 1990): 296–307. © 1990 by the University of North Texas. Reprinted by permission.

"*The Red Badge of Courage*: The Purity of War" by James M. Cox. From *Southern Humanities Review* 25, no. 4 (Fall 1991): 305–320. © 1991 by Auburn University. Reprinted by permission.

"'Nobody seems to know where we go': Uncertainty, History, and Irony in *The Red Badge of Courage*" by John E. Curran, Jr. From *American Literary Realism 1870–1910* 26, no. 1 (Fall 1993): 1–12. © 1993 by McFarland & Company, Inc. Reprinted by permission.

"The Emblematics of Invulnerability in *The Red Badge of Courage*" by Joseph Urbas. From *Q/W/E/R/T/Y* 4 (October 1994): 255–63. © 1994 by Joseph Urbas. Reprinted by permission.

"The Army Motif in *The Red Badge of Courage* as a Response to Industrial Capitalism" by Daniel Shanahan. From *Papers on Language & Literature* 32, no. 4 (Fall 1996): 399–409. © 1996 by the Board of Trustees of Southern Illinois University. Reprinted by permission.

Index